Vision Board Book: Manifesting Your Dream Life

A Clip Art Journey for Inspired Women, Luxury/Soft Life Edition

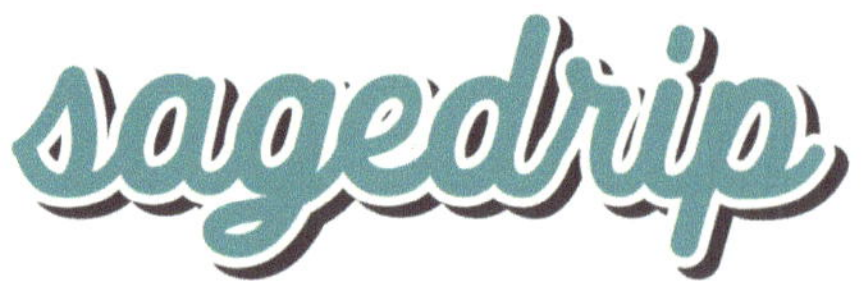
sagedrip

Foreword:

Welcome, ladies, to the first steps of your transformative journey with "Vision Board Book: Manifesting Your Dream Life - A Clip Art Journey for Inspired Women, Luxury Edition." This book is not just an assortment of beautiful images; it is a gateway to a world of possibility, a world where your dreams and aspirations take tangible form and inspire you towards a more fulfilling, radiant life.

Whether you are dreaming of exotic travels, a luxurious lifestyle, nurturing self-care and meditation rituals, enriching relationships, or genuine friendships, this book is designed to awaken your deepest desires and help manifest them into reality. Each image within these pages holds the potential to spark your imagination, ignite your ambition, and serve as a stepping stone on your path to success.

Creating your vision board with the provided clip art is a dynamic, creative process. Here are some steps to guide you through:

1. **Reflect**: Begin by reflecting on your aspirations for the upcoming year. What areas of your life are you most eager to enrich?
2. **Choose Your Images**: Delve into the pages of this book and select images that resonate with your goals. Remember, there's no right or wrong choice here; pick what speaks to your heart.
3. **Assemble Your Vision Board**: Arrange your chosen images on a board or in a journal. You can group them by theme or scatter them for a more abstract approach.
4. **Secure Your Images**: Once you're happy with the arrangement, secure the images with glue or tape.
5. **Reflect and Affirm**: Take a moment to absorb the collective power of your vision board. With each glance, let it serve as a vivid reminder of your goals and the beautiful journey that awaits you.
6. **Display Your Vision Board**: Position your vision board somewhere you'll see it daily. Let it be a constant source of motivation and inspiration.

Remember, your vision board is a personal, powerful tool for visualizing your future and empowering your present. It represents not just your goals, but the passion, dedication, and resilience you bring to achieving them.

"Visionary Vistas" is more than just a book. It is a journey, a guide, and a friend. It is the seed of your dreams and the canvas of your future. So, open your heart, ignite your spirit, and let's embark on this journey of manifestation together.
May each page turn become a step towards your dream life.

It's been a joy to create this unique book for you. Now it's your turn to create, to dream, and to manifest. Go get the life you deserve!!

-Sage Drip

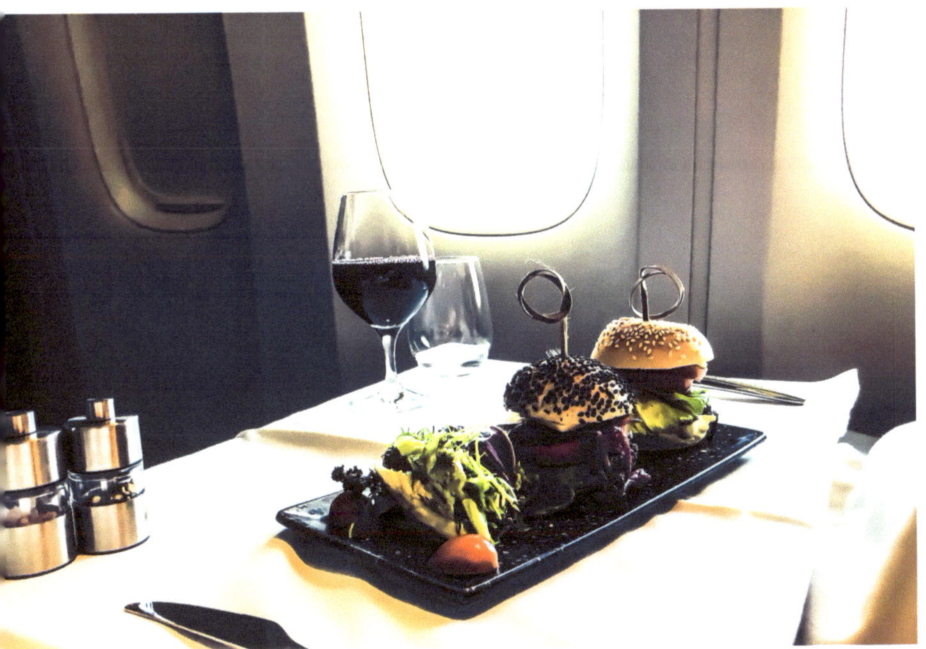

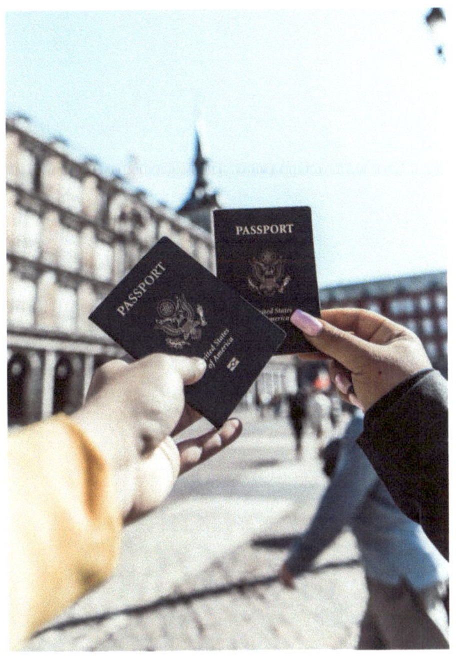
PASSPORT
PASSPORT

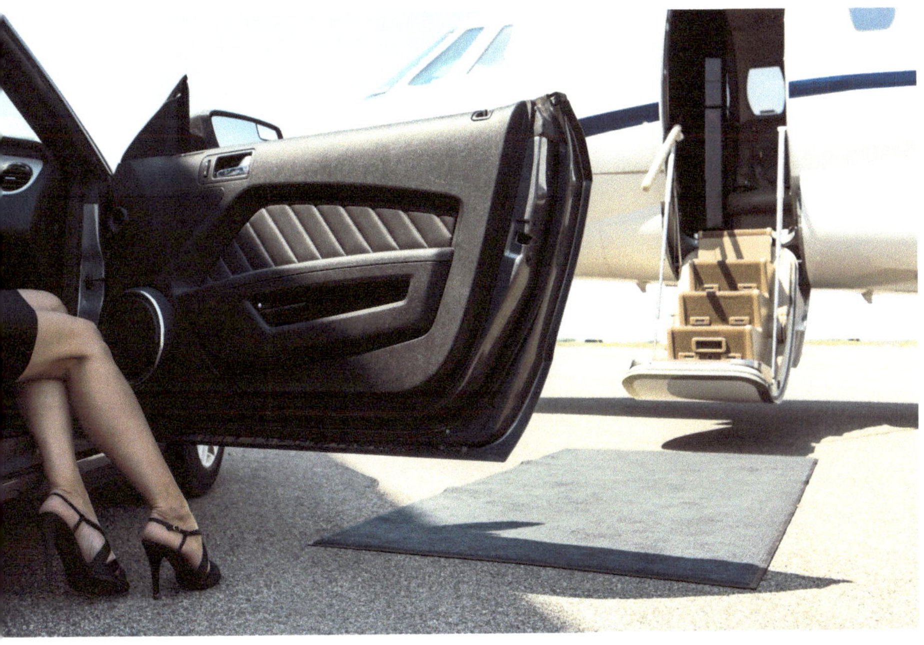

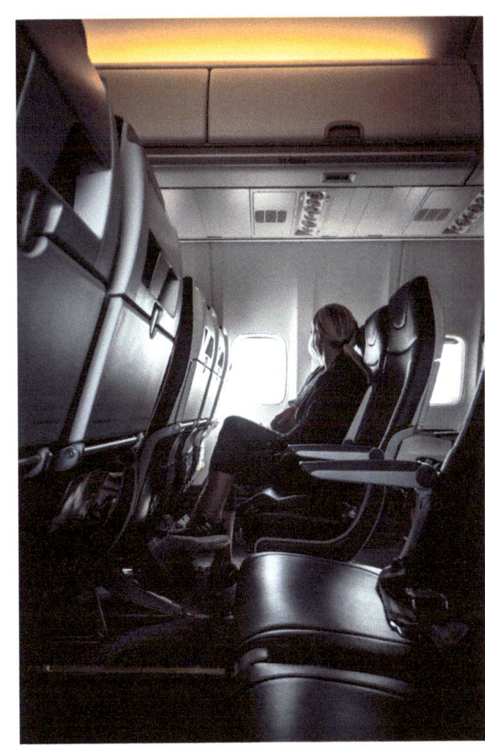

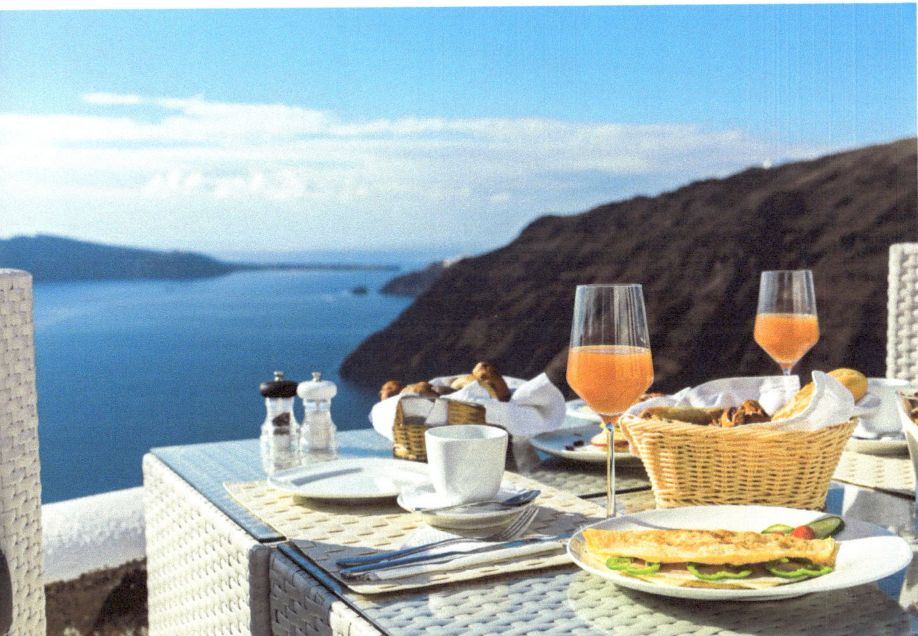

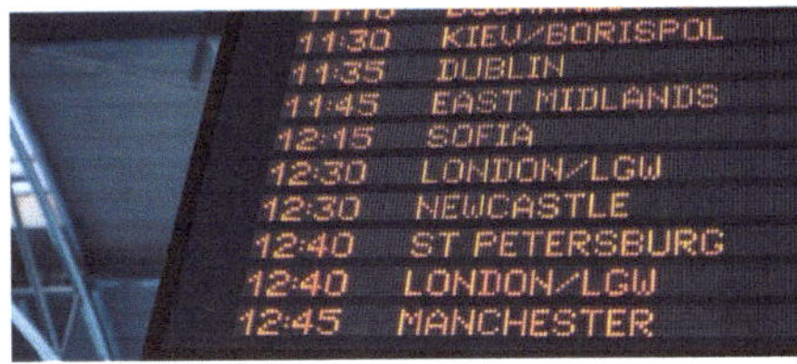
11:30 KIEV/BORISPOL
11:35 DUBLIN
11:45 EAST MIDLANDS
12:15 SOFIA
12:30 LONDON/LGW
12:30 NEWCASTLE
12:40 ST PETERSBURG
12:40 LONDON/LGW
12:45 MANCHESTER

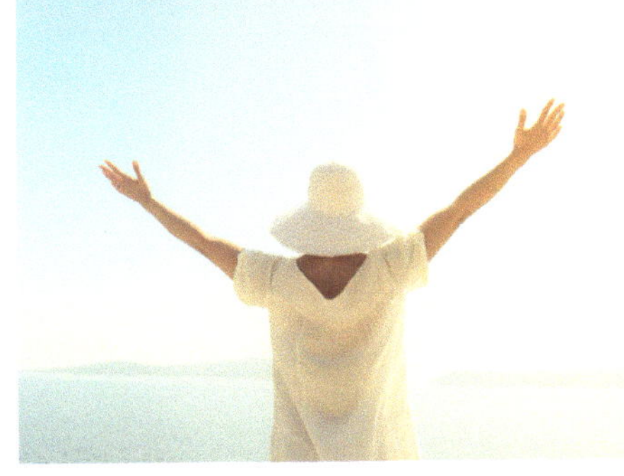

Work
Travel
Save
Repeat

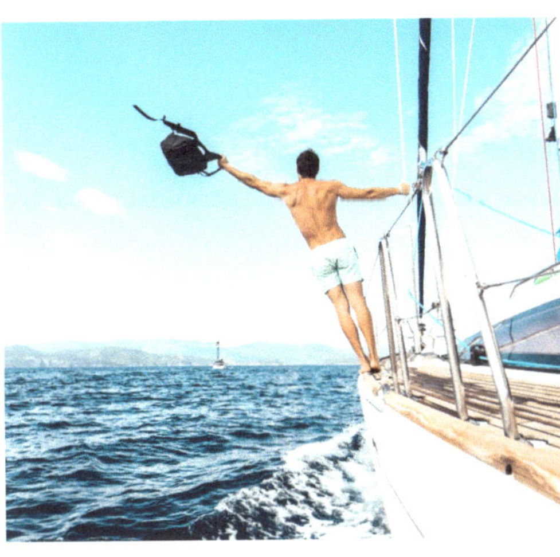

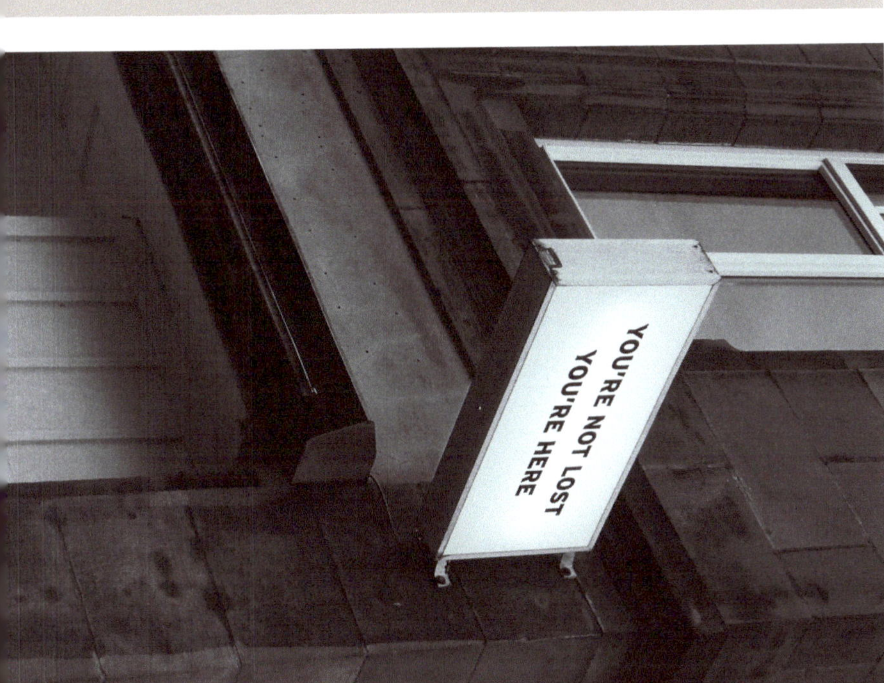

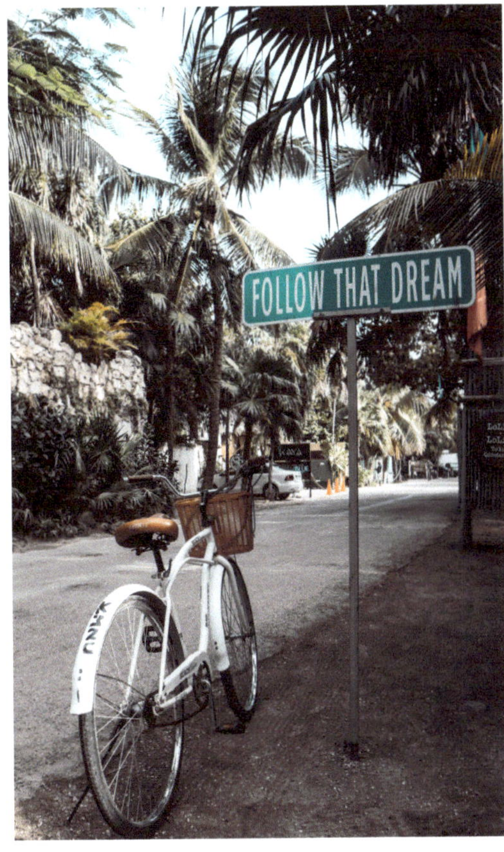

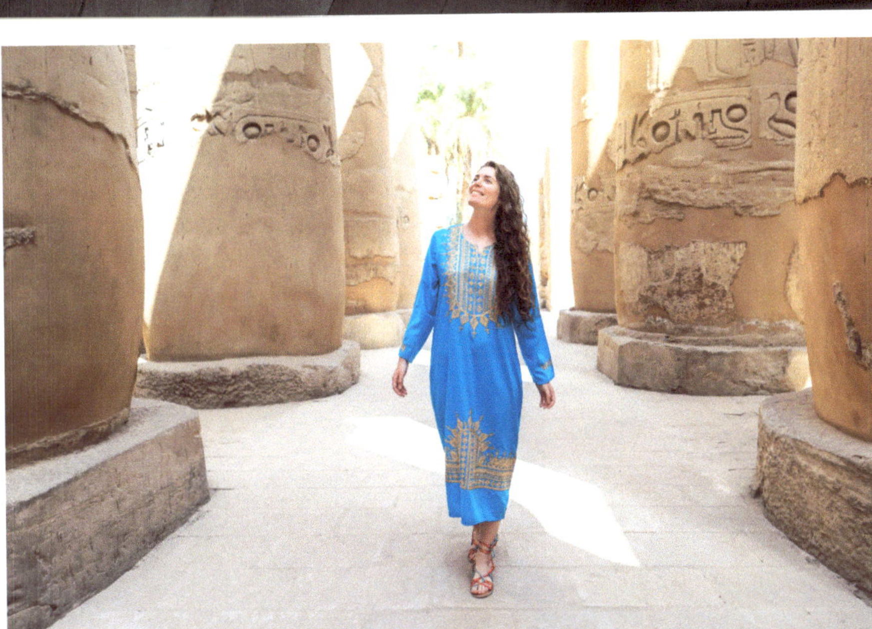

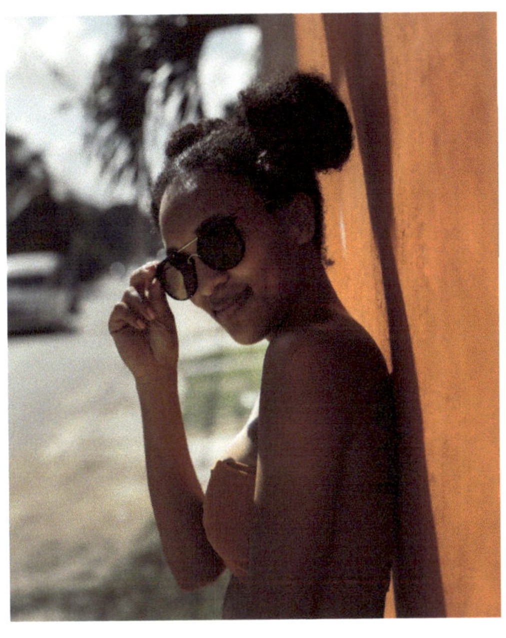

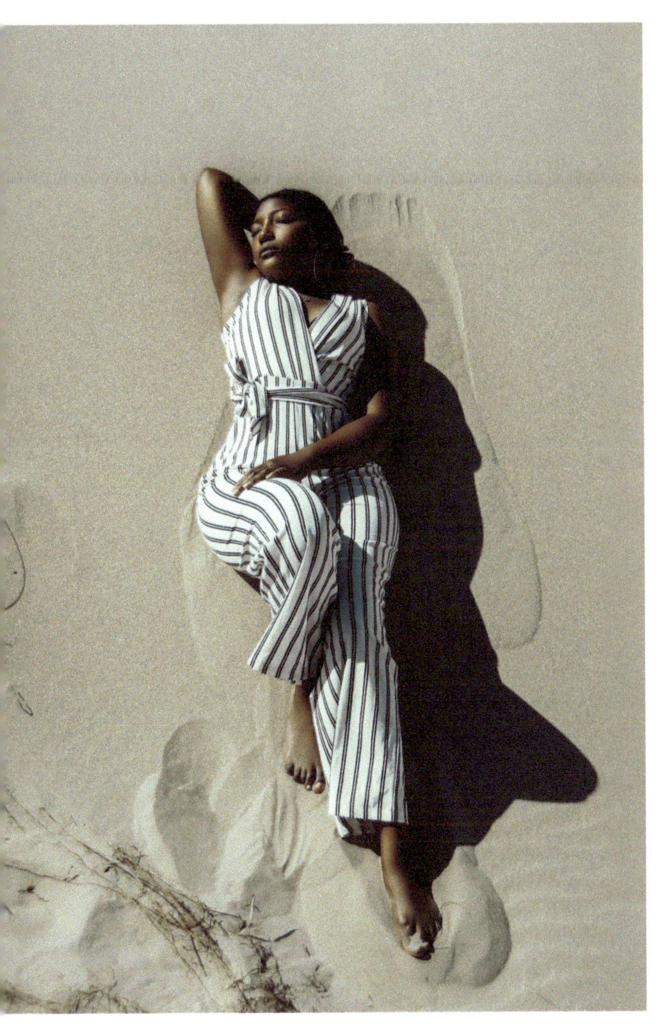
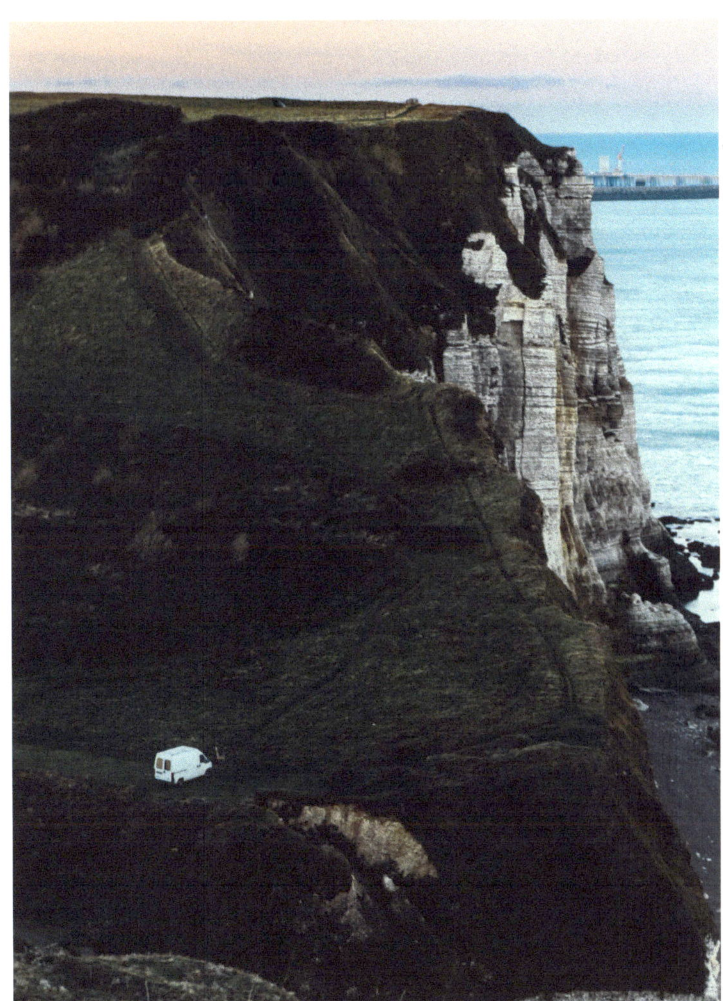
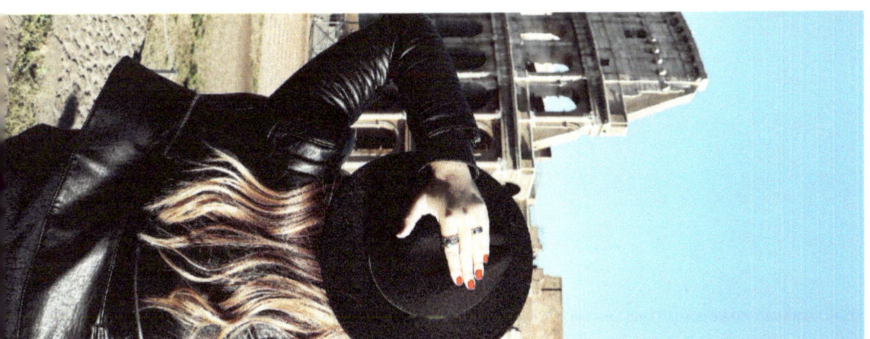
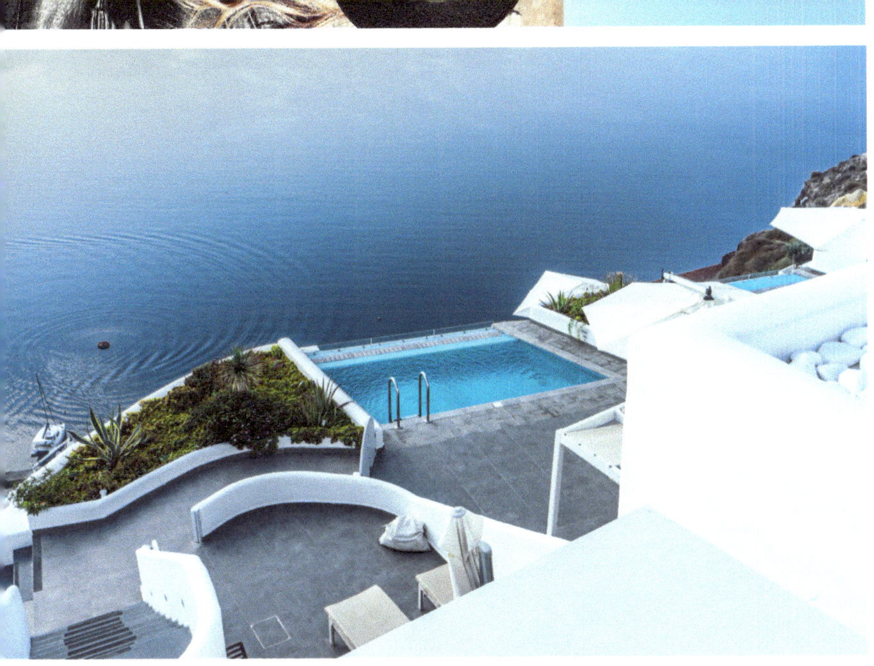
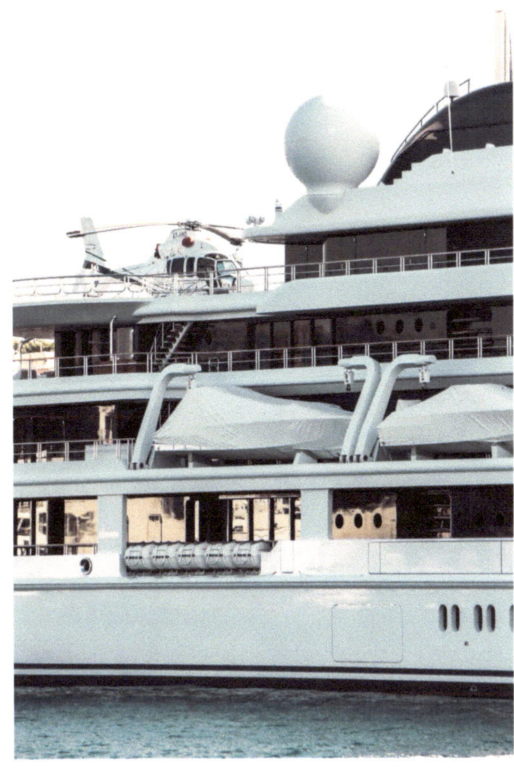

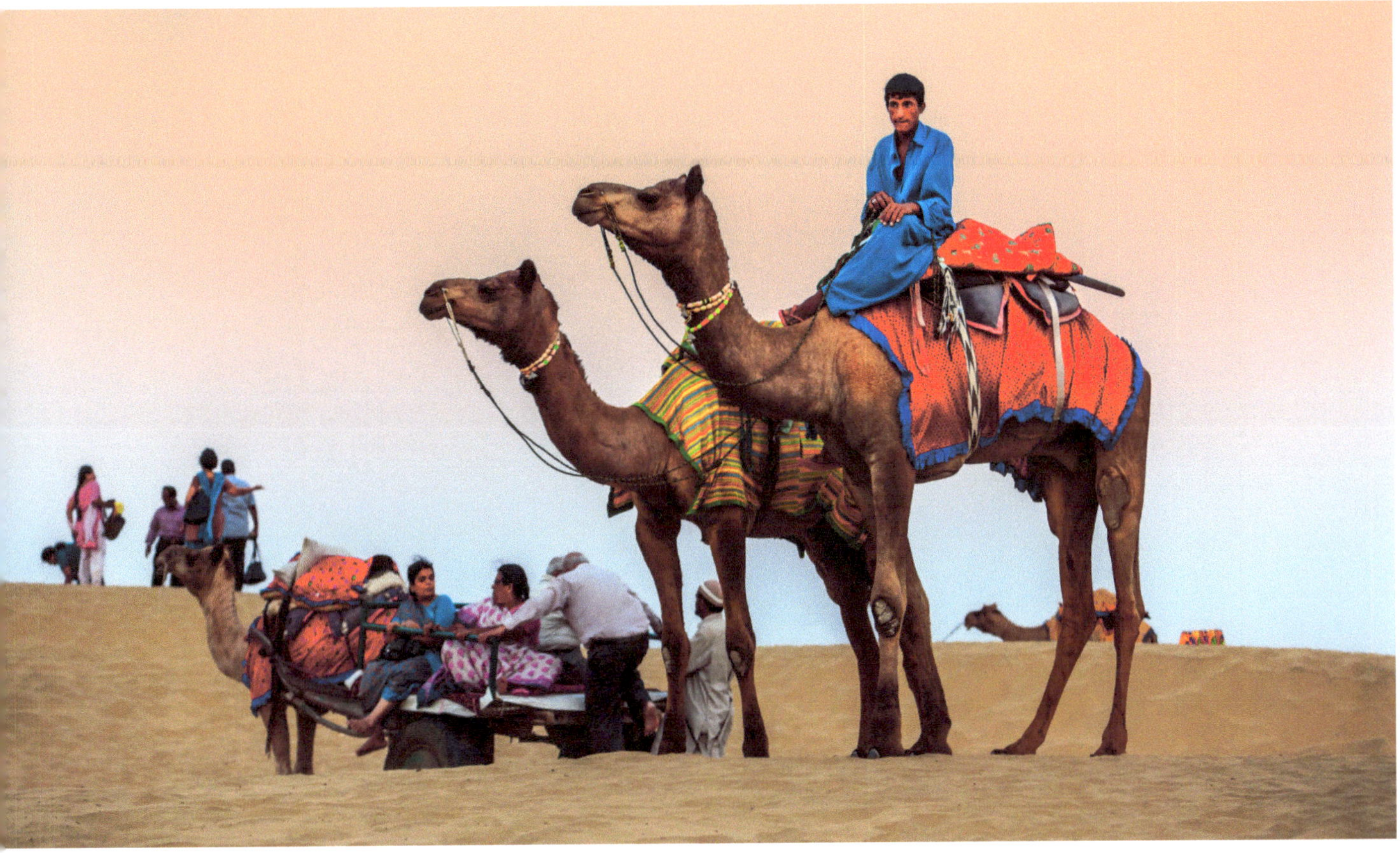

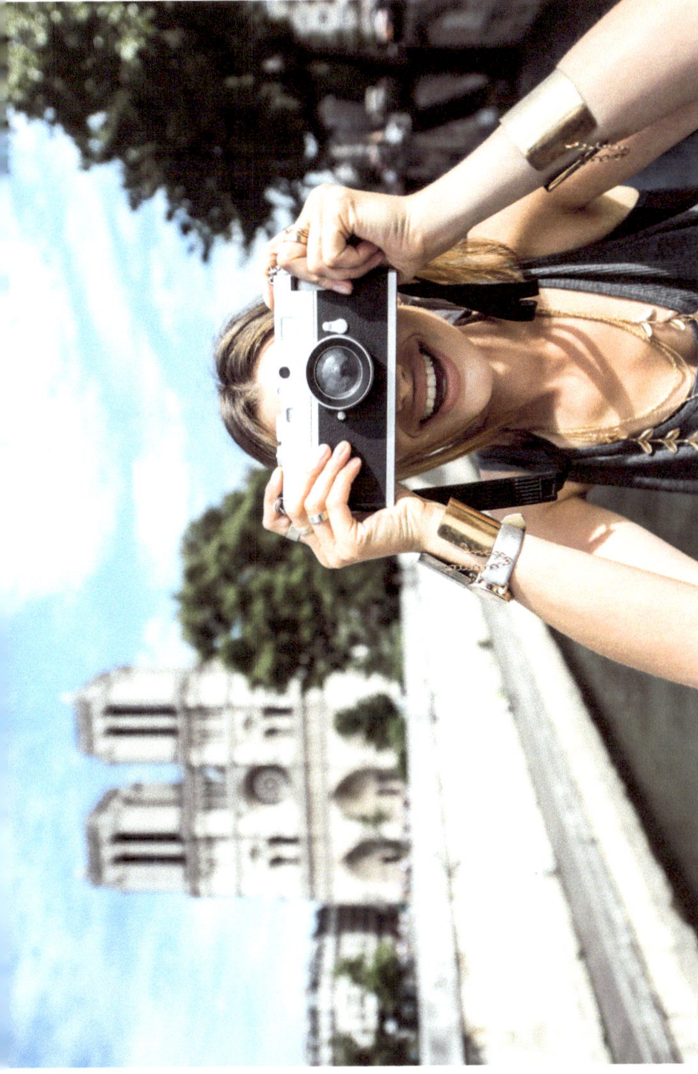

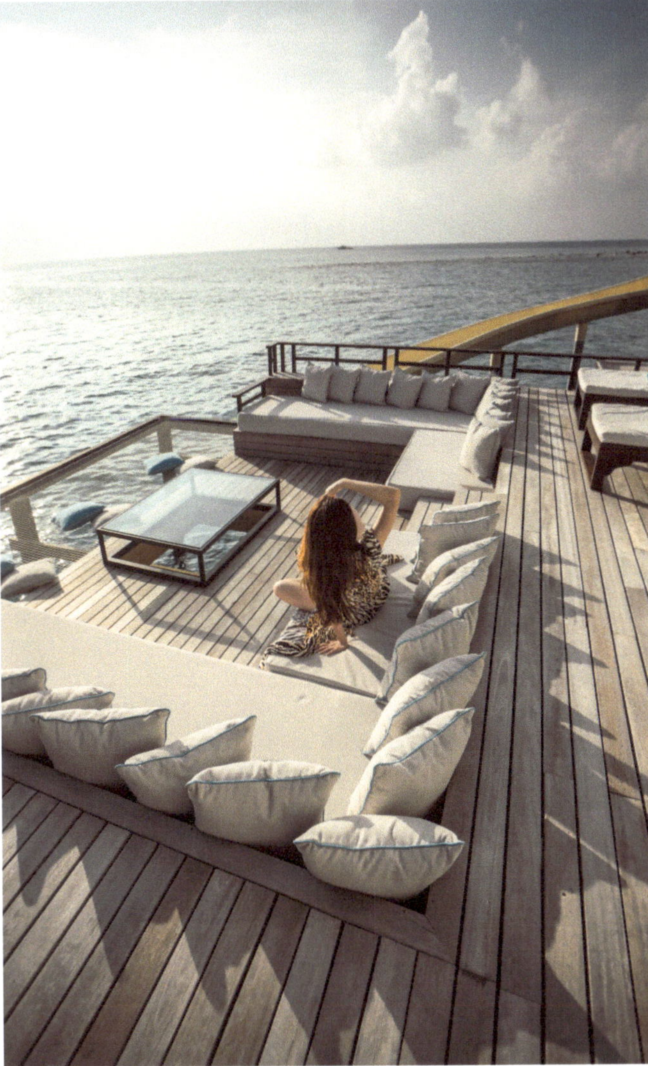

Travel is my therapy

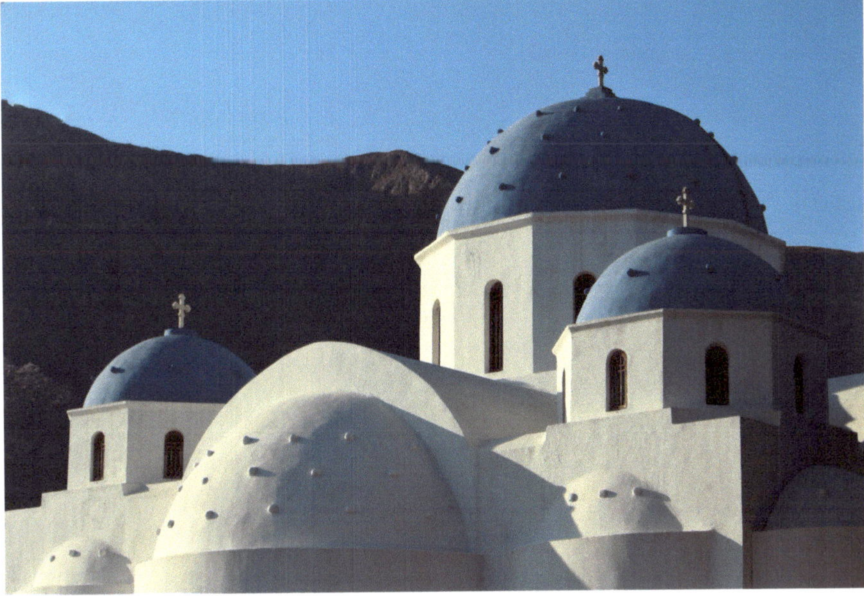

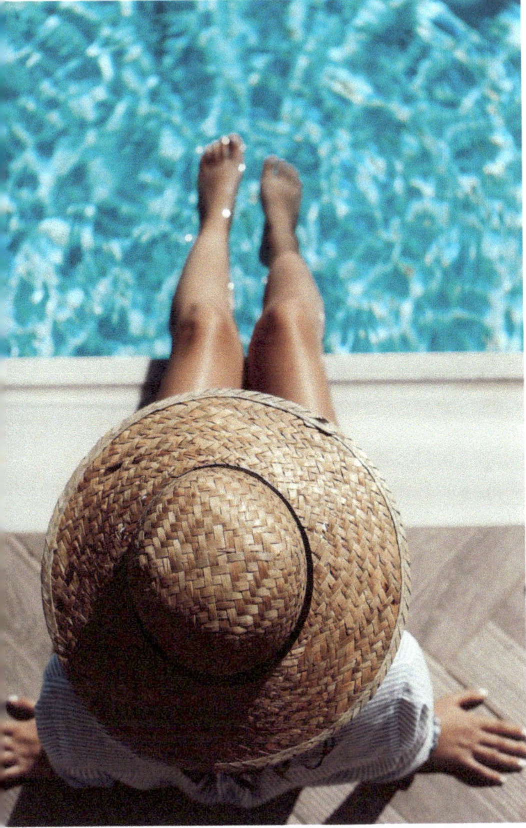

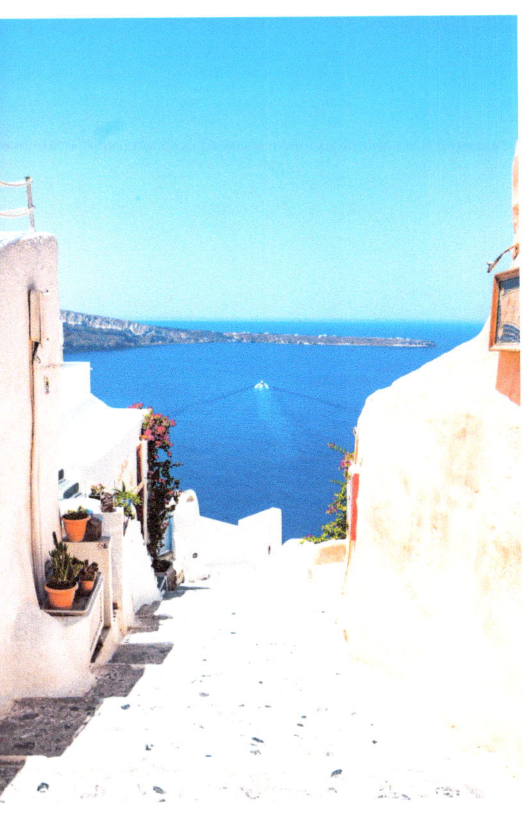

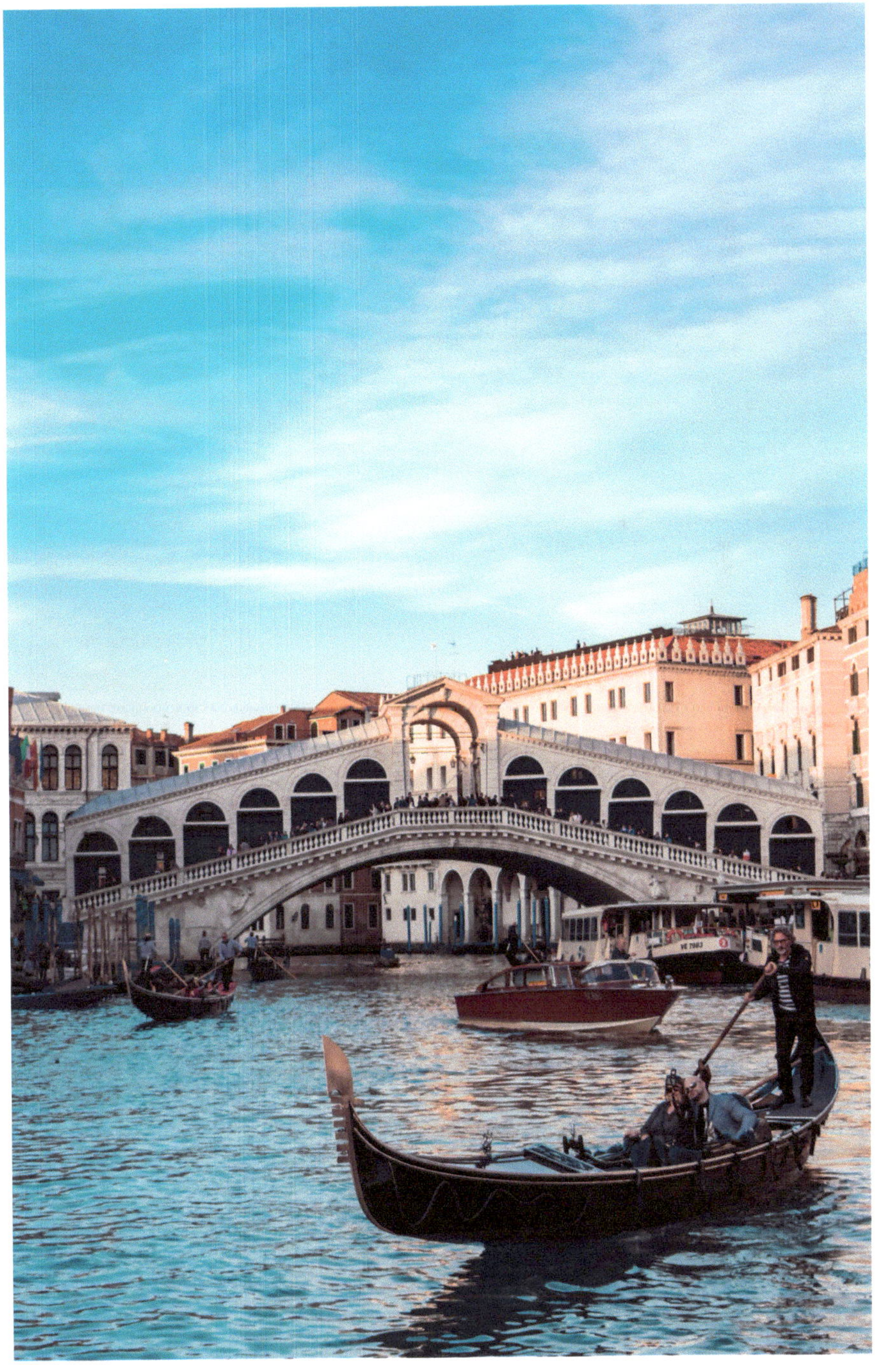

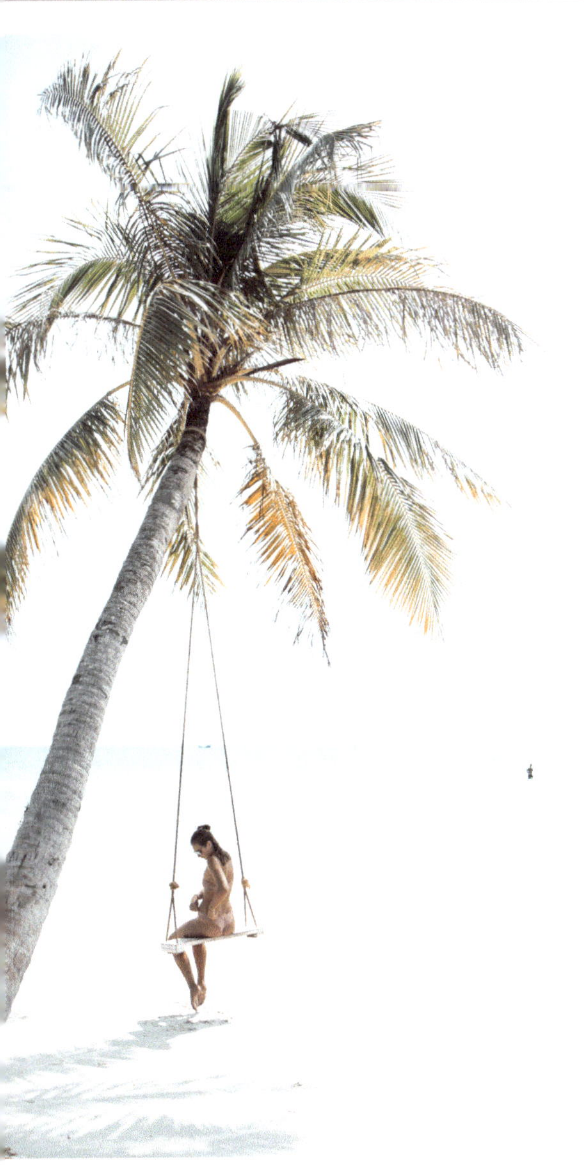

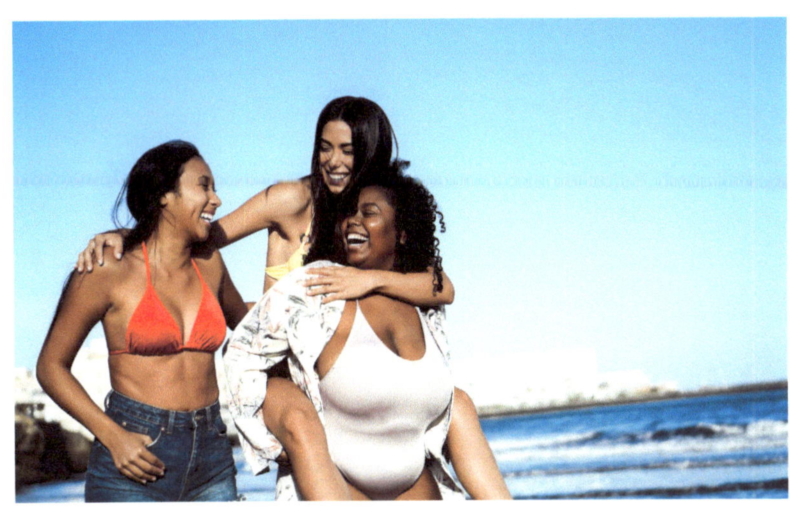

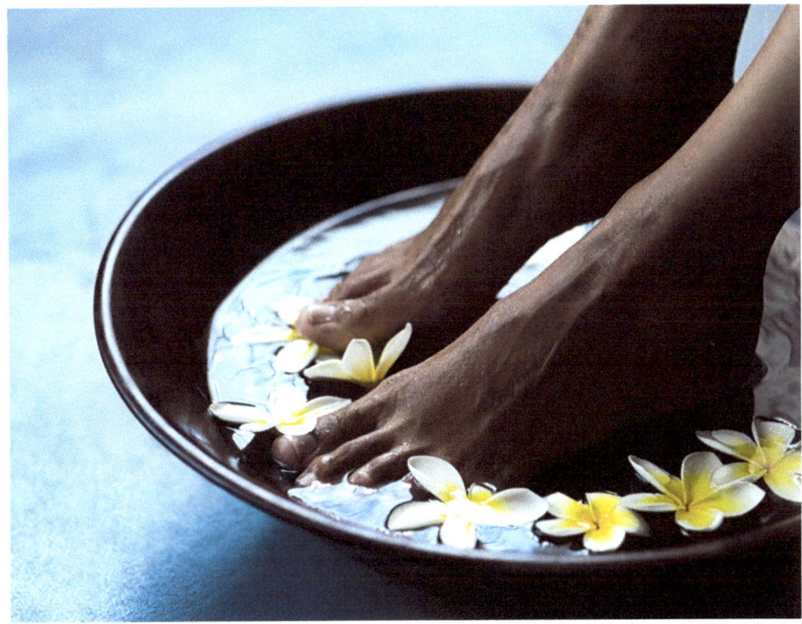

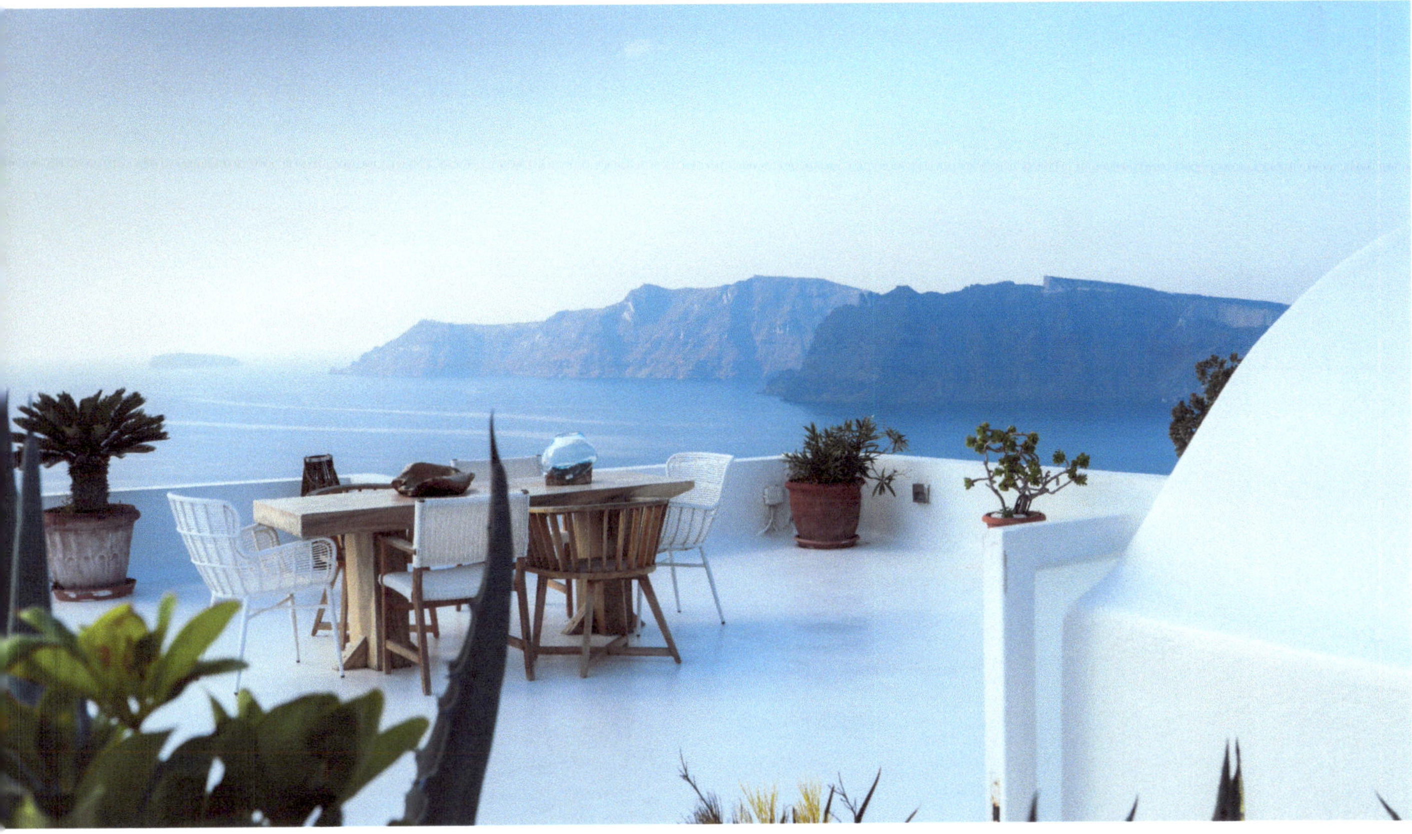

Self Care Isn't Selfish

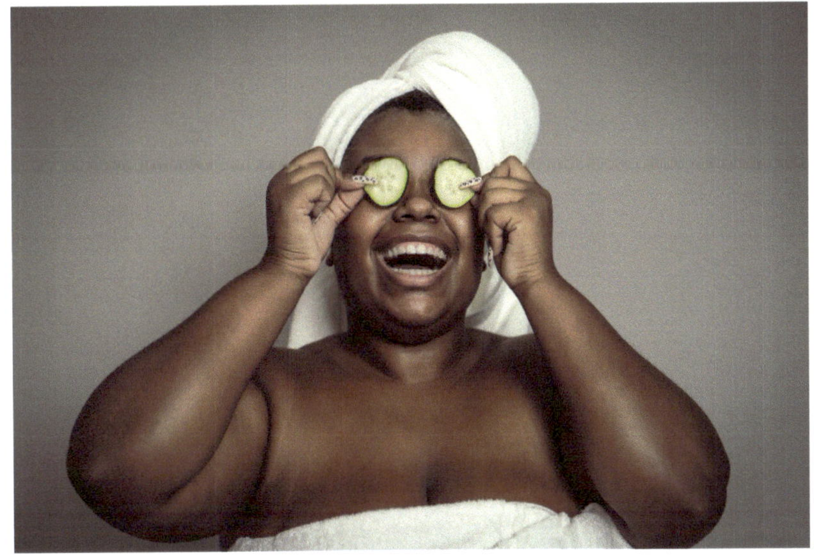

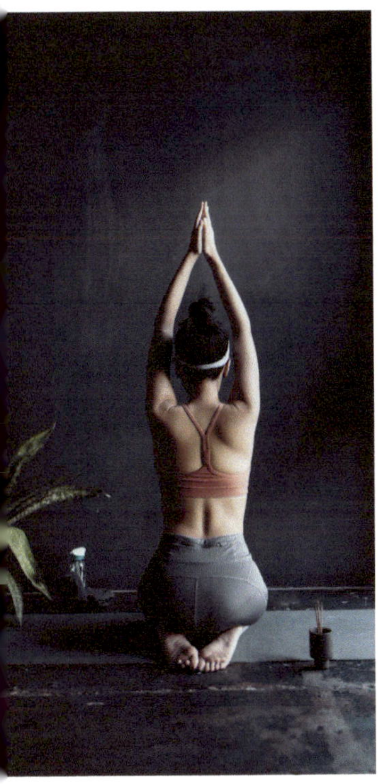

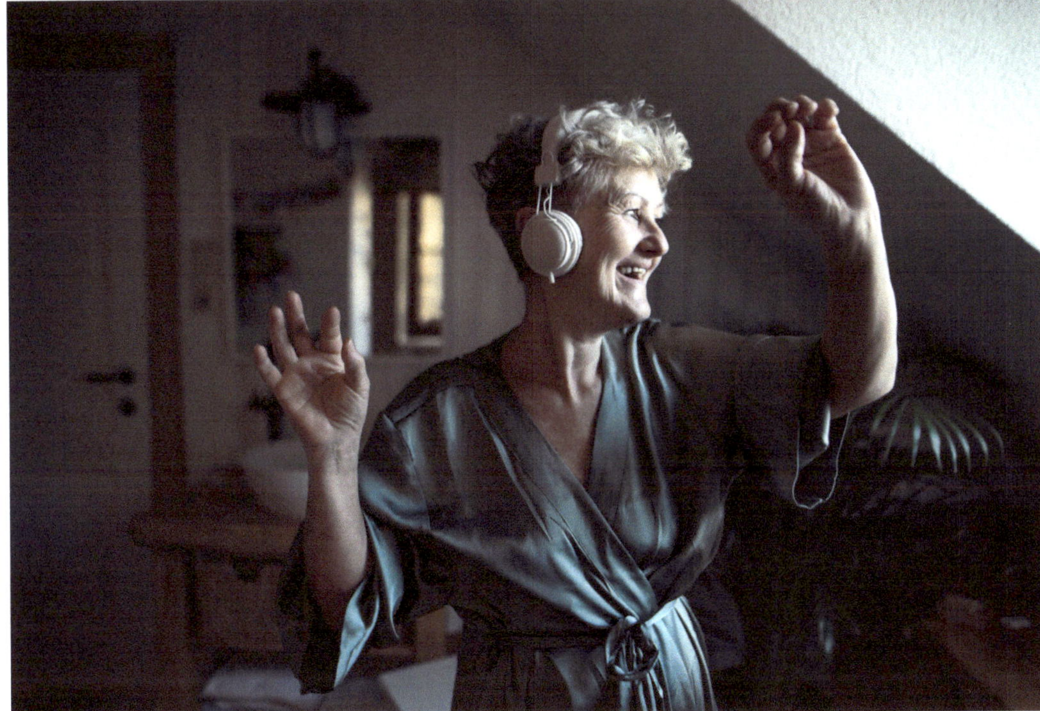

"I don't need a fan club. I've got myself."
- Ted Lasso TV Show

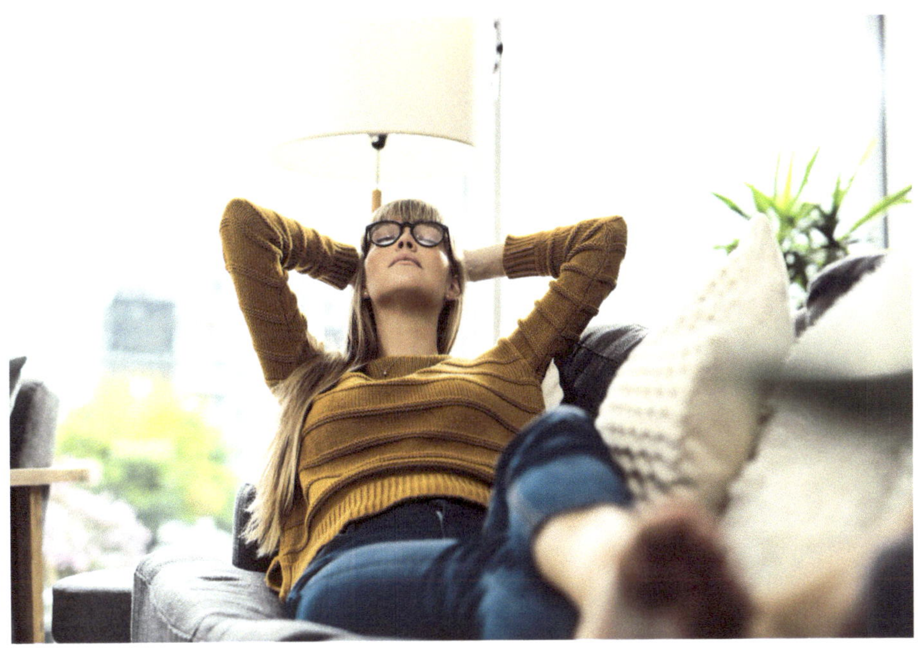

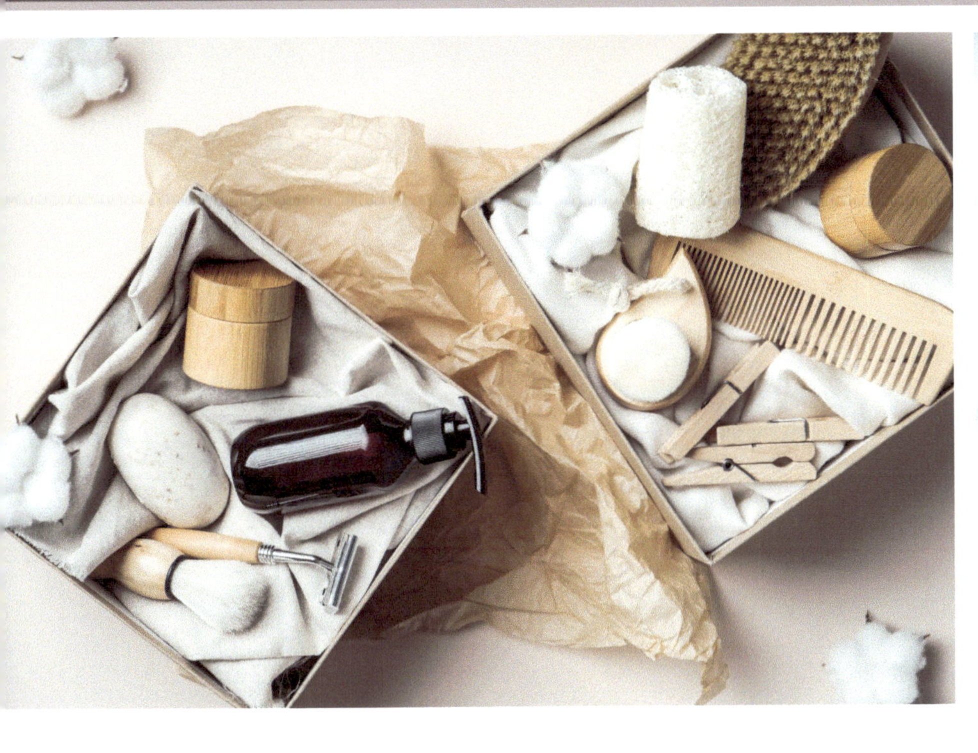
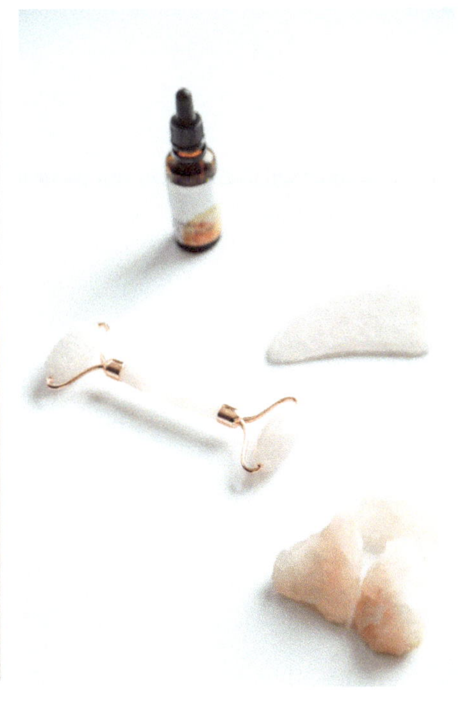
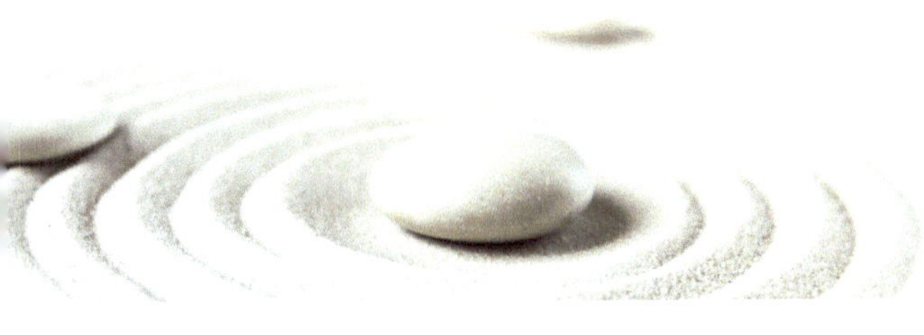
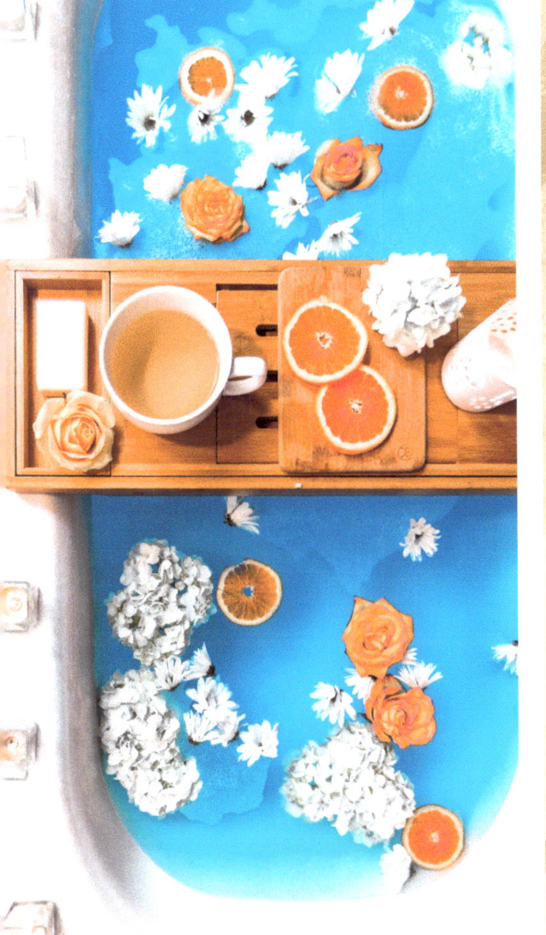

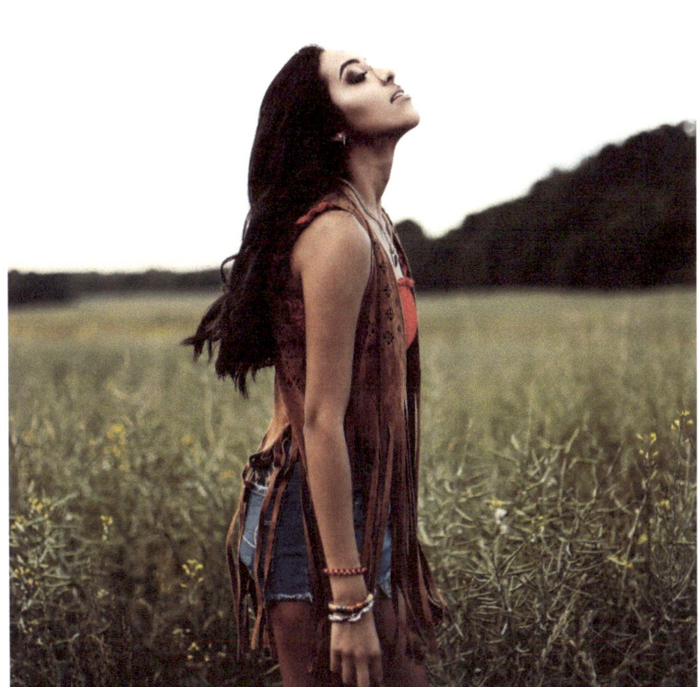

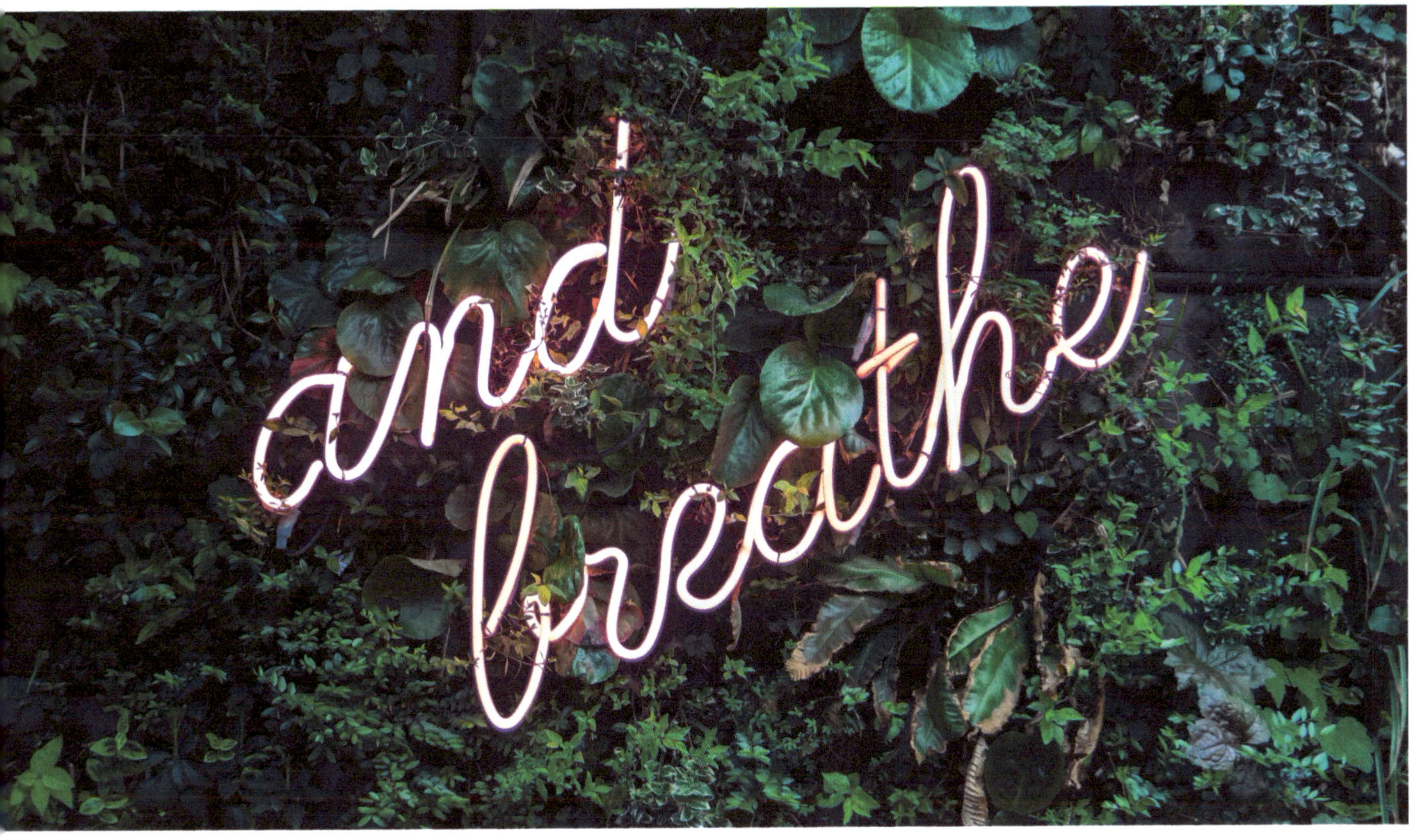

and breathe

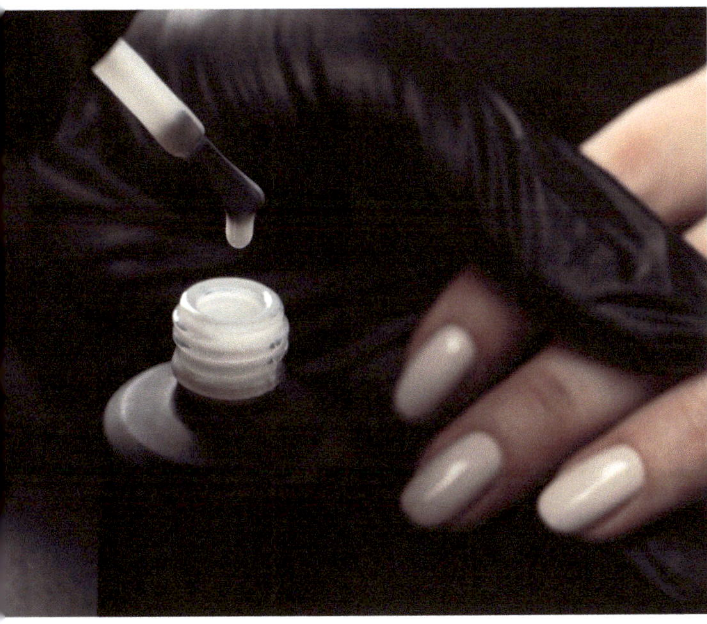

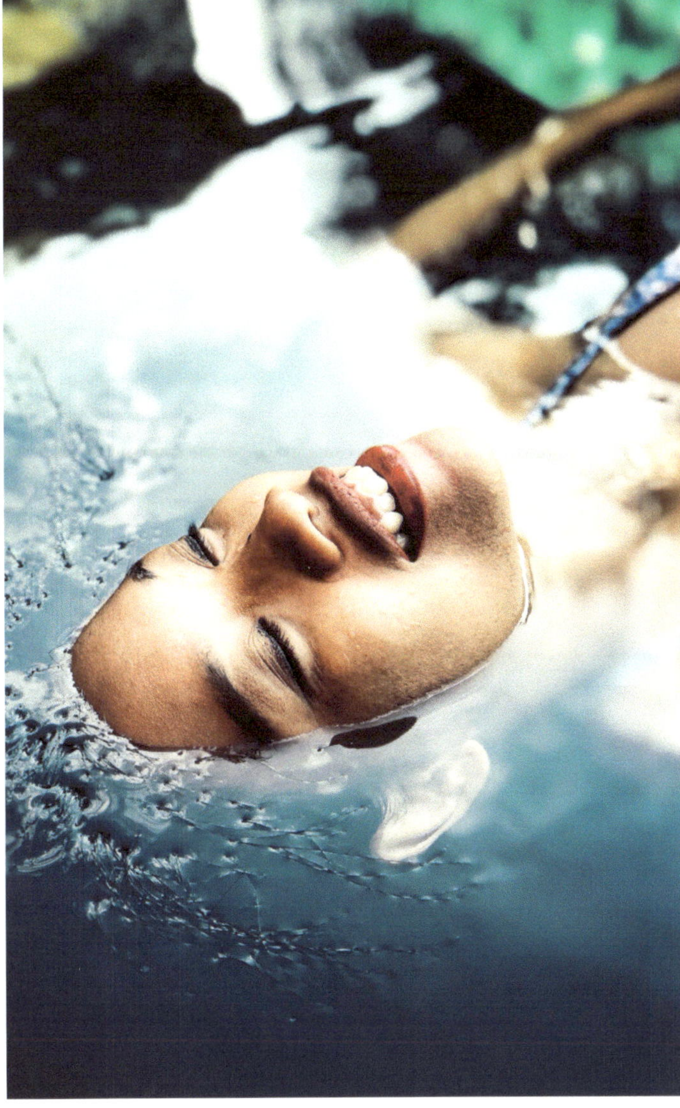

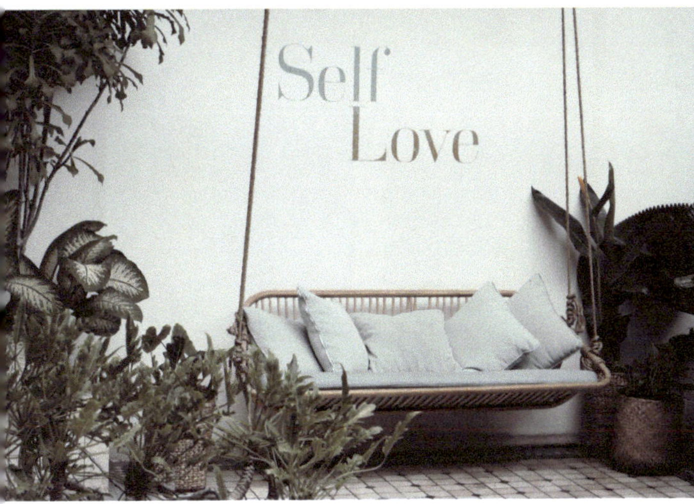

"Life moves pretty fast. If you don't stop and look around once in a while, you could miss it." -
Ferris Bueller's Day Off (1986)

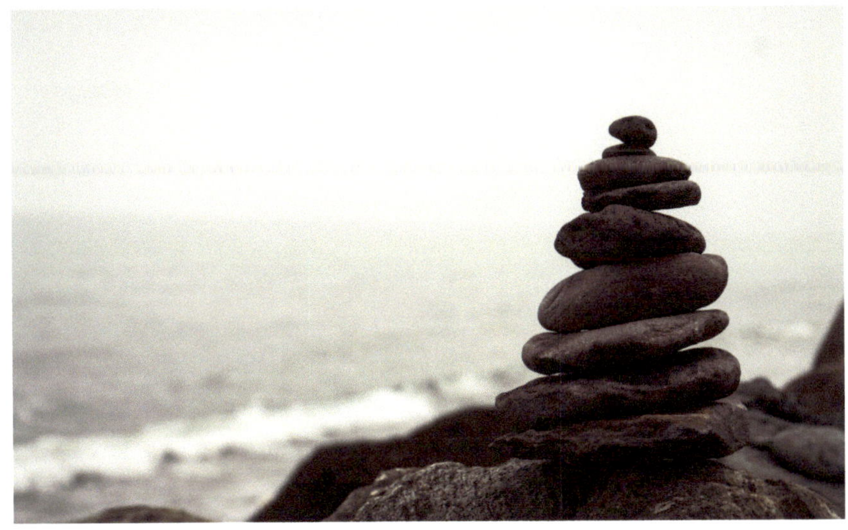

"Be yourself; everyone else is already taken."
-Oscar Wilde

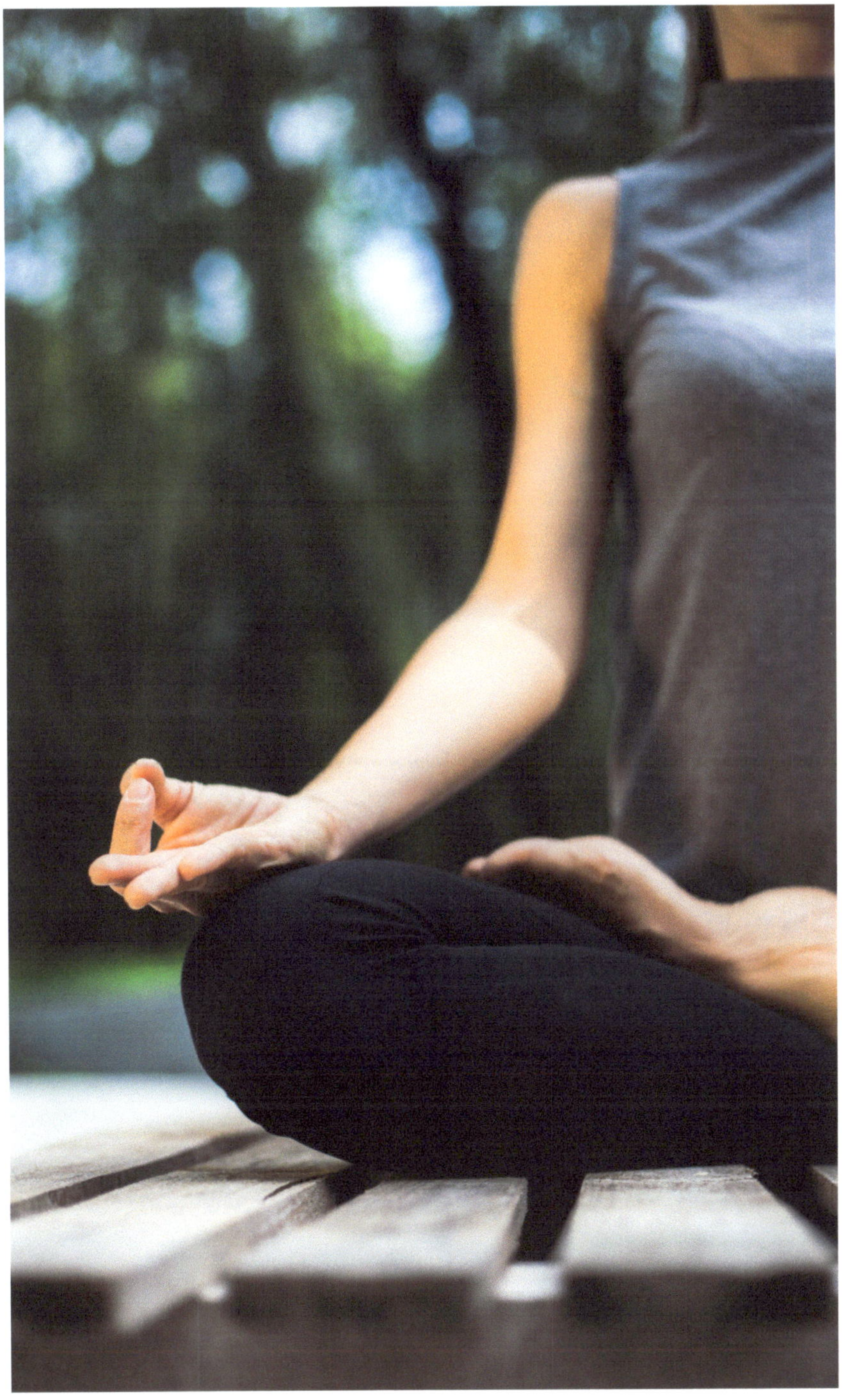

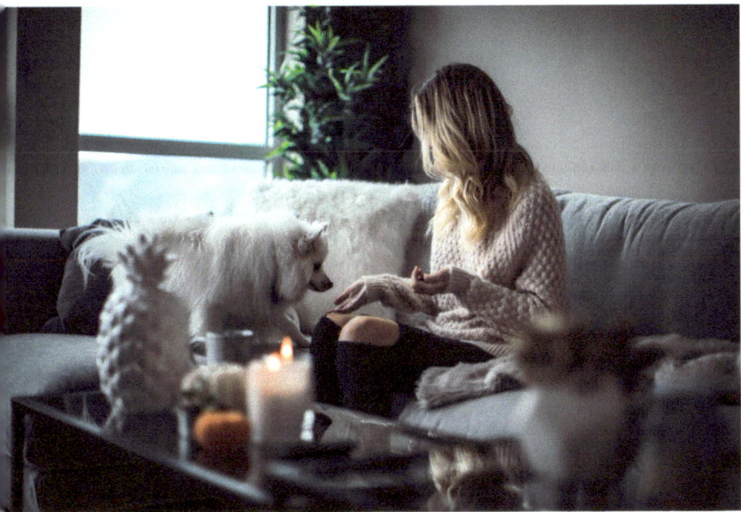

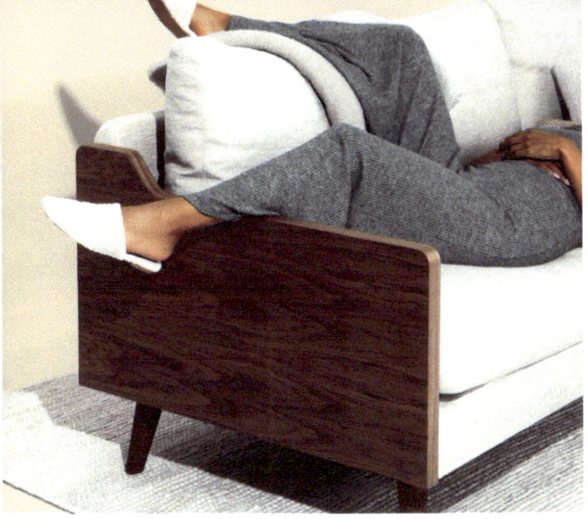

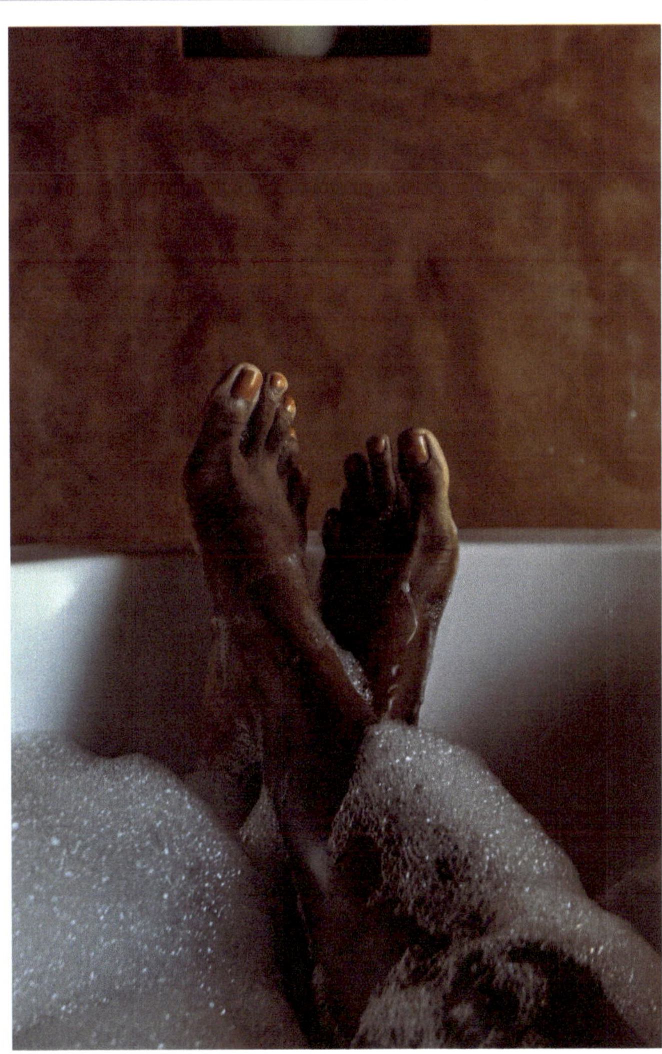

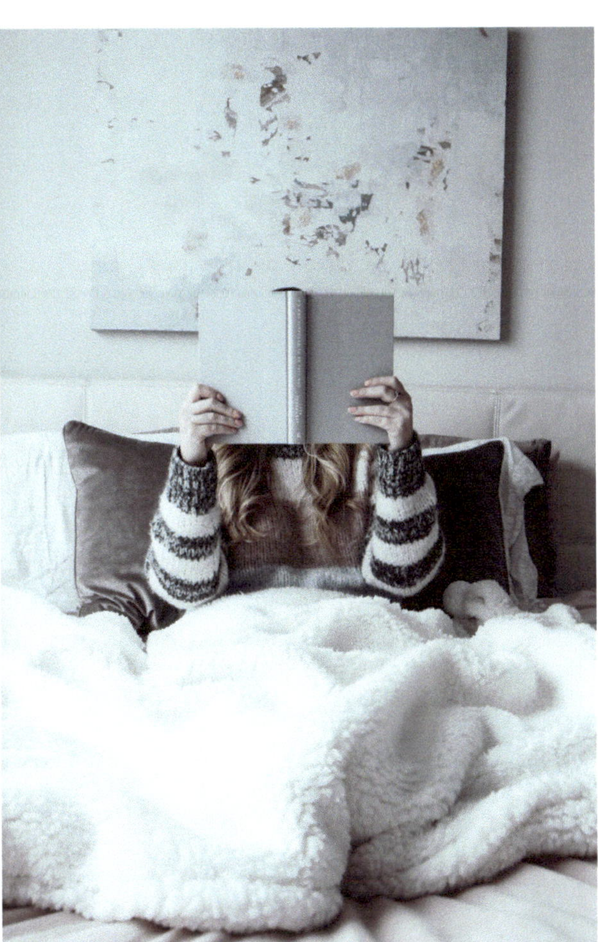

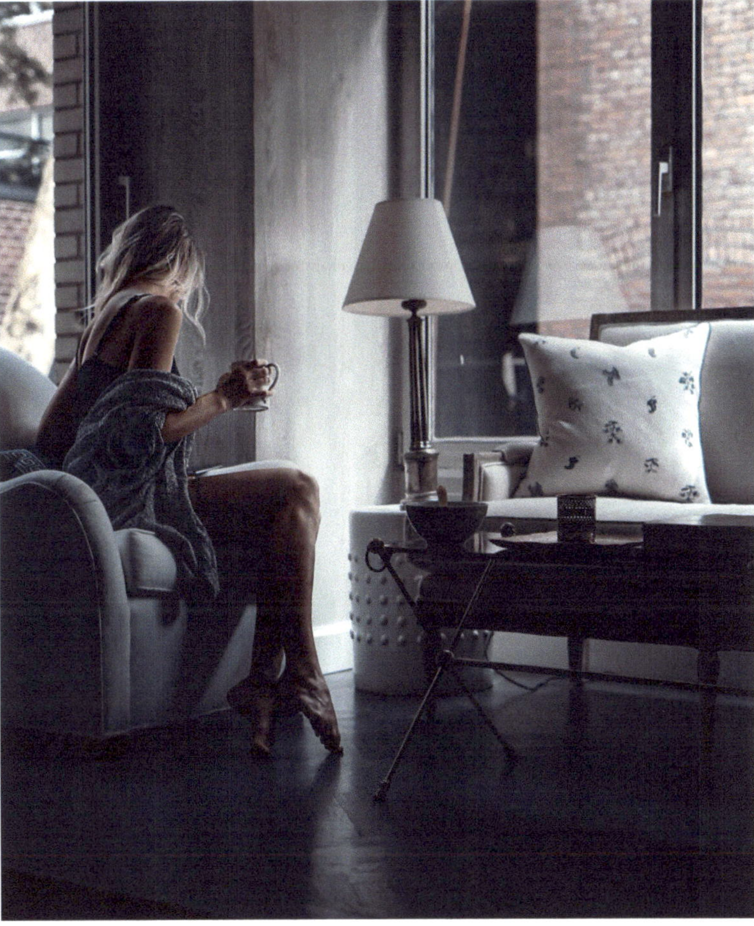

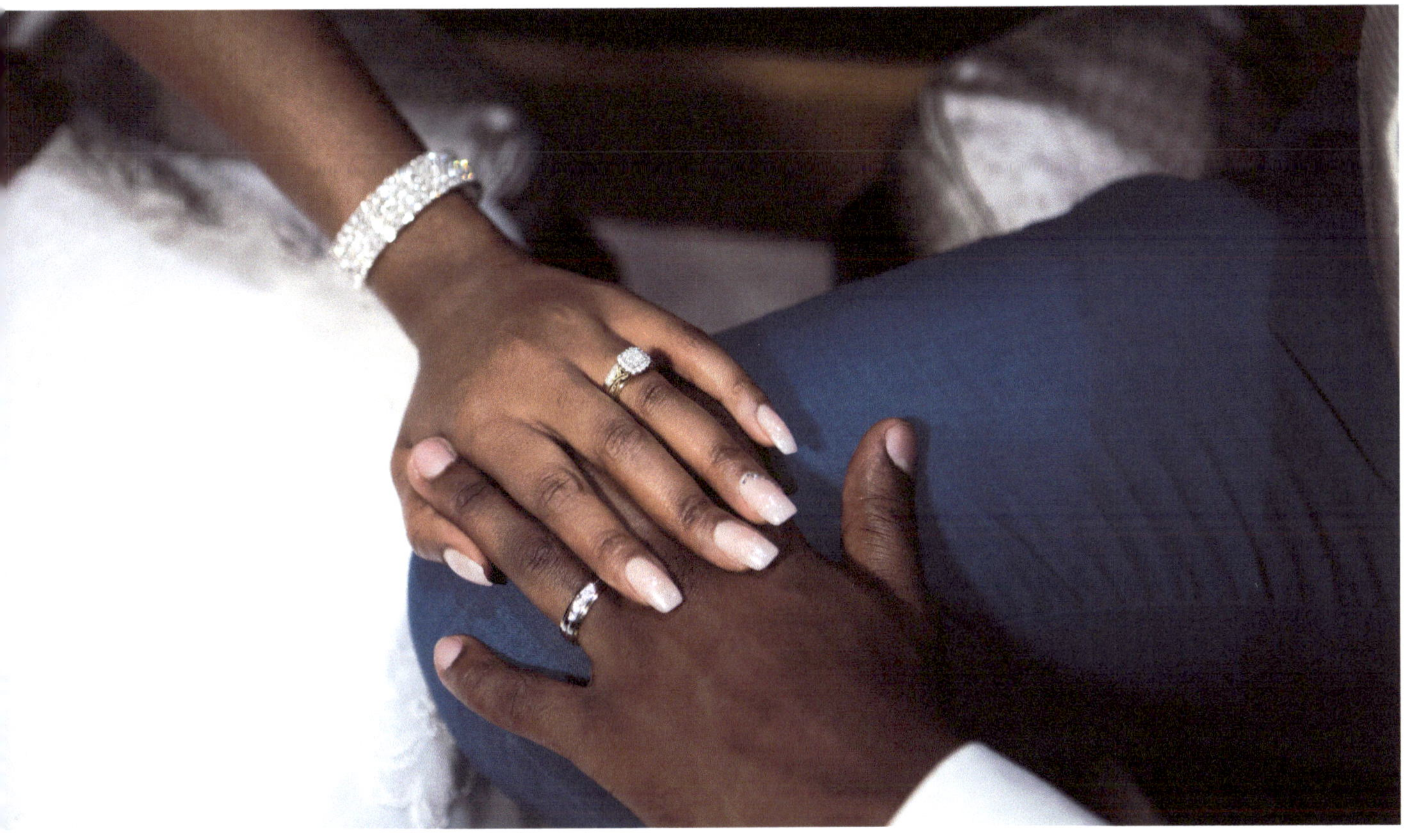

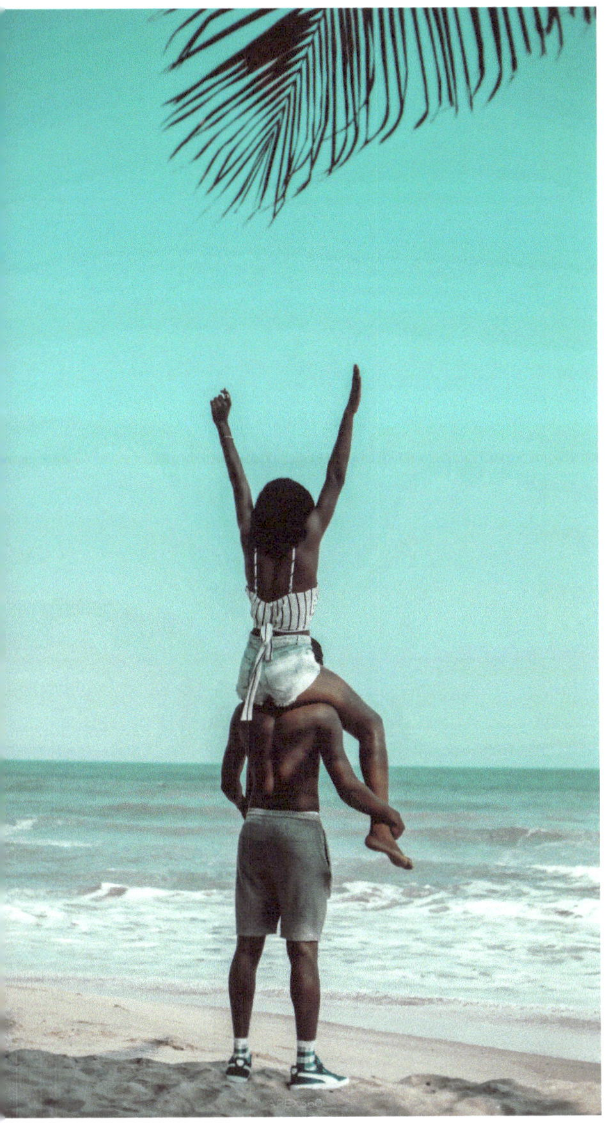

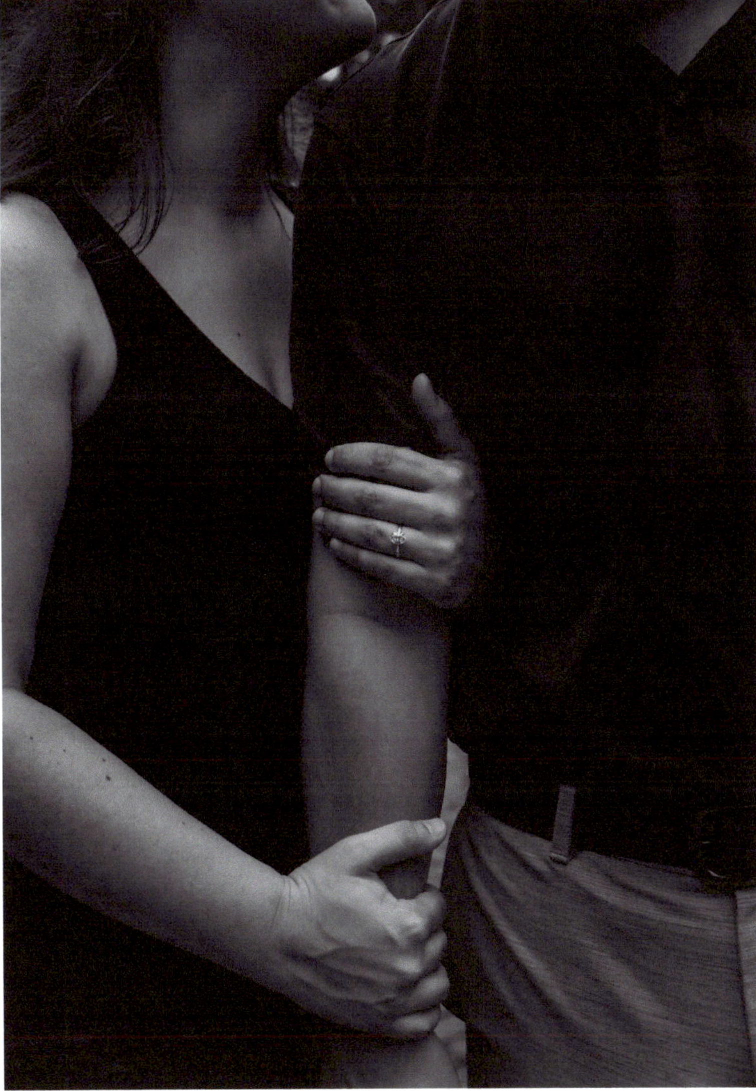

"Trust your intuition and be guided by love."

-Charles Eisenstein

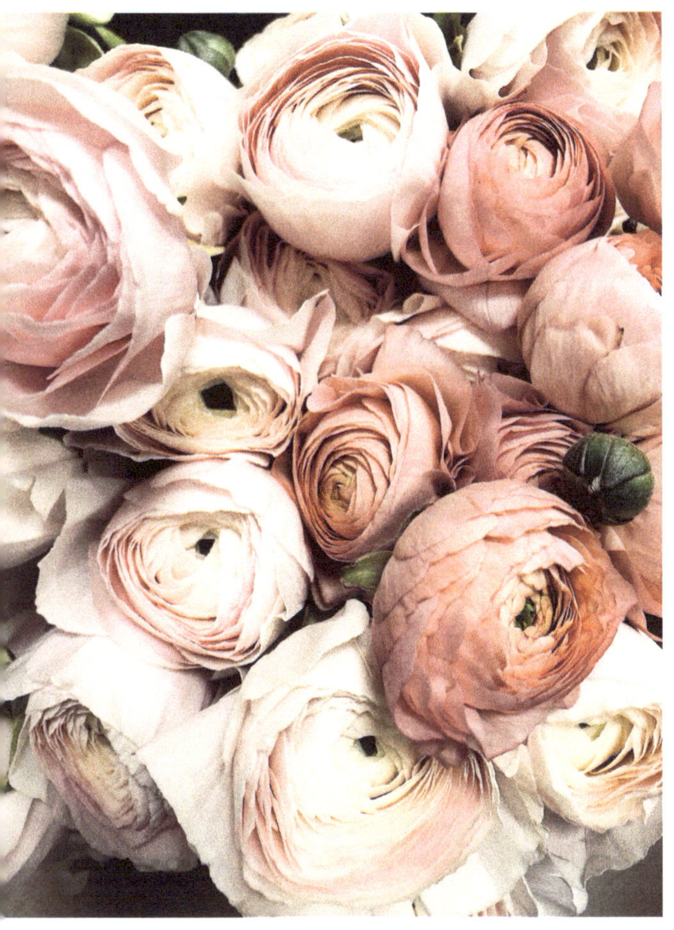
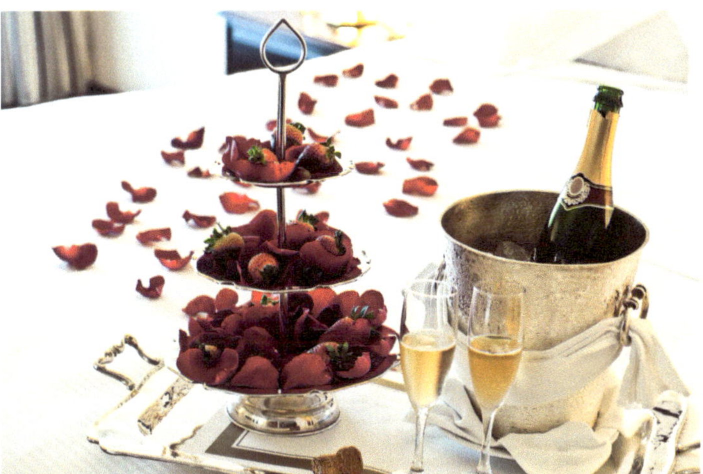
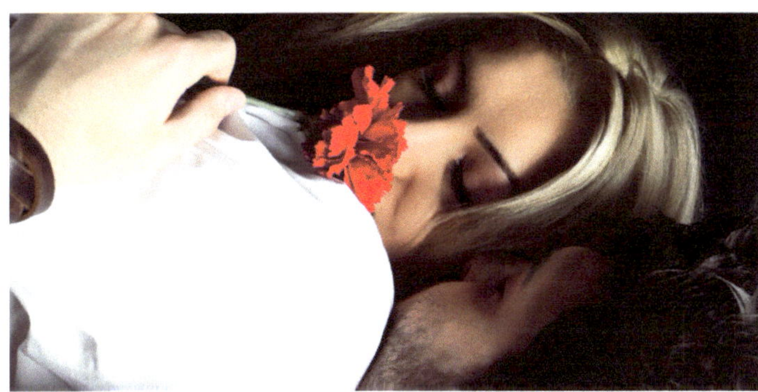
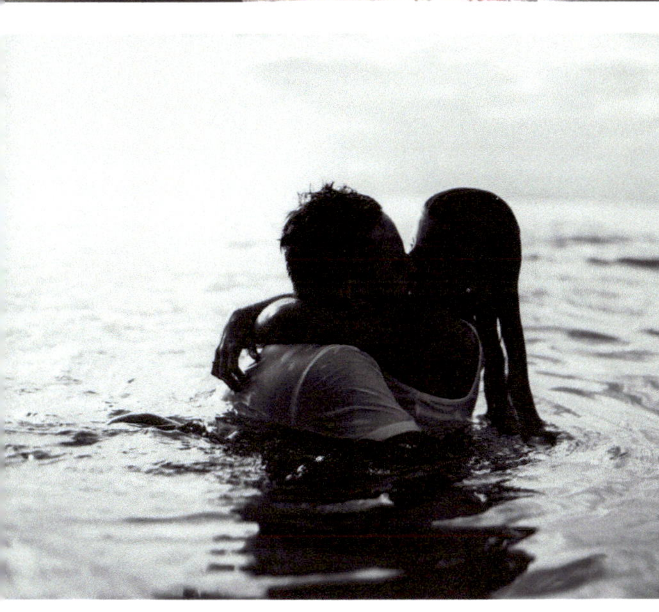
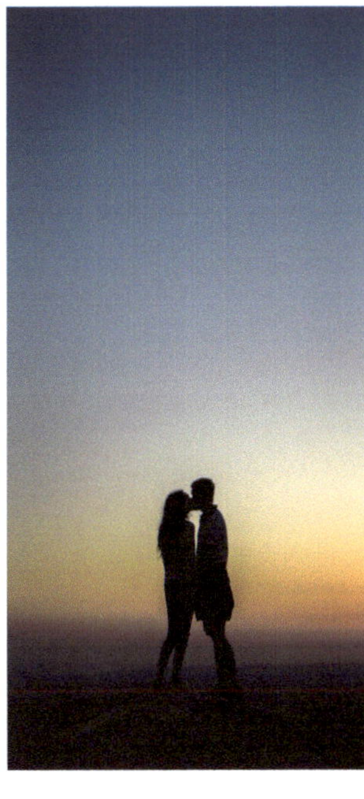
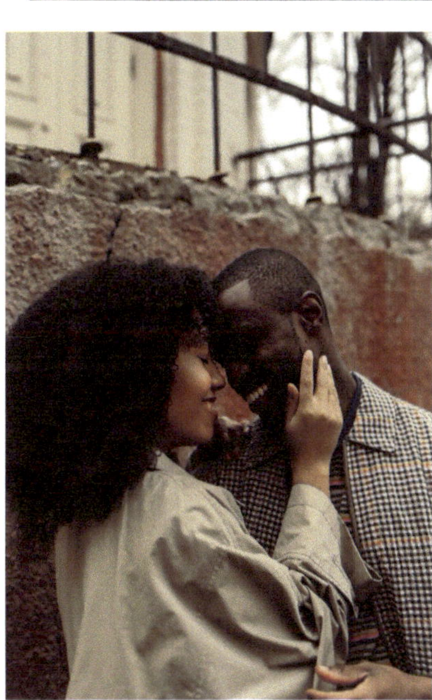

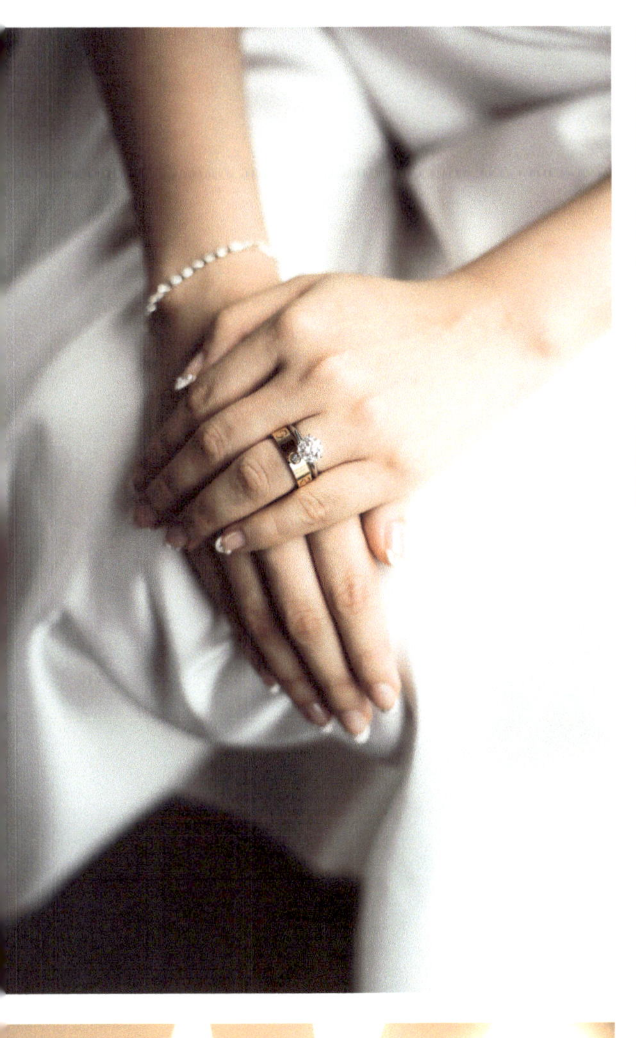
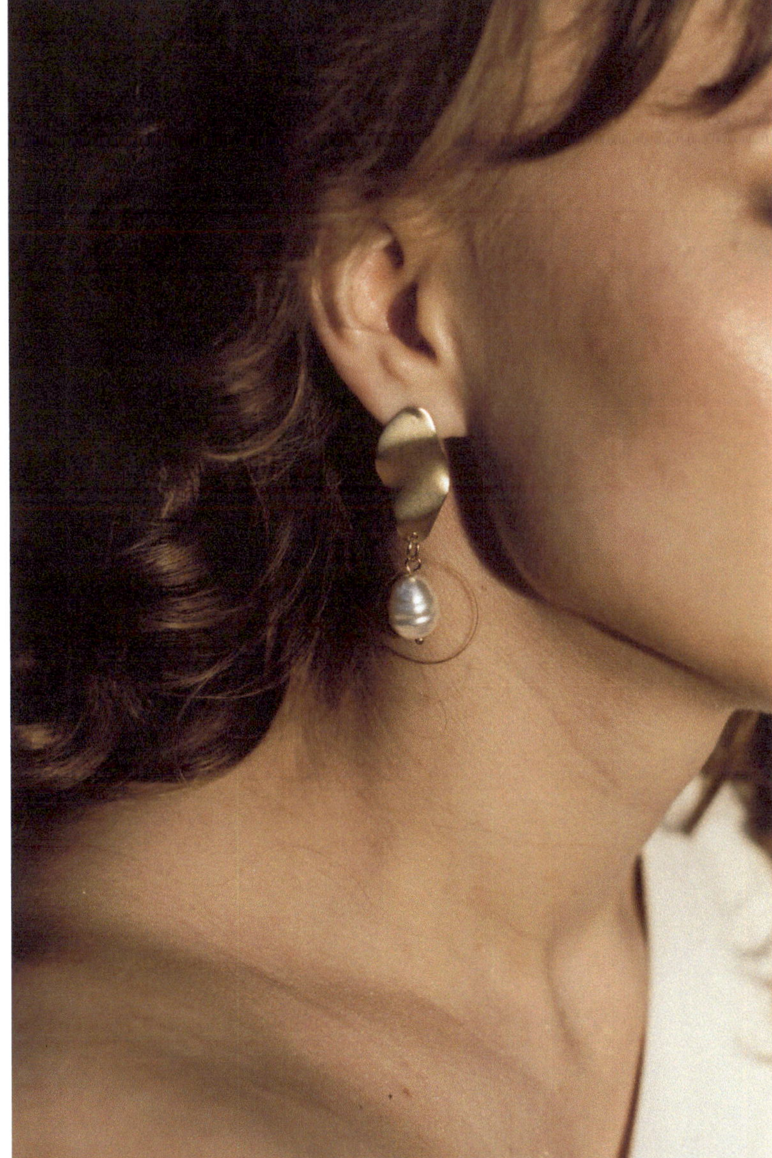
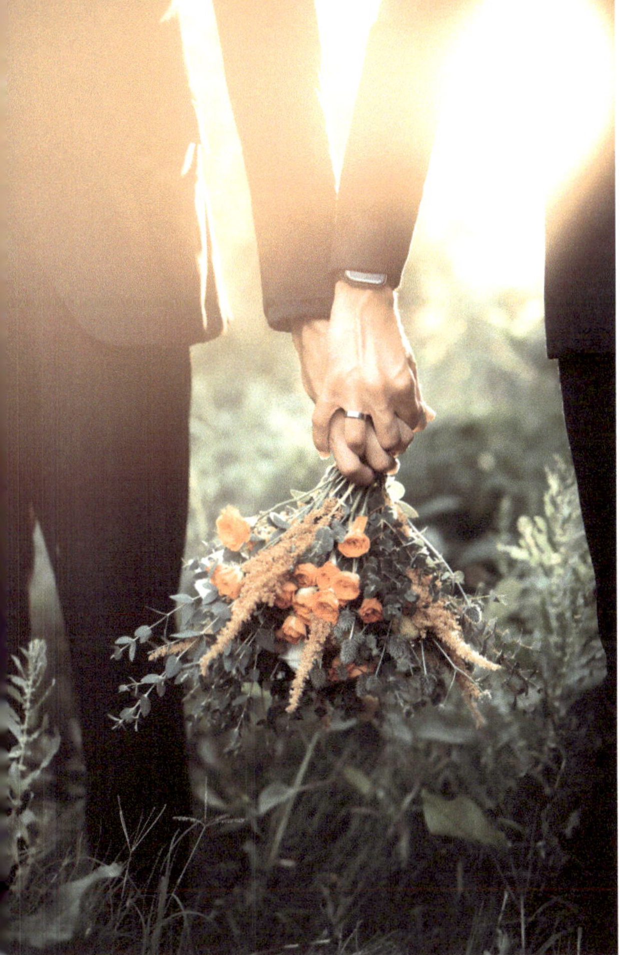
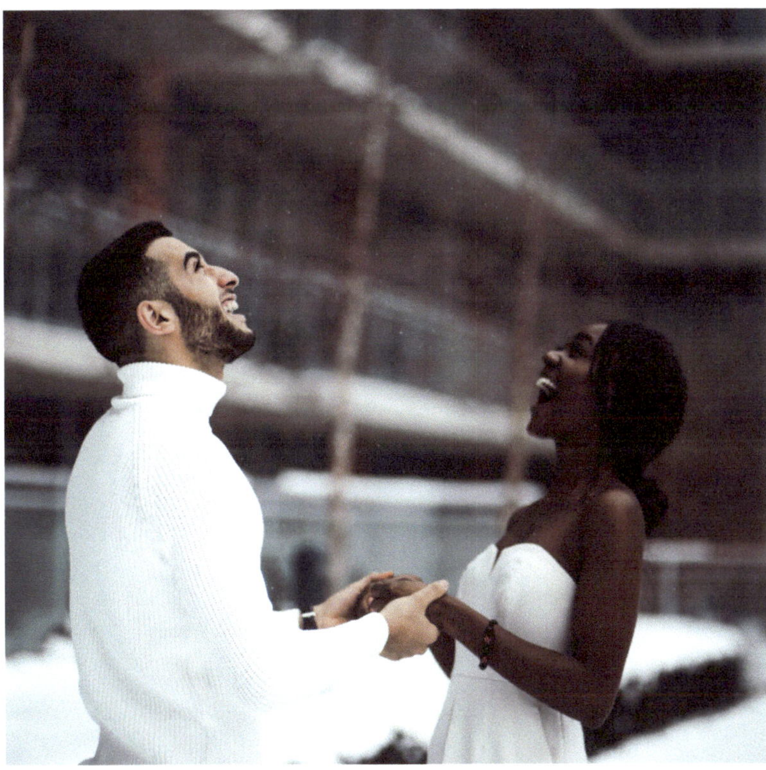

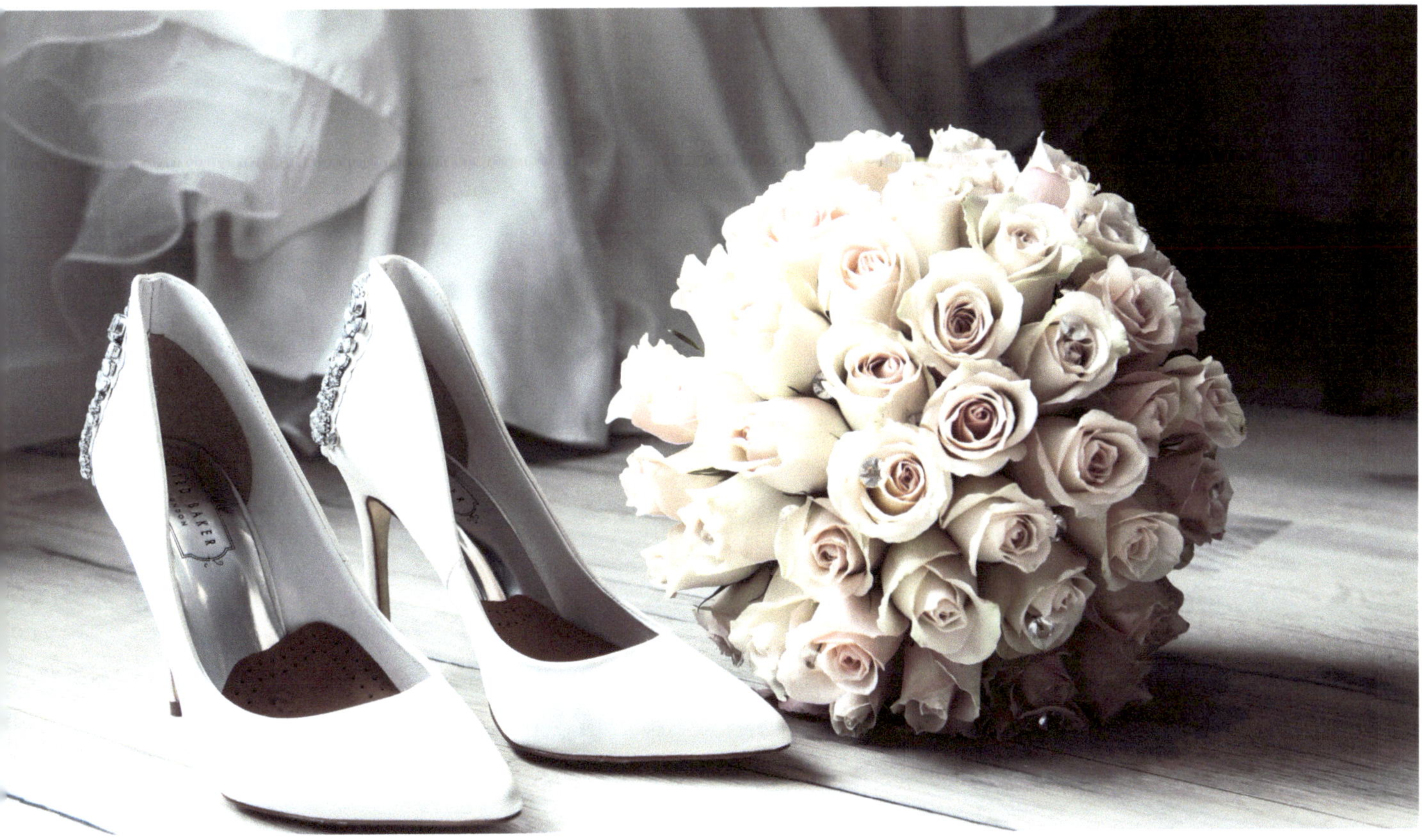

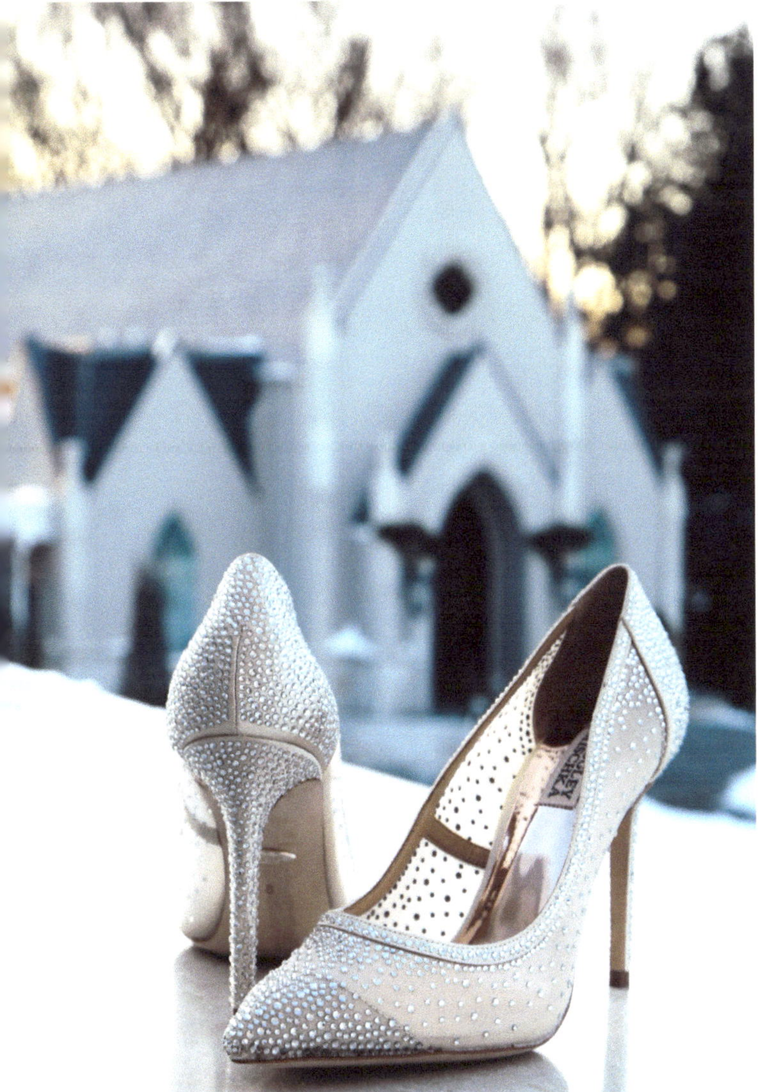

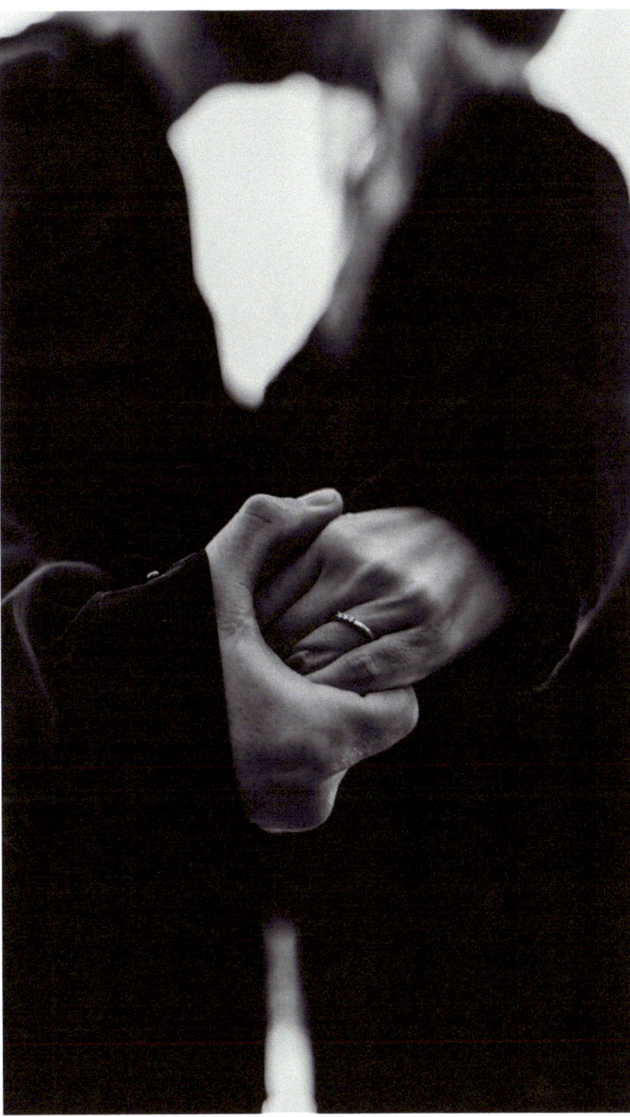

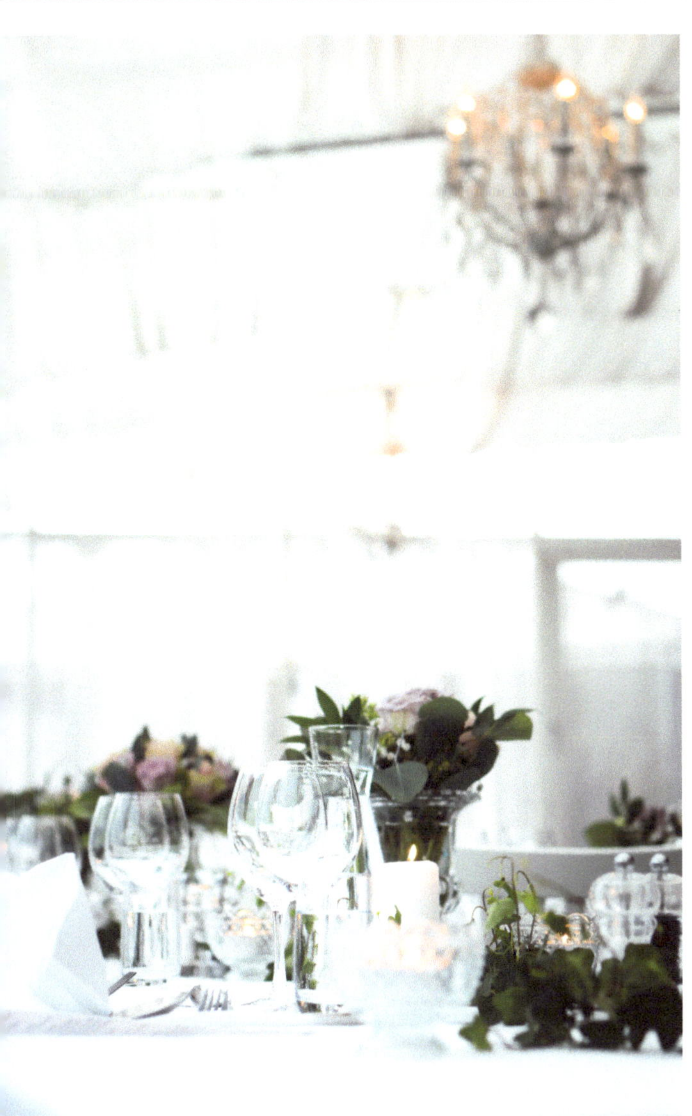
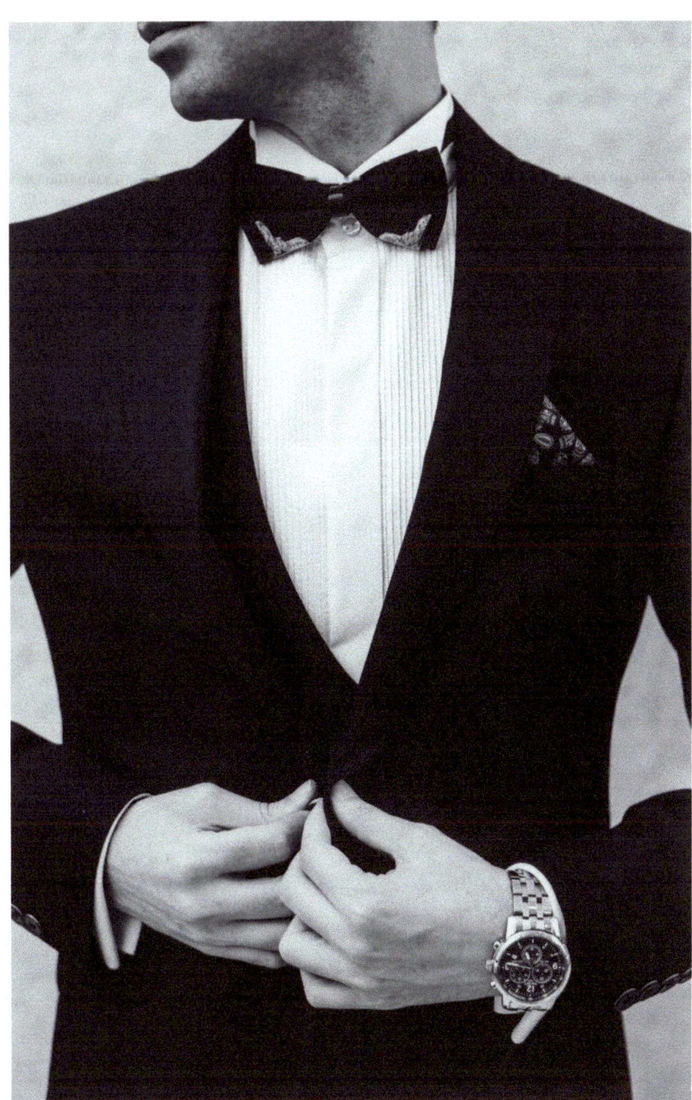
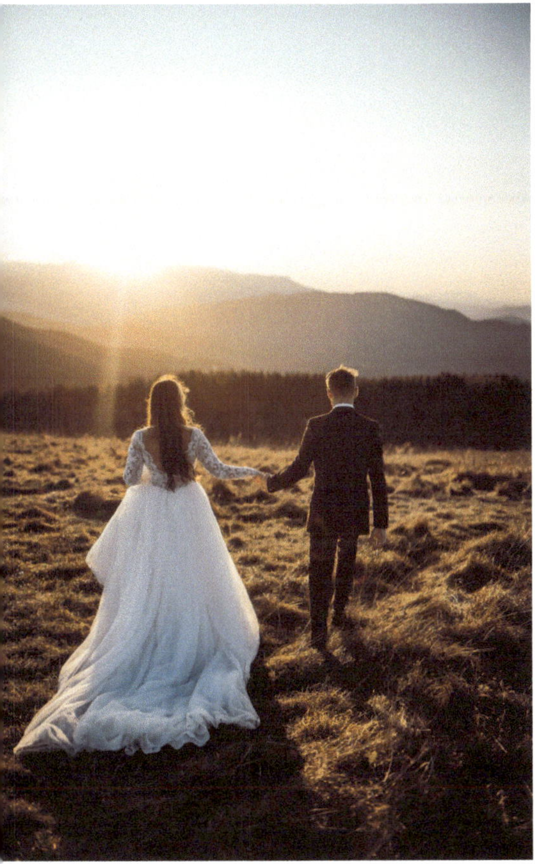
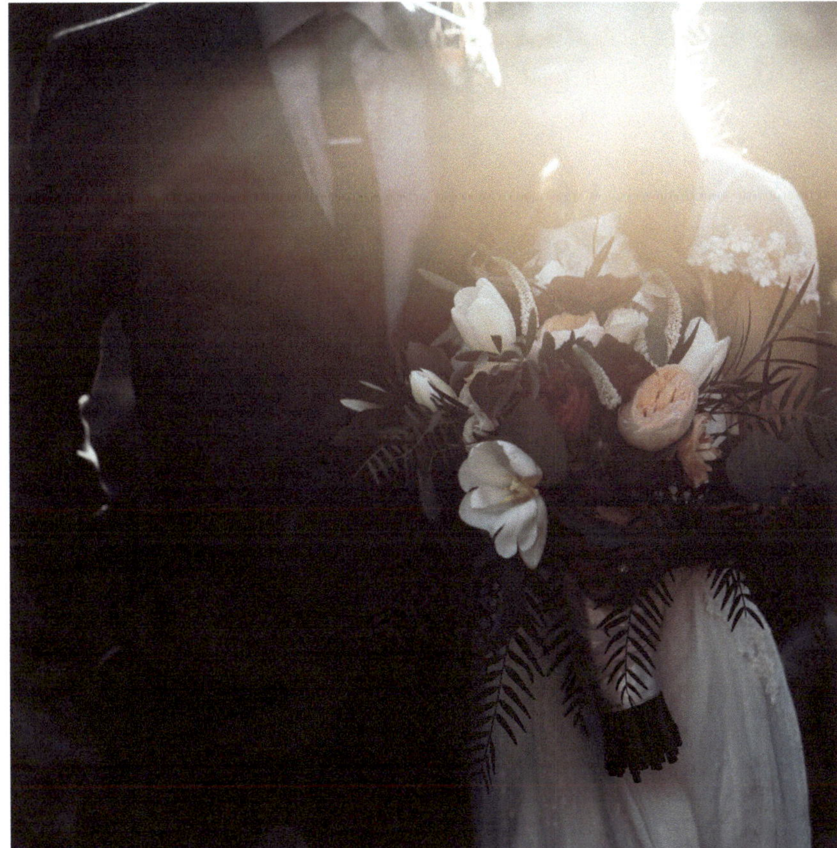

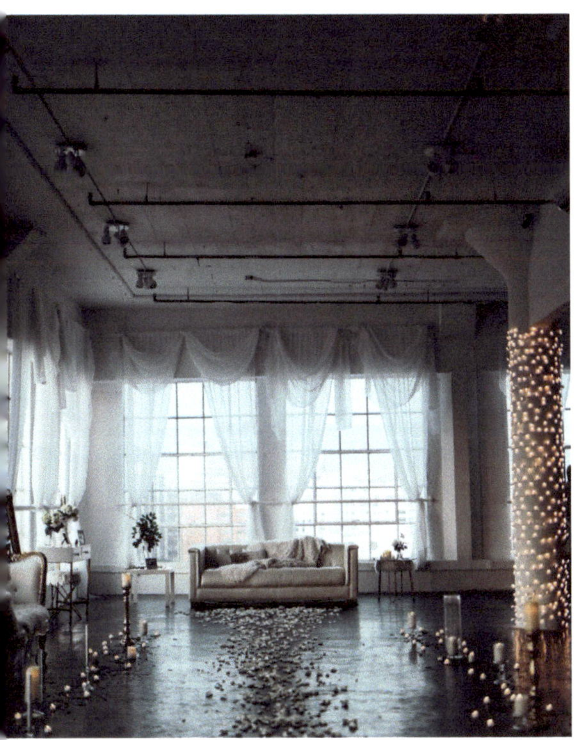

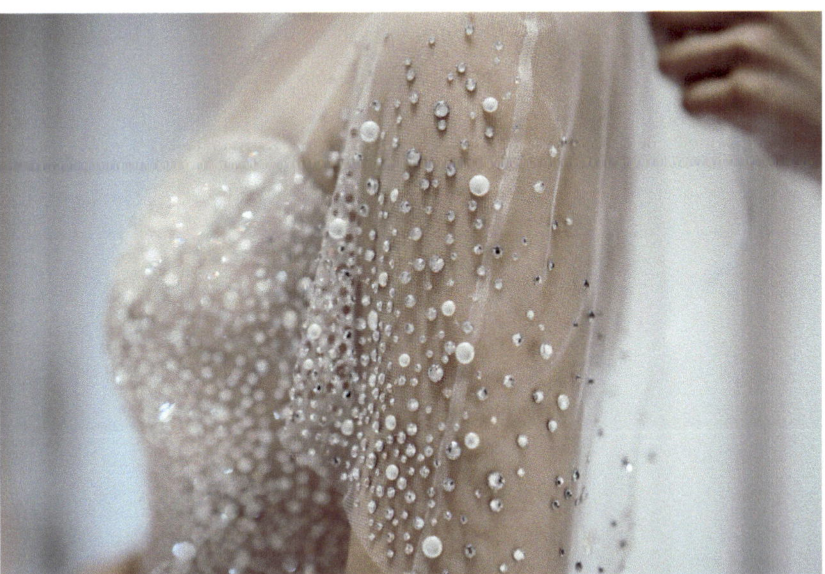

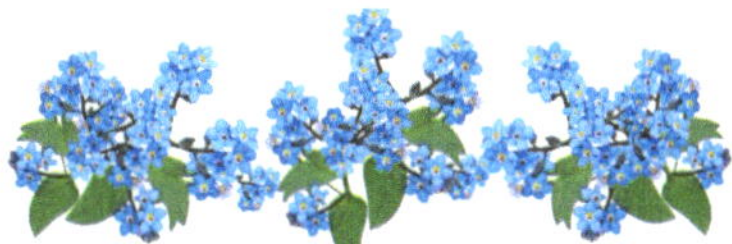

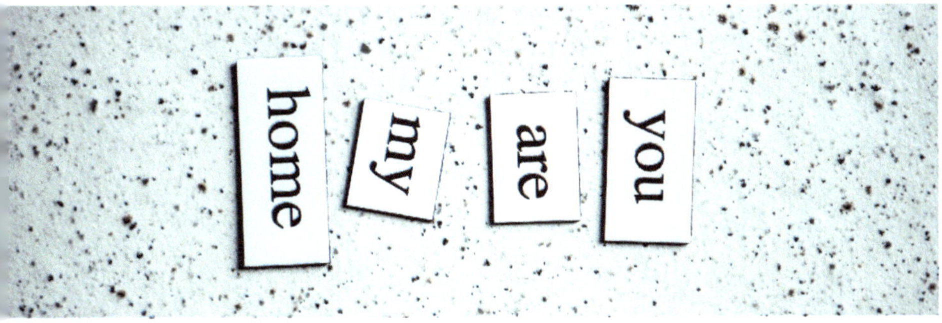

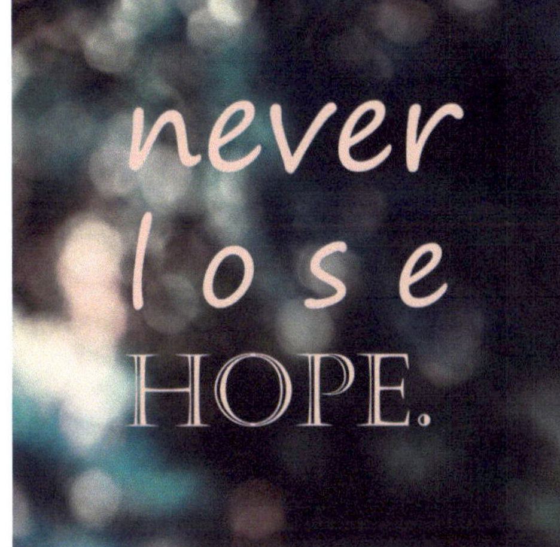
never
lose
HOPE.

you
are
my
home

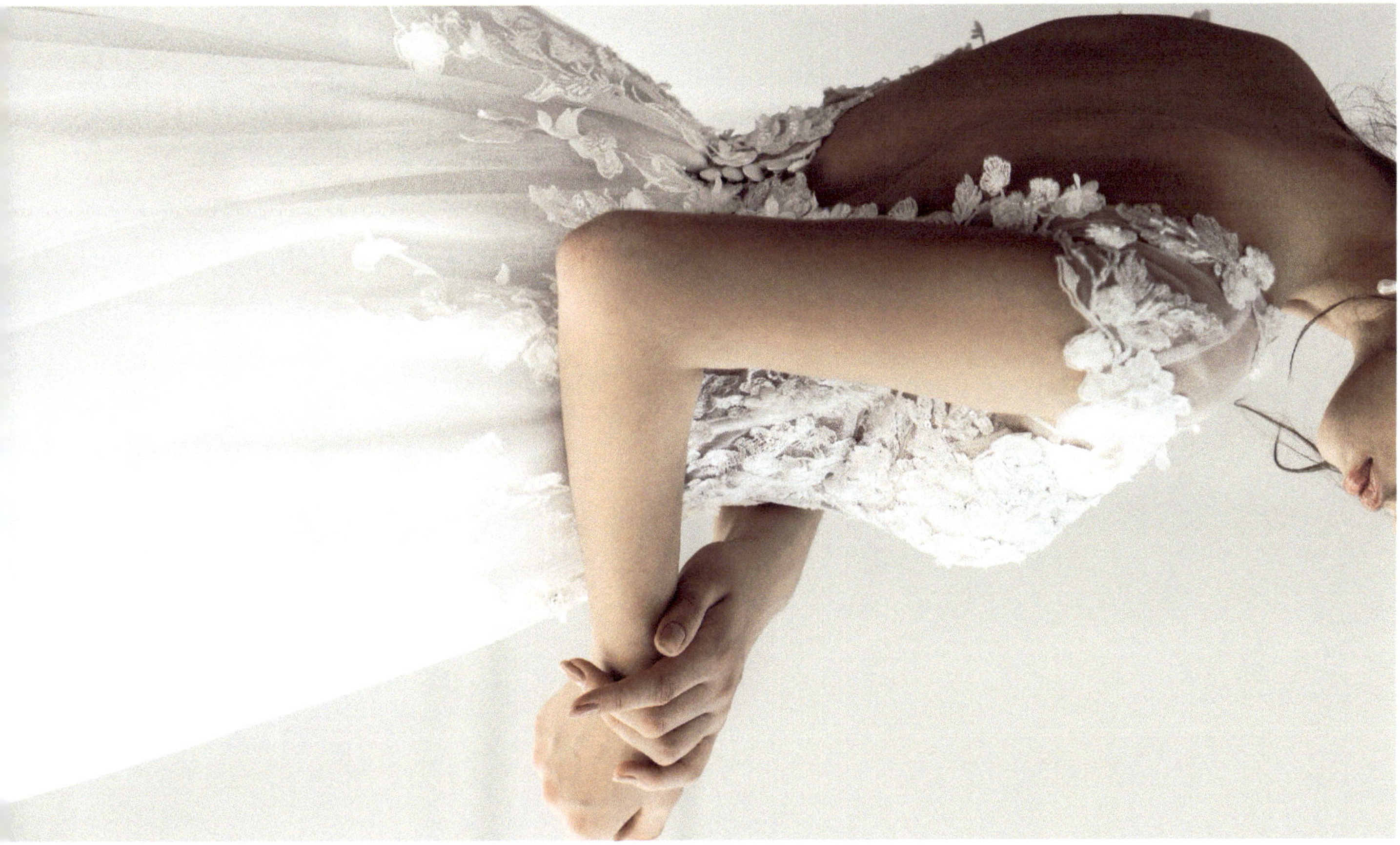

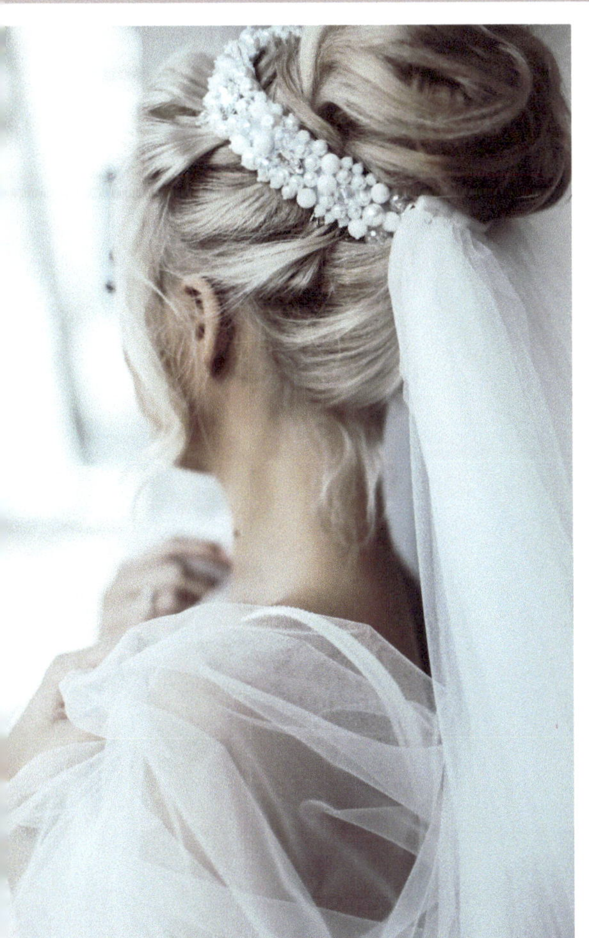
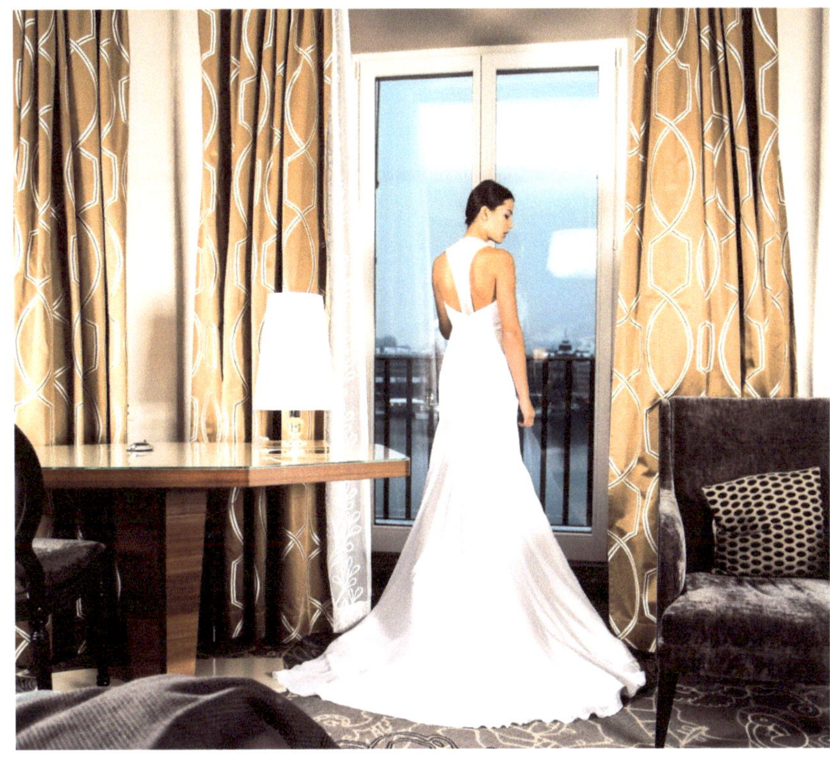
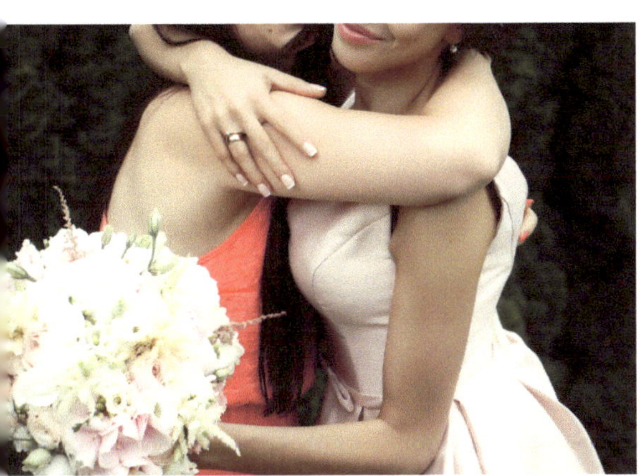
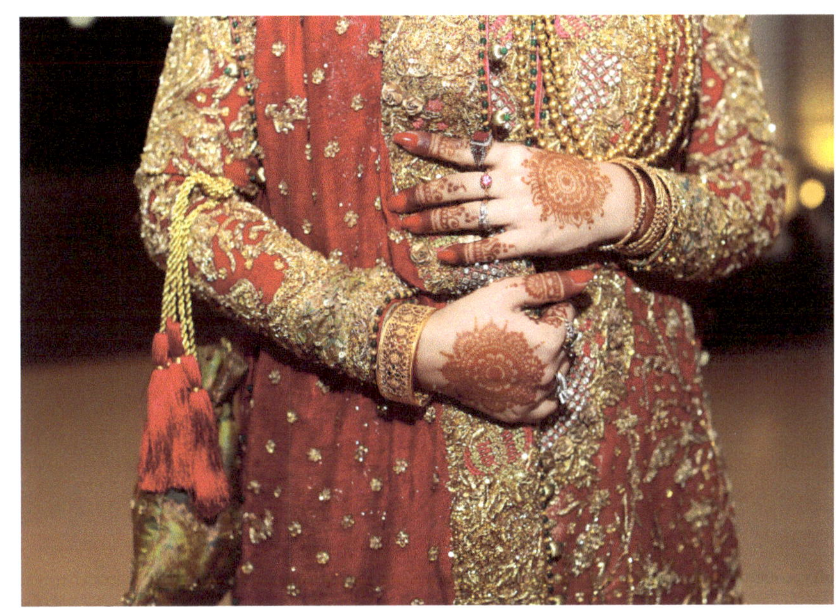
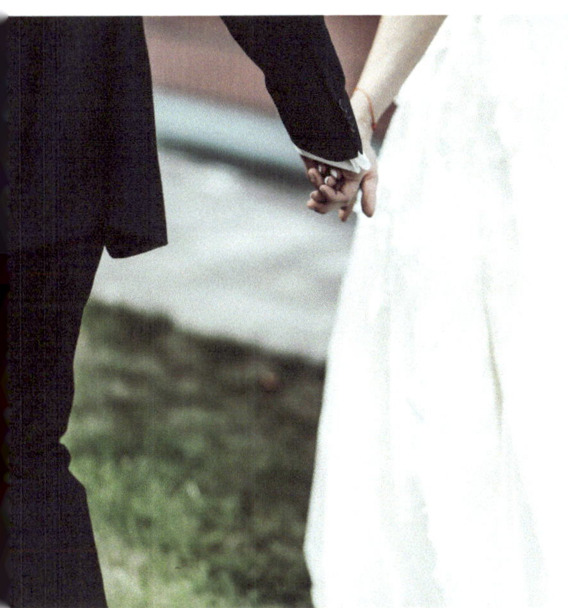
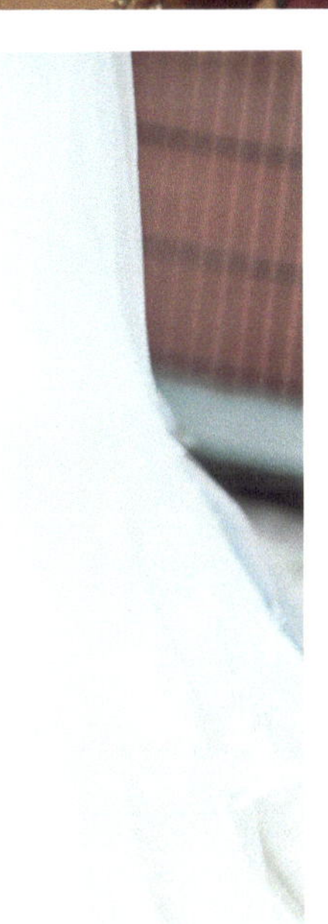
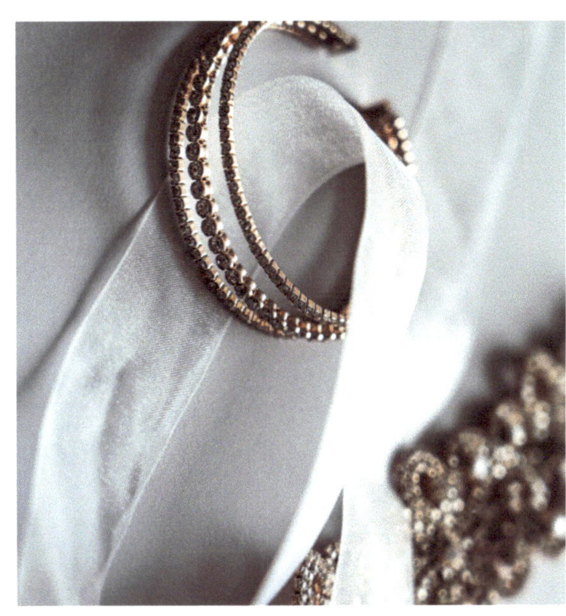

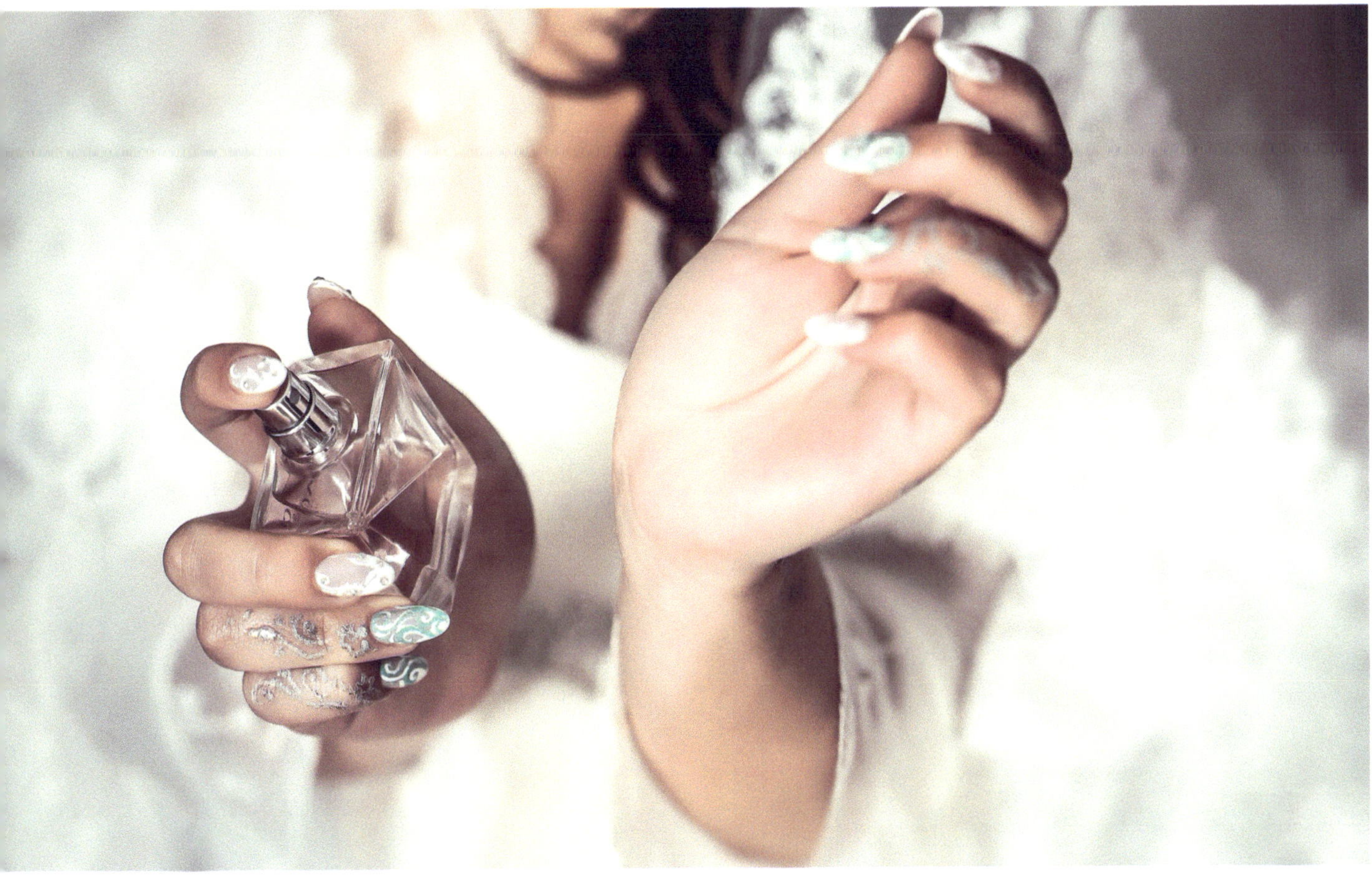

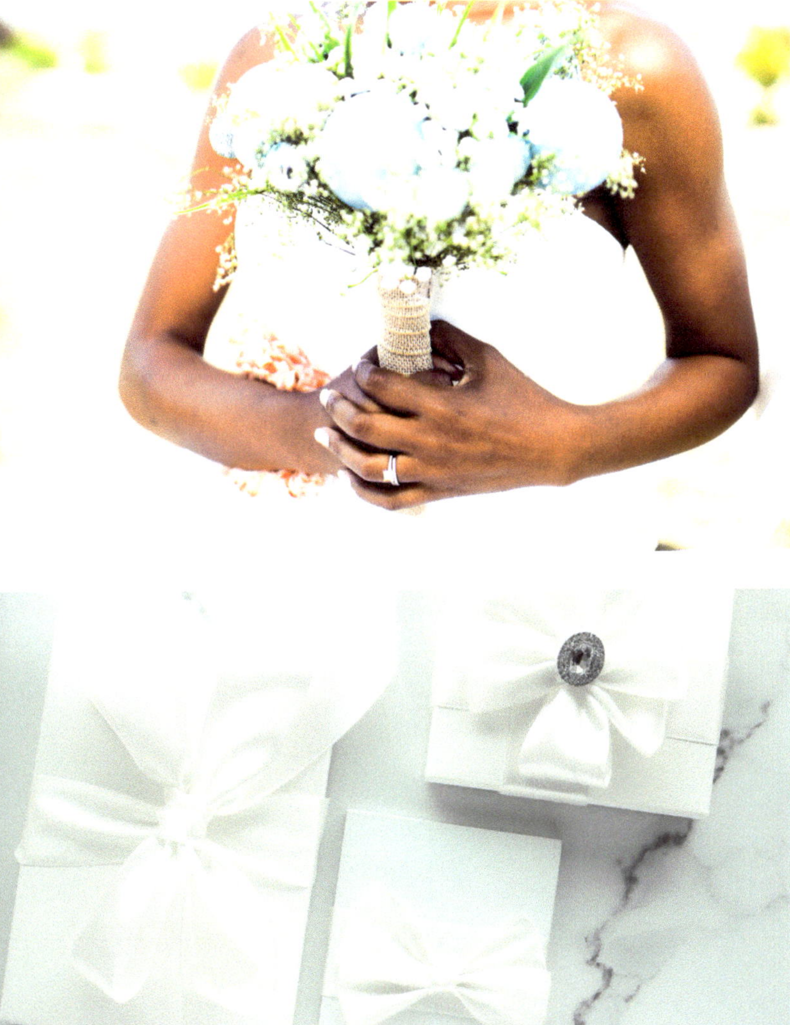

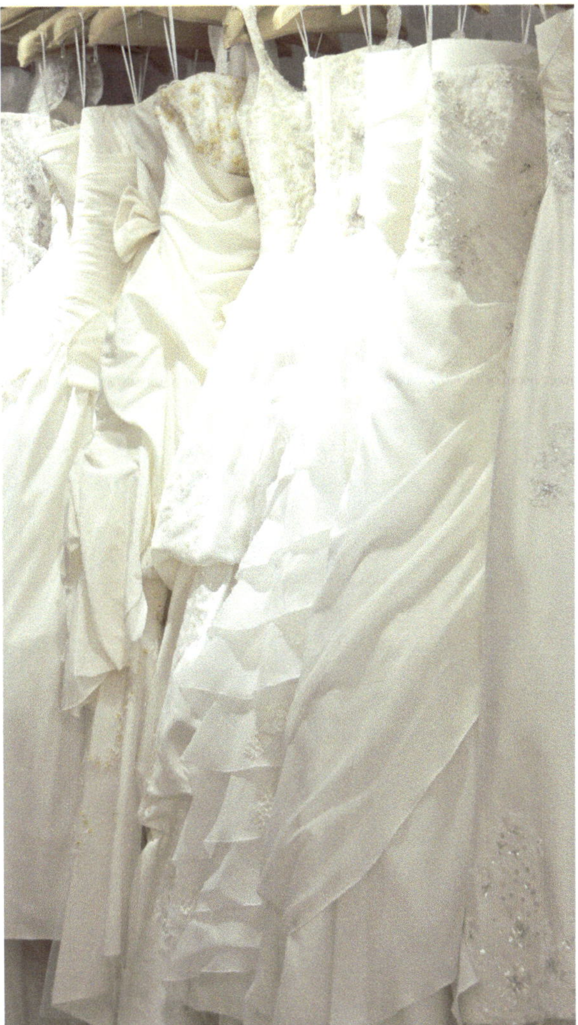

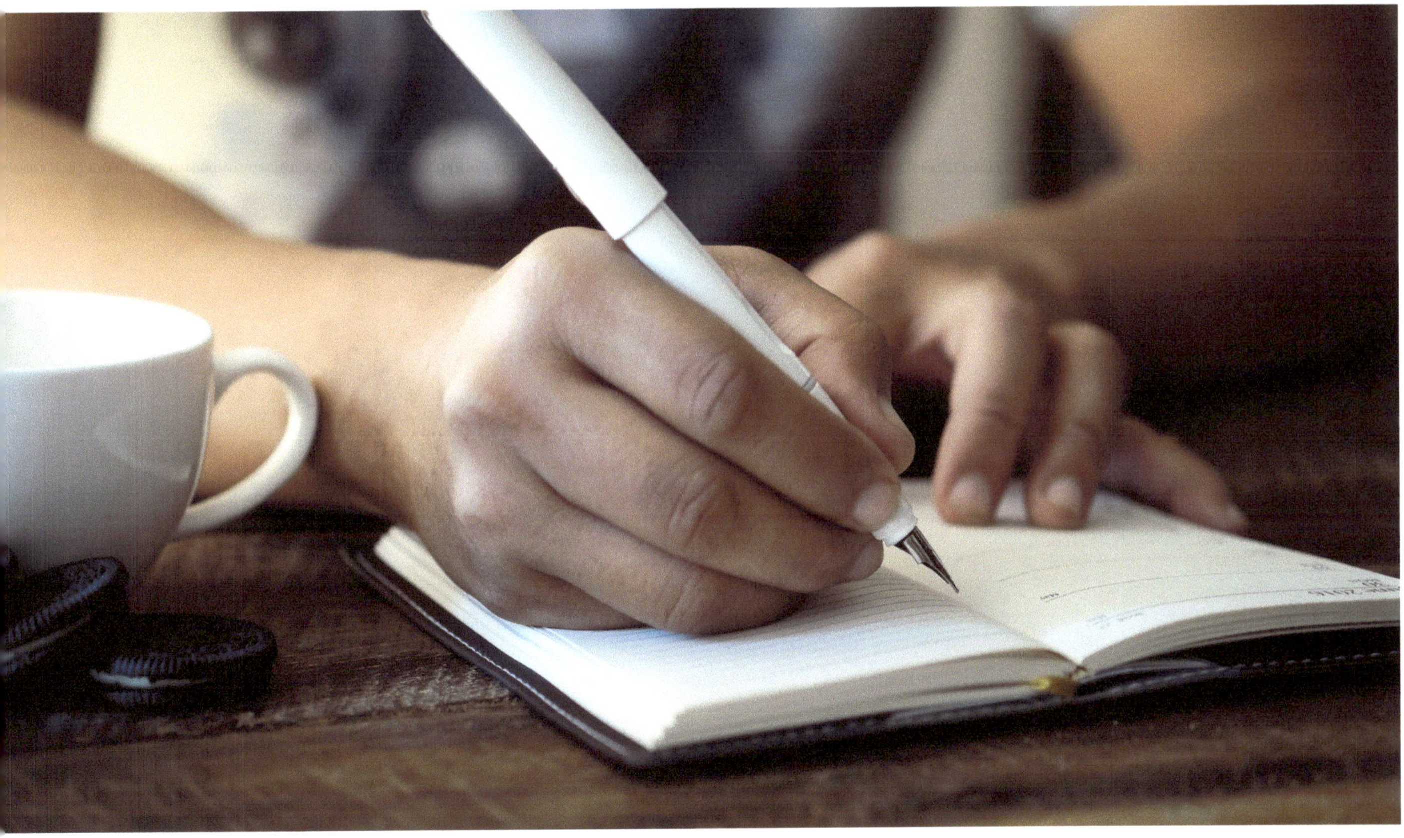

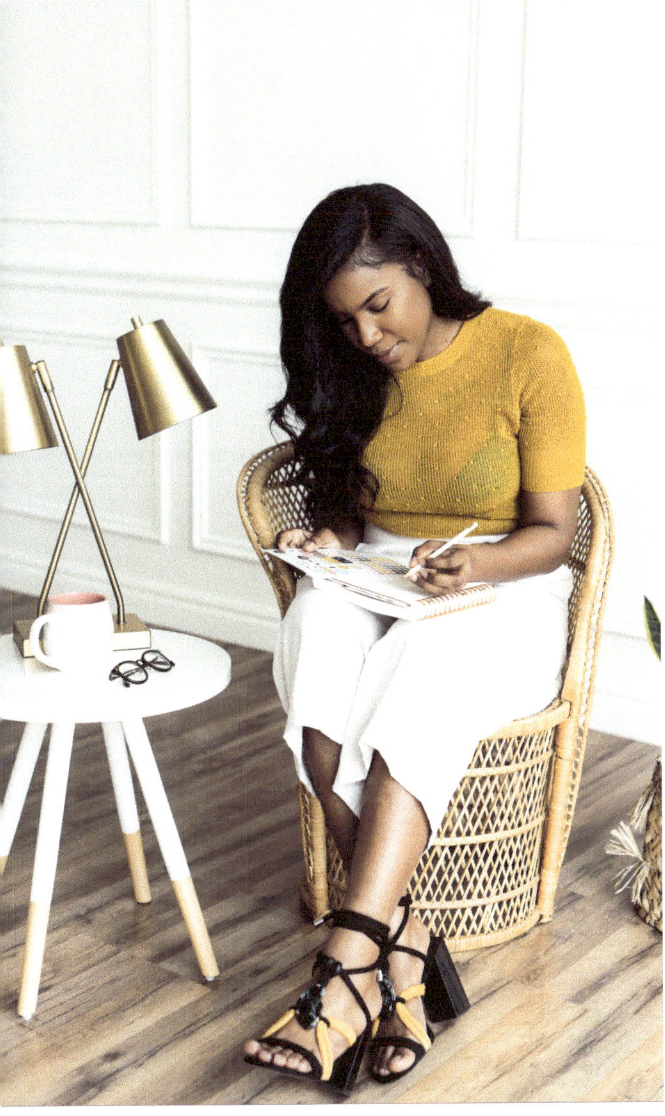

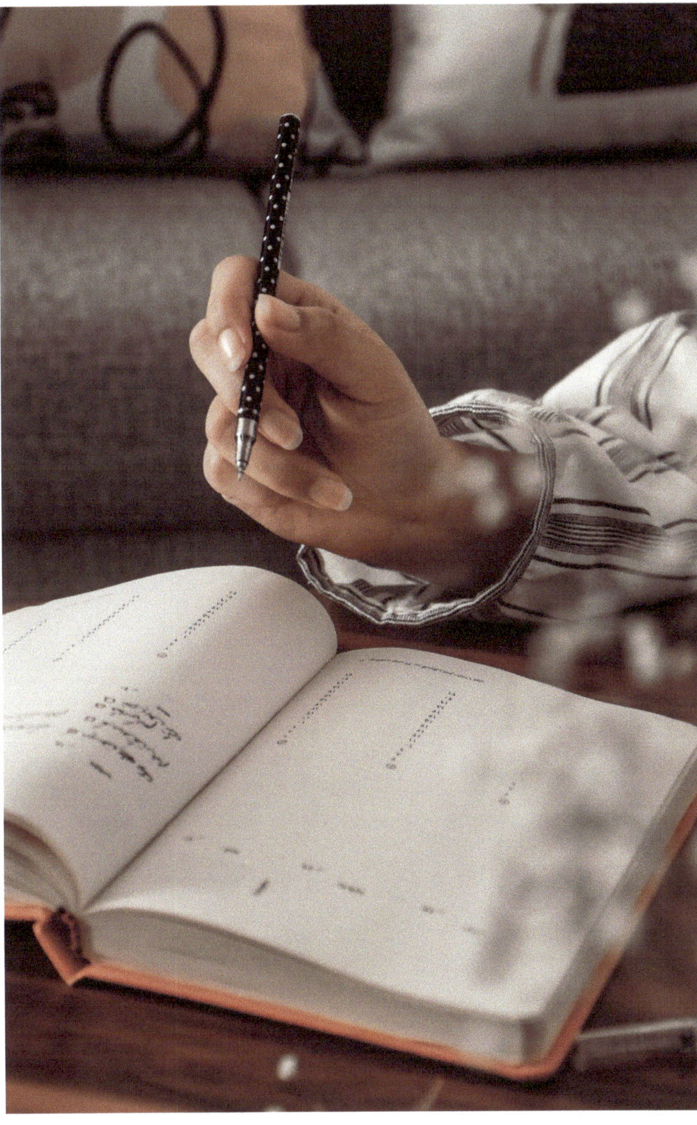

A journal is your completely unaltered voice."

-Lucy Dacus

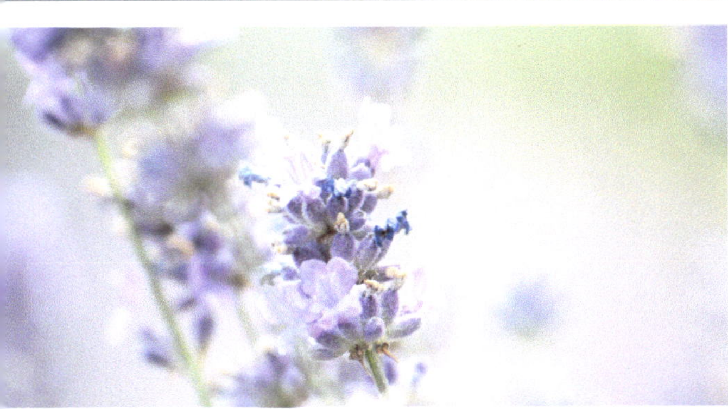

"A goal without a plan is just a wish."

-Antoine de Saint-Exupery

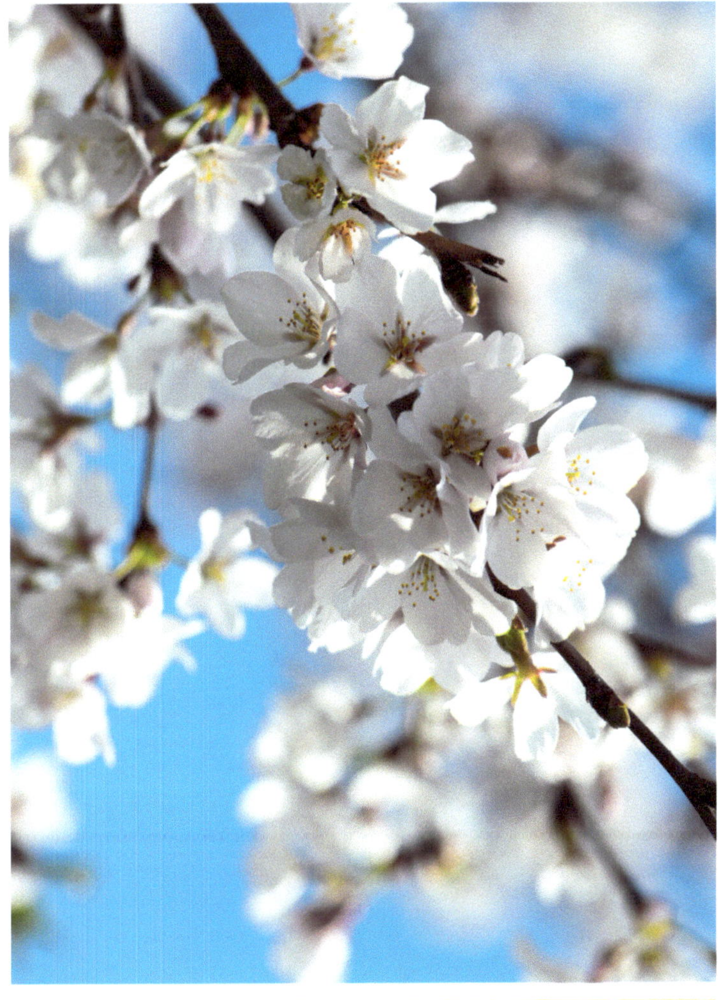

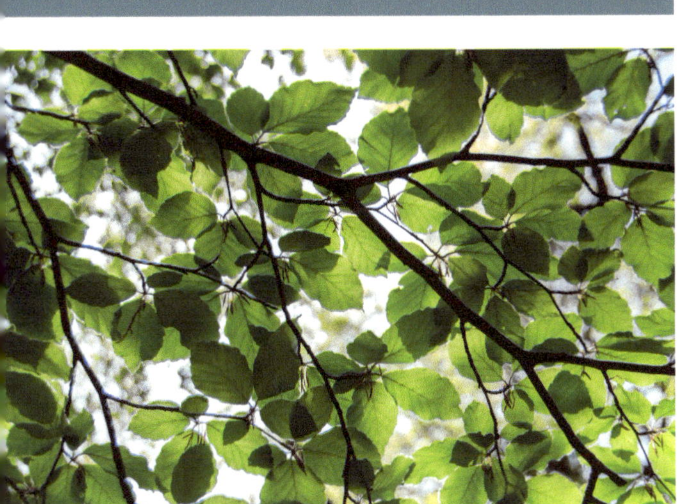

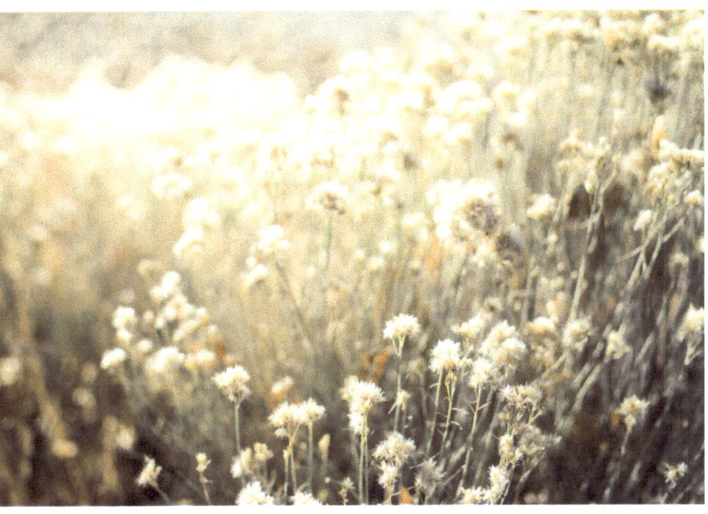

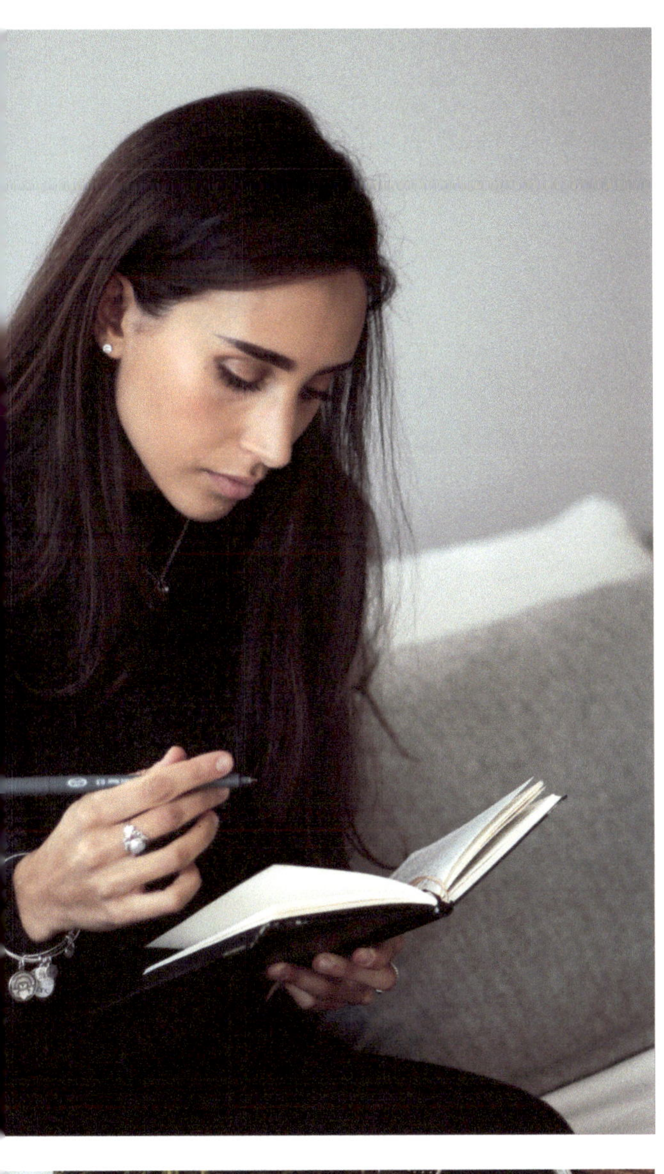

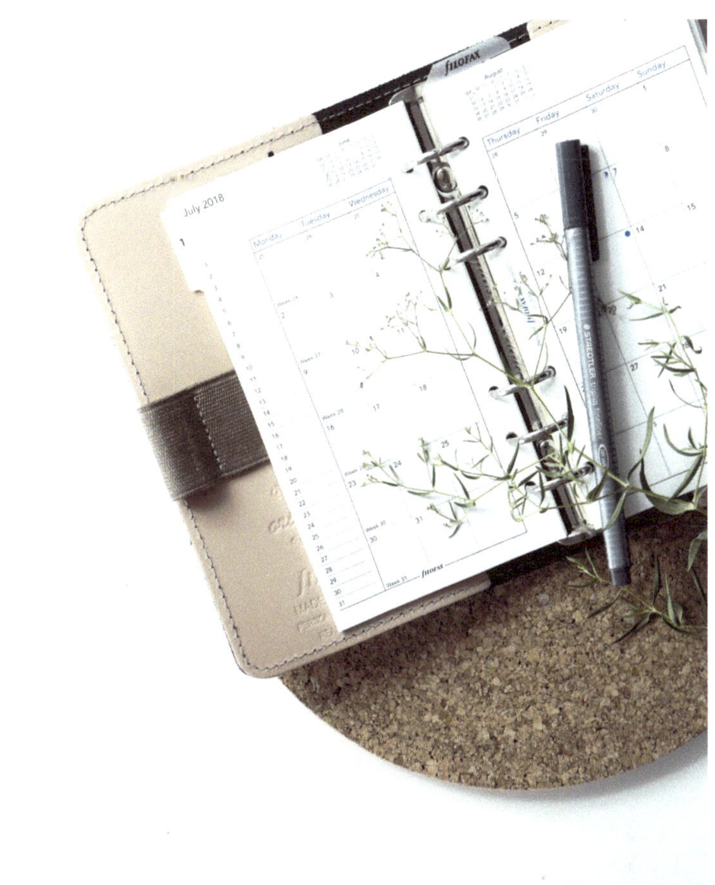
filofax
July 2018

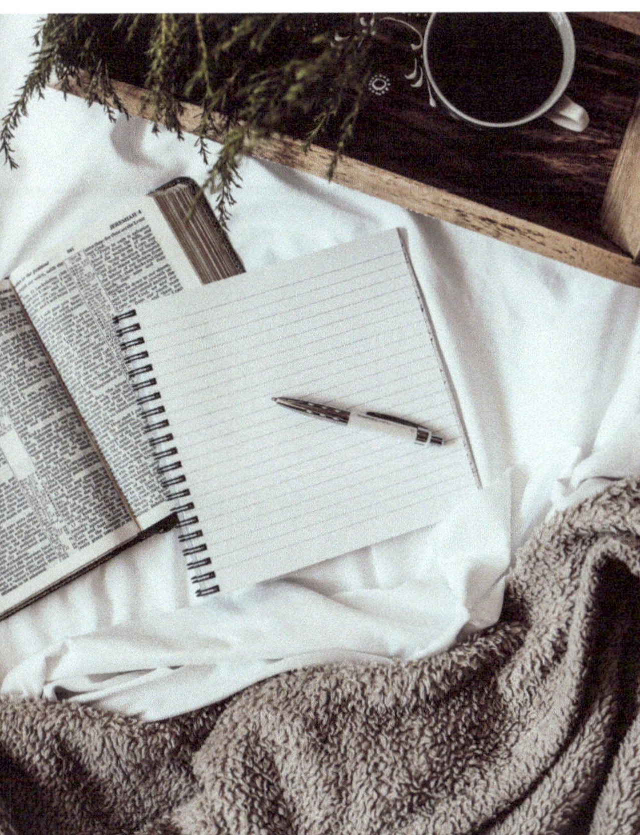

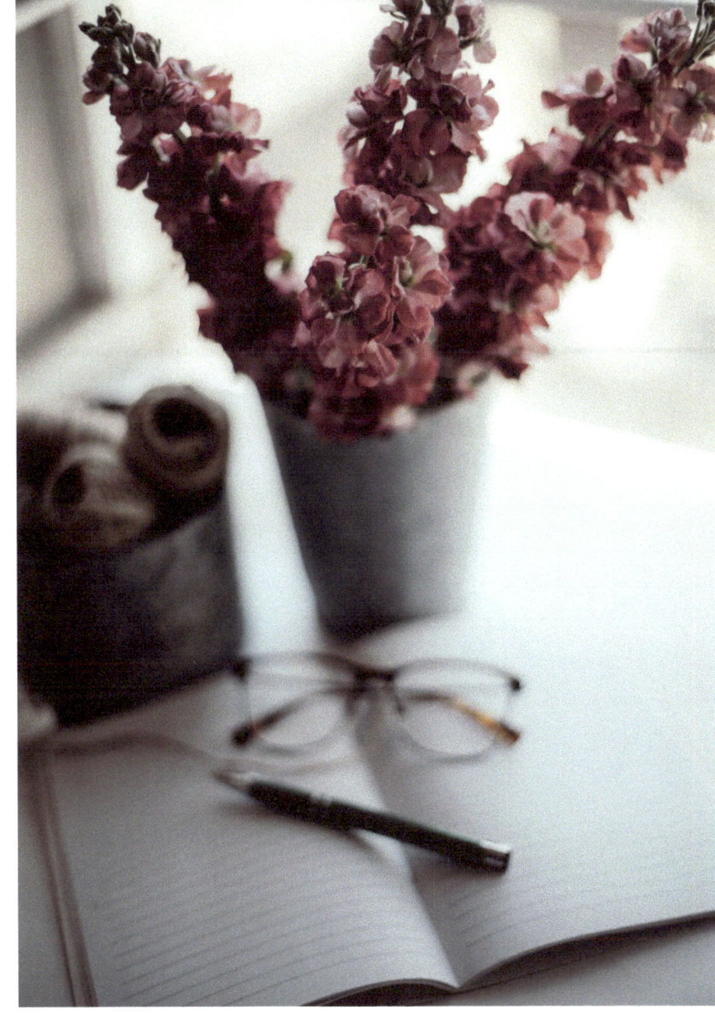

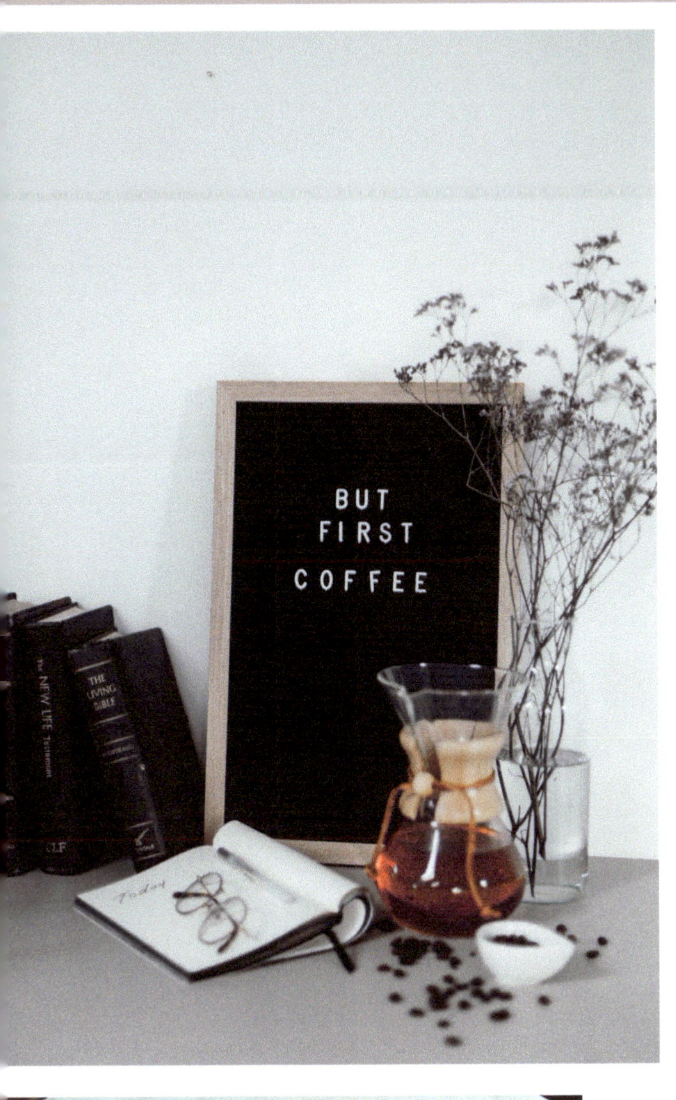
BUT
FIRST
COFFEE

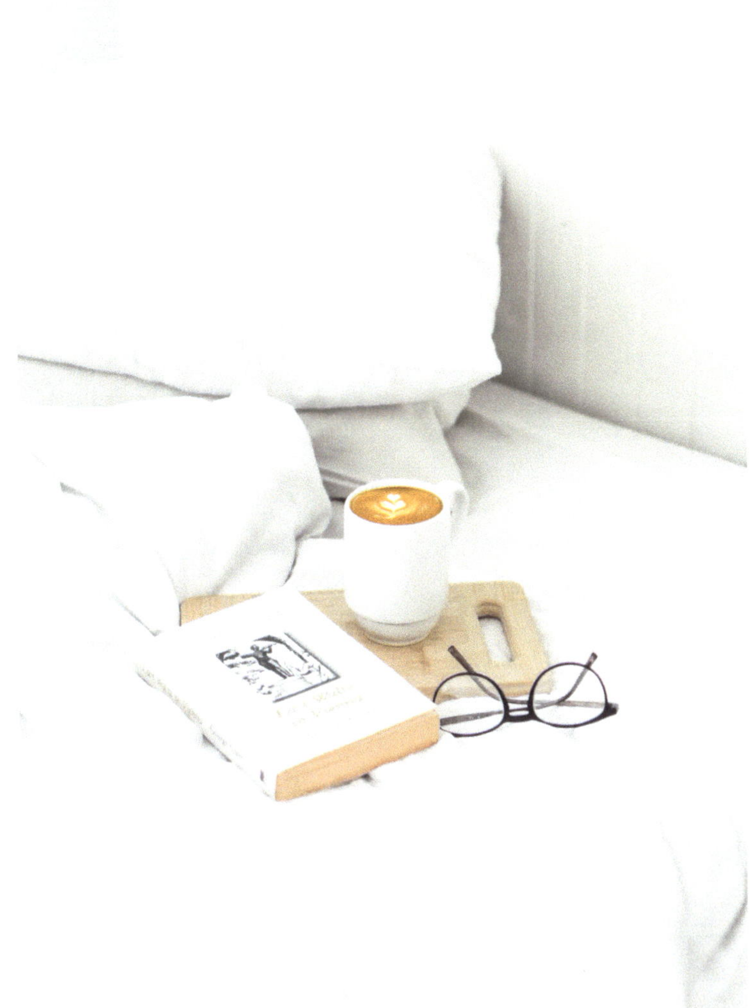

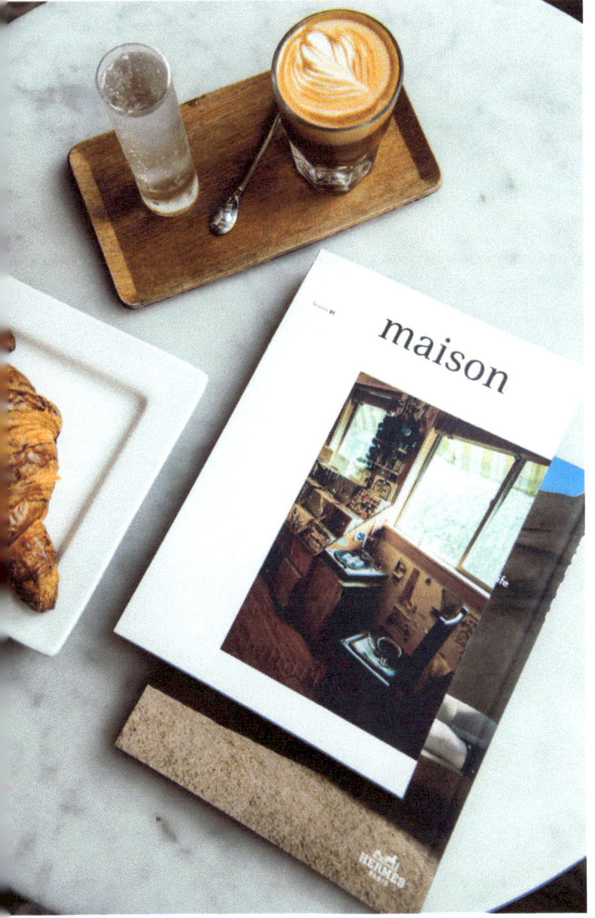
maison

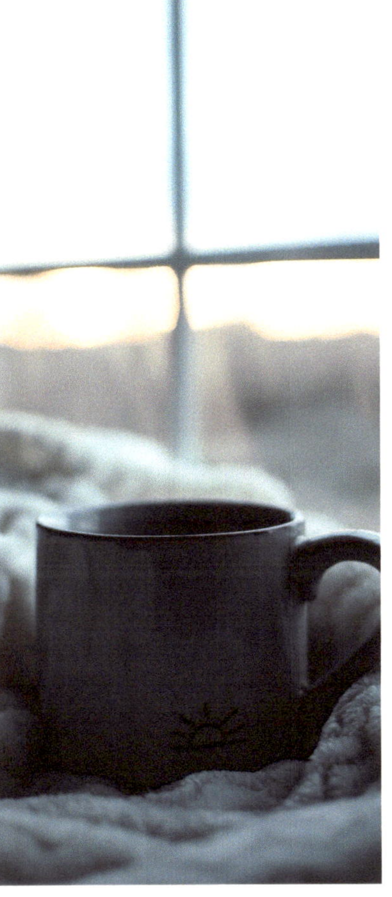

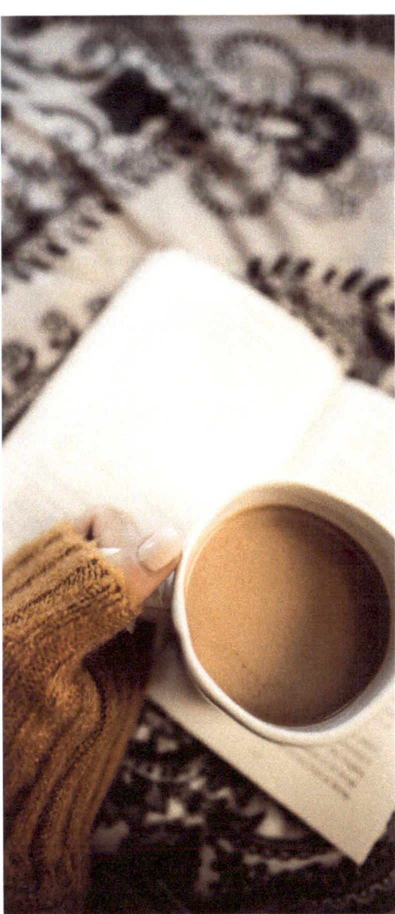

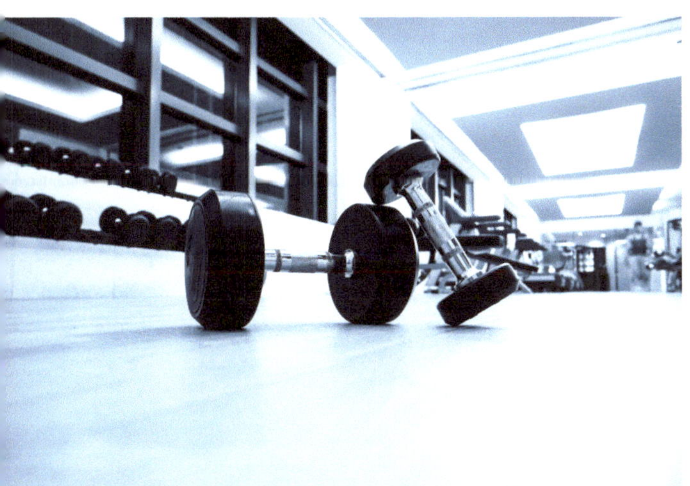

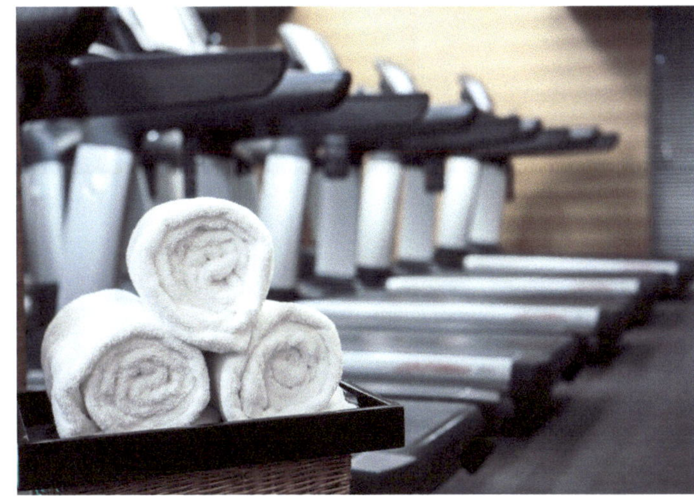

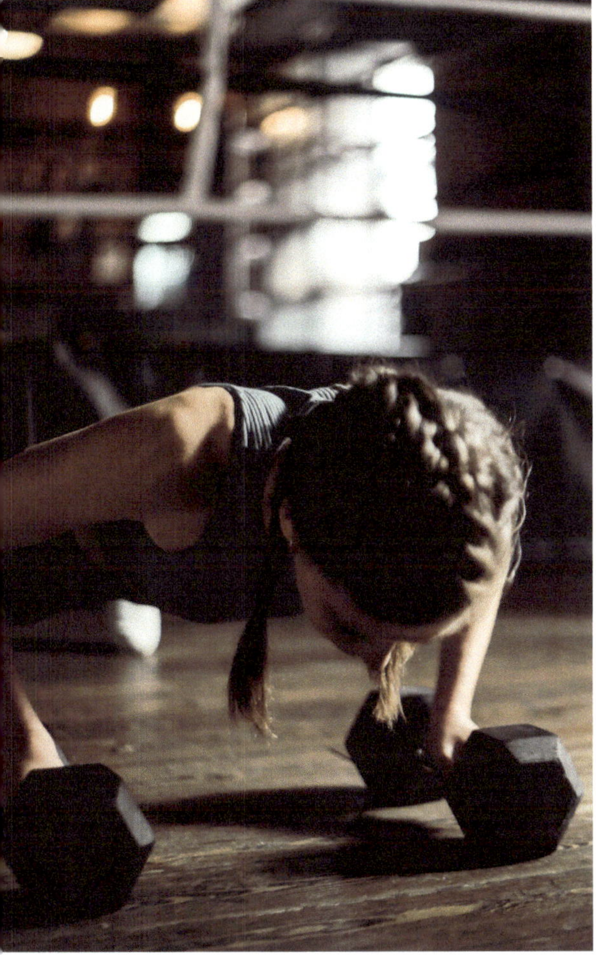

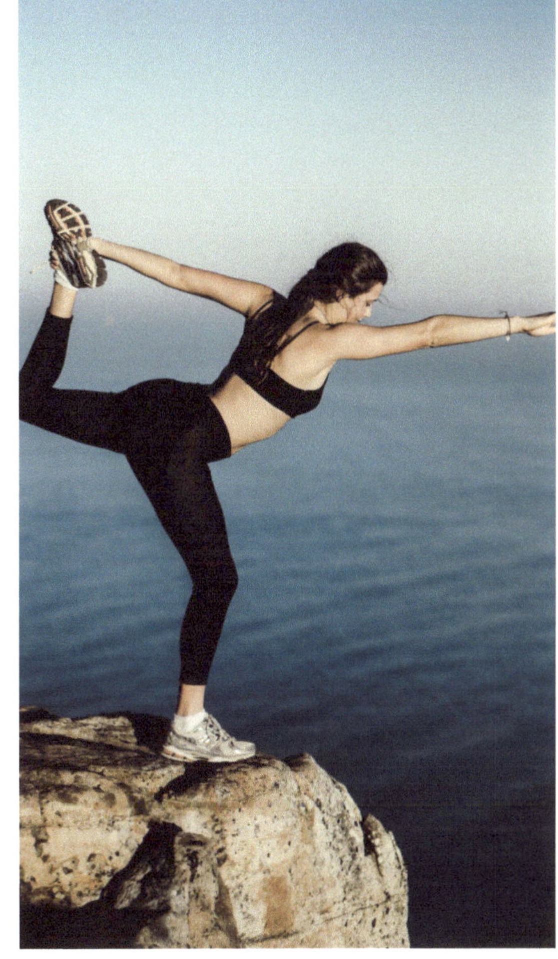

Mind, Body, Spirit

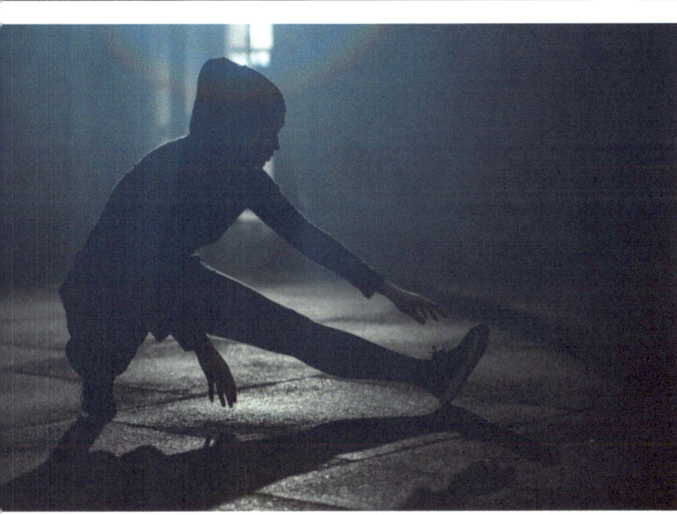

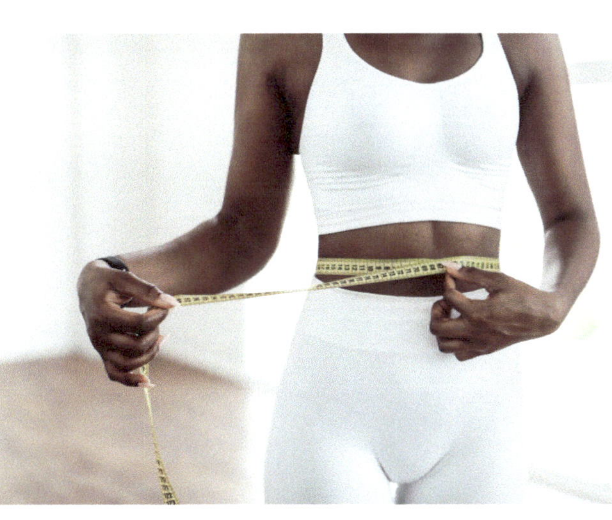

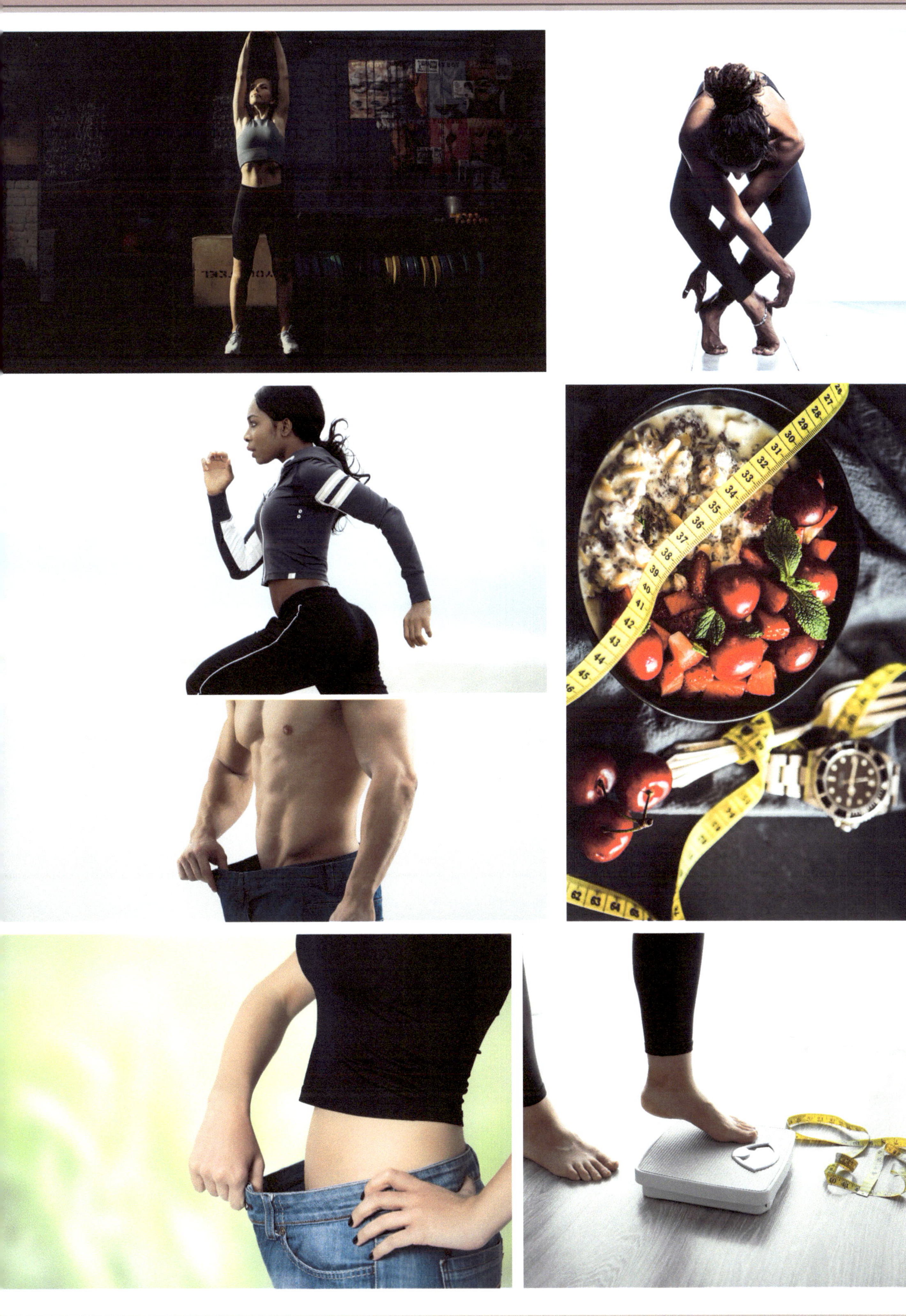

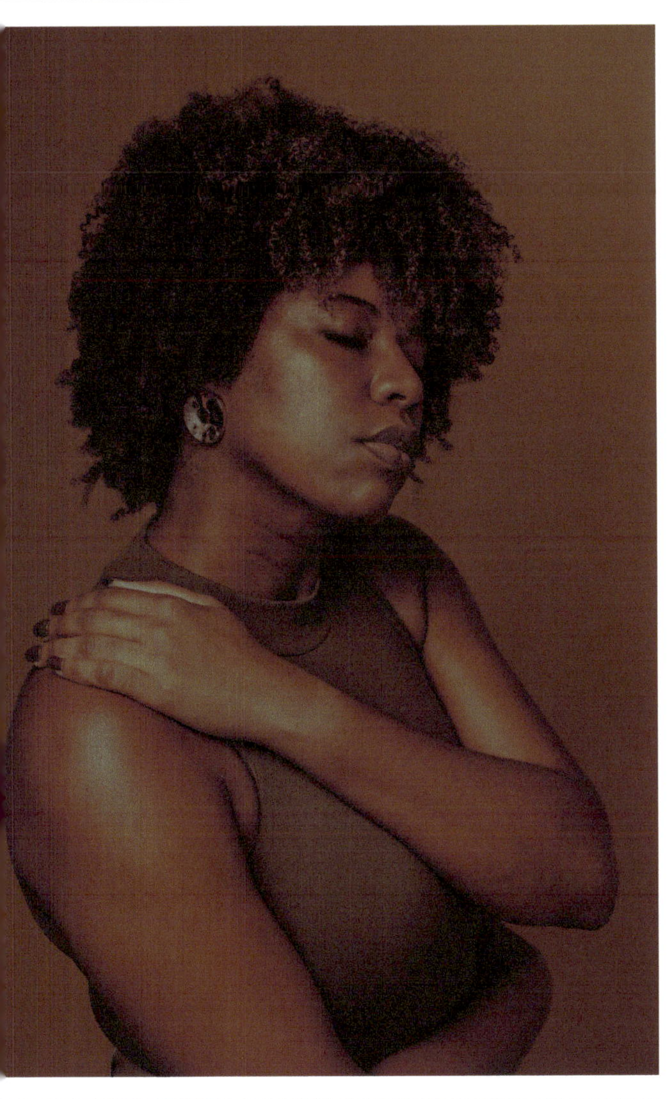
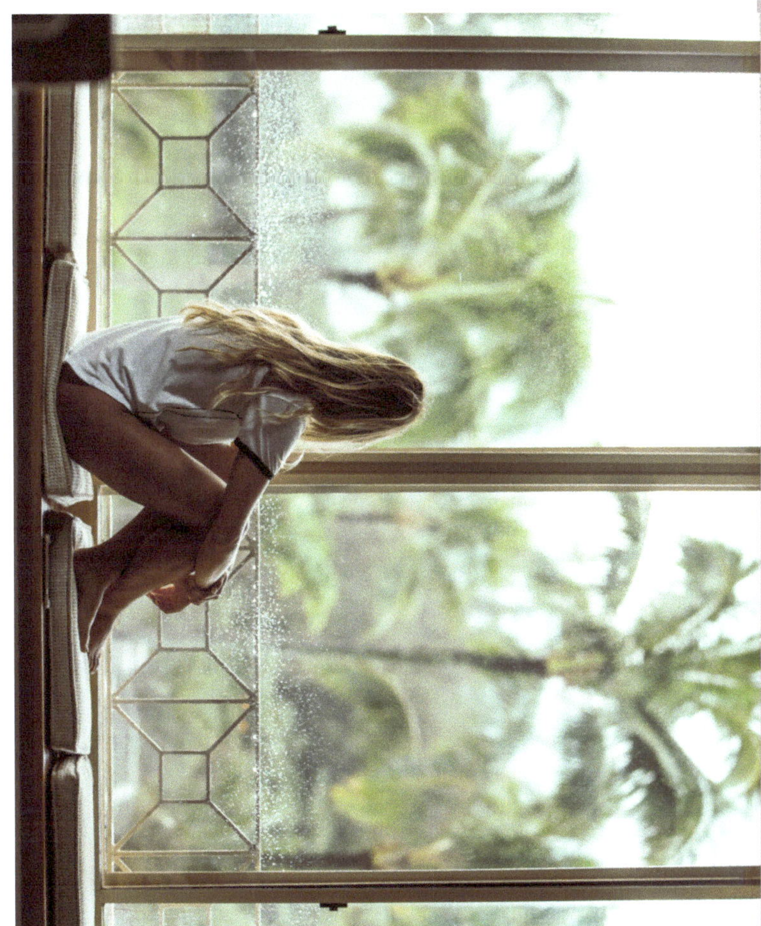
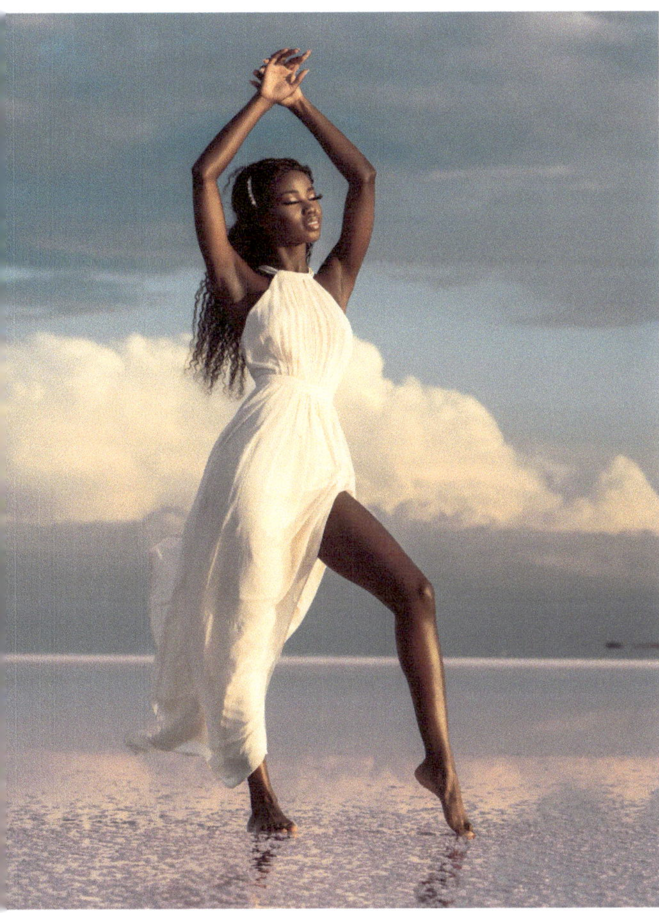
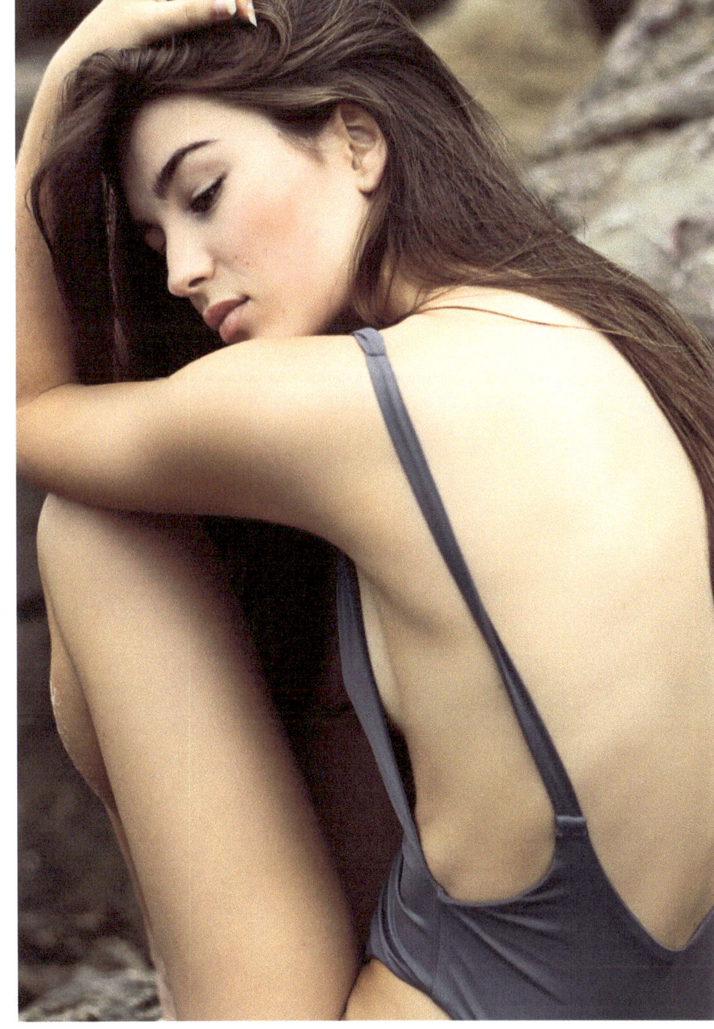

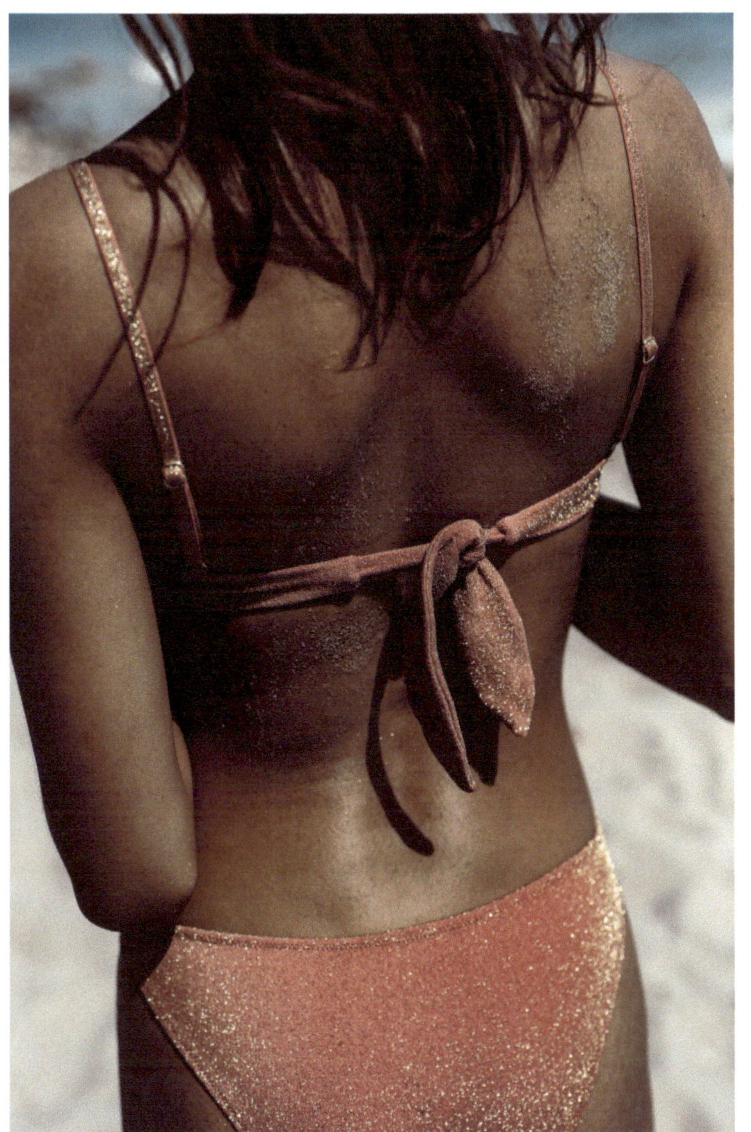

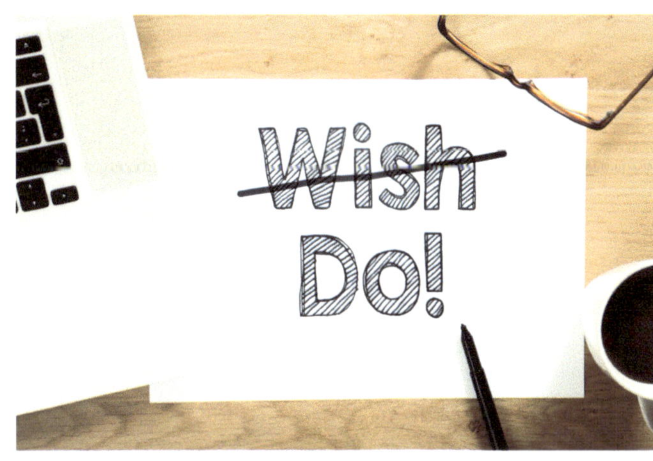
Wish
Do!

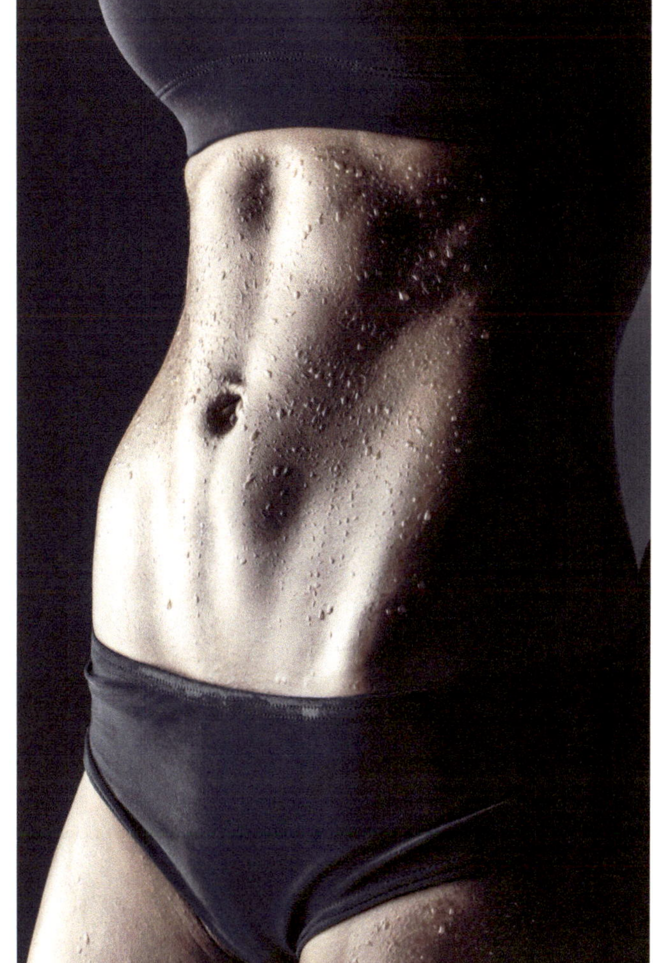

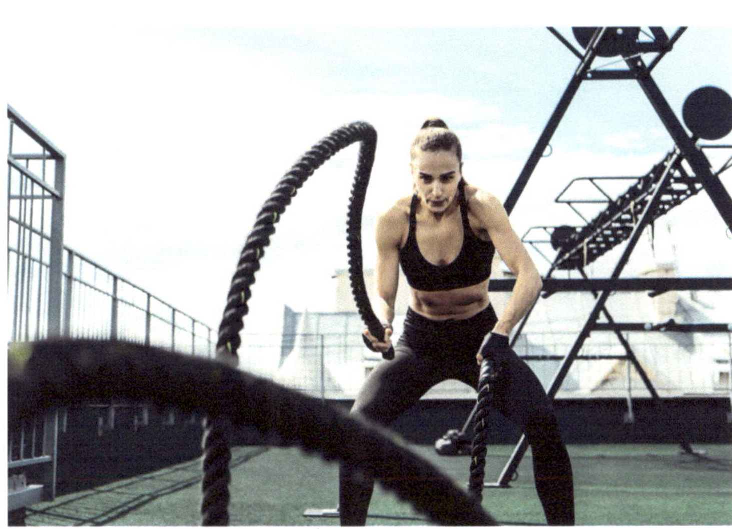

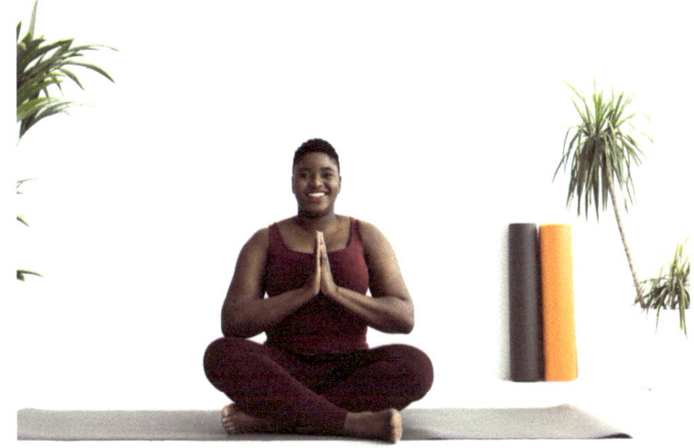

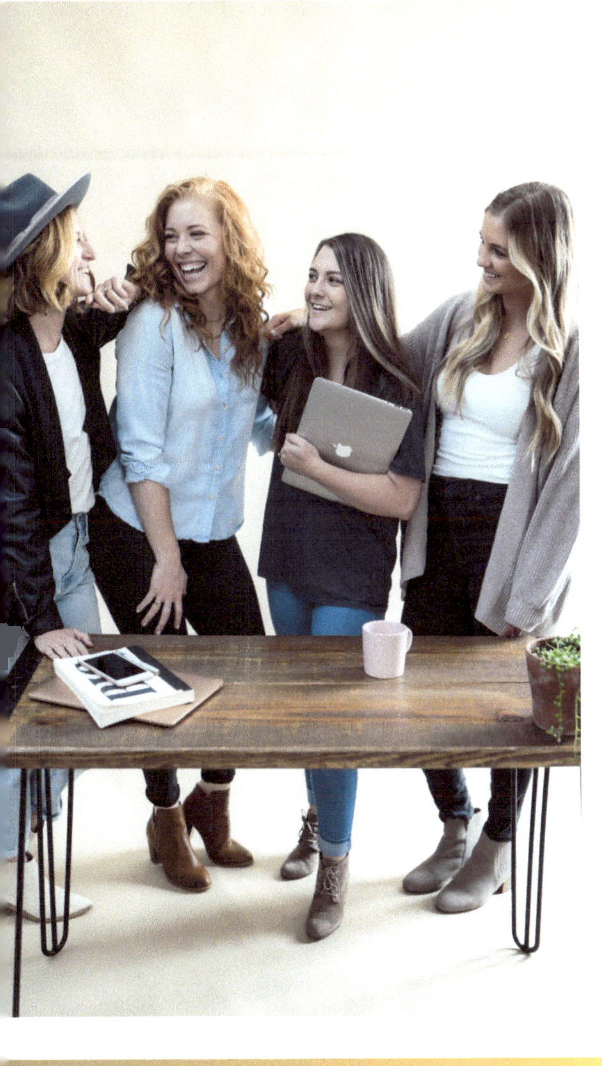

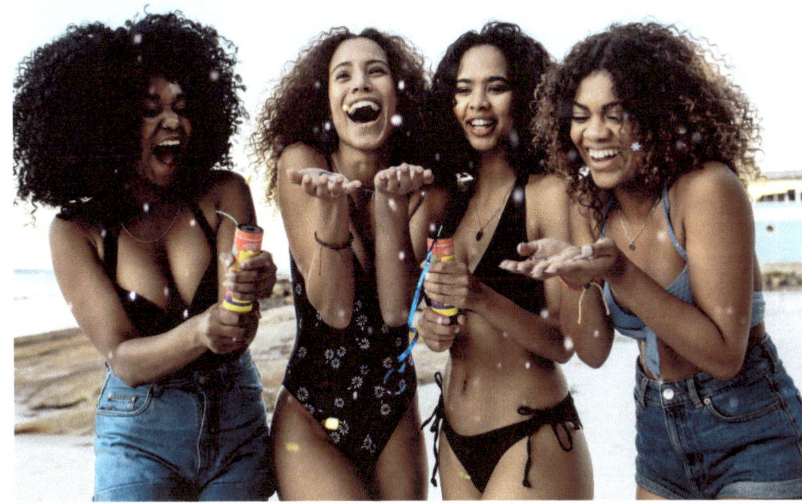

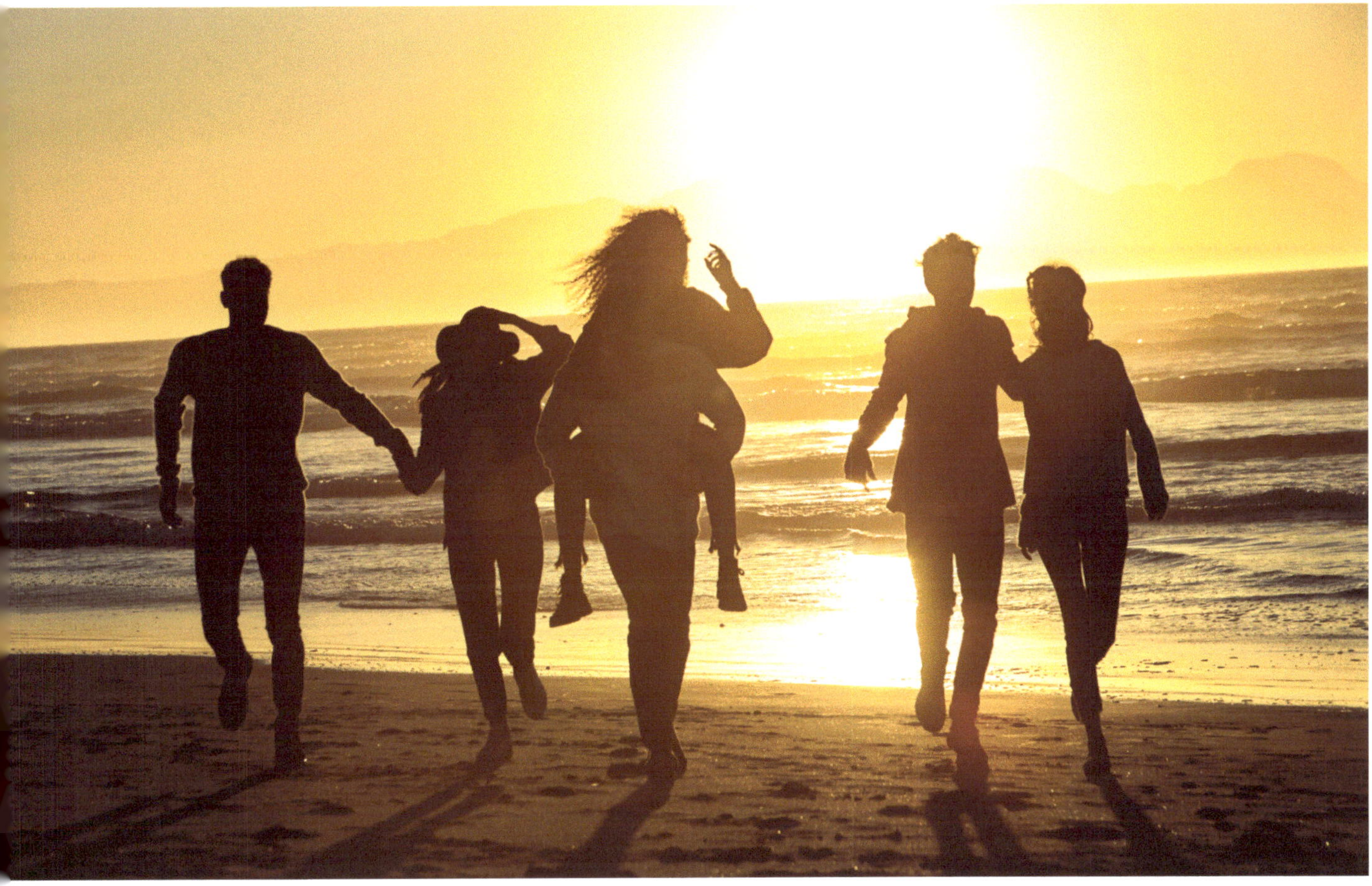

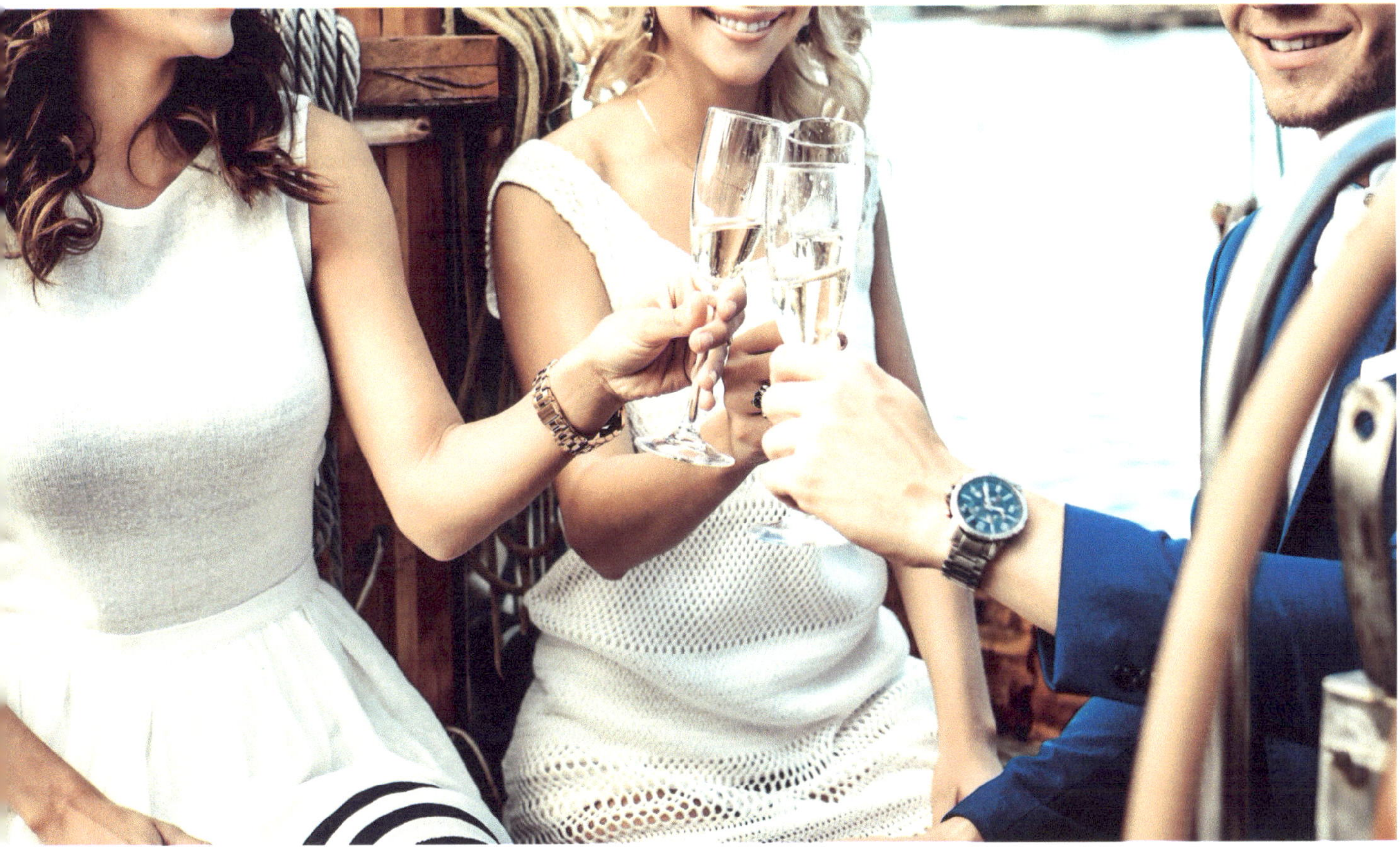

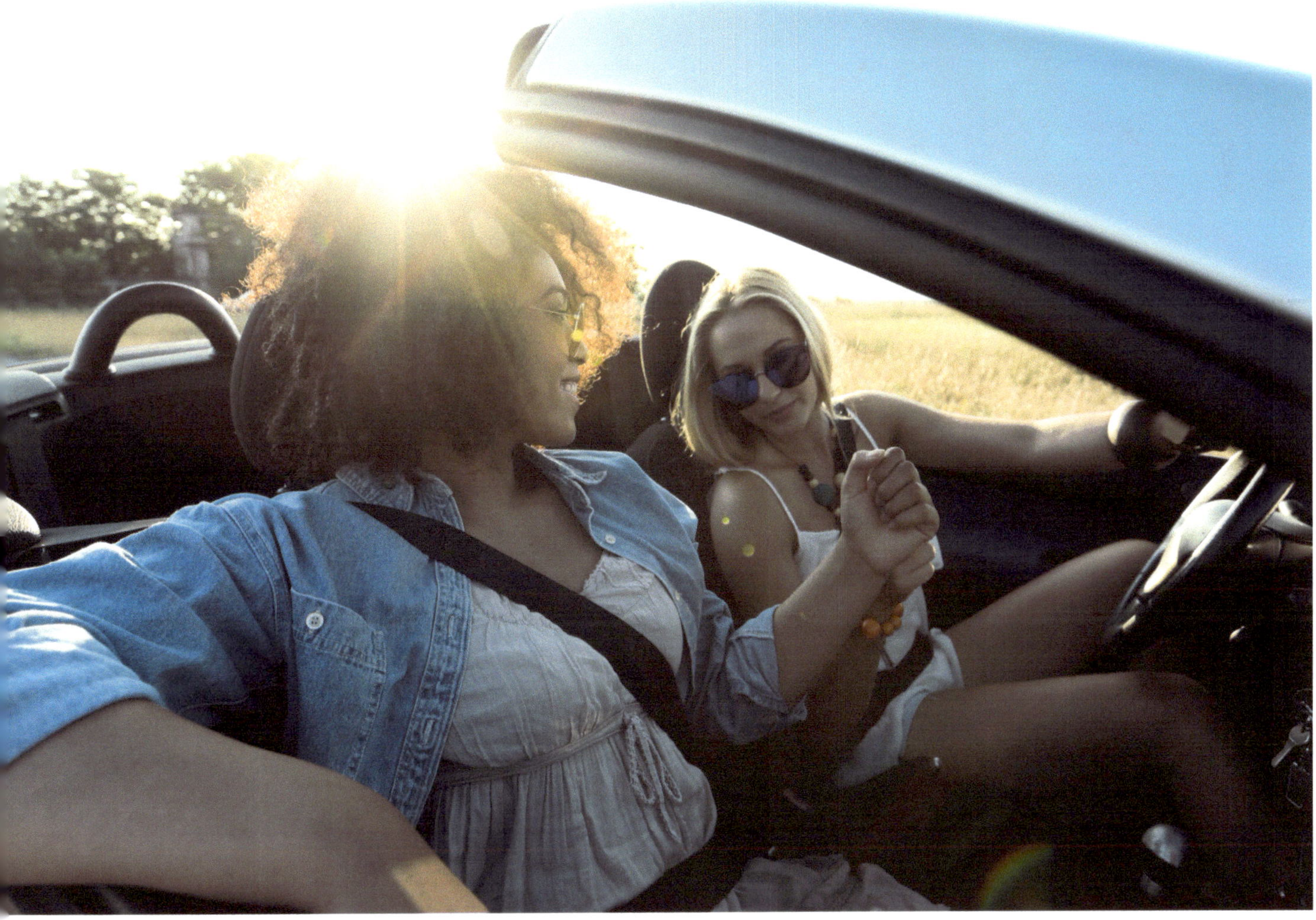

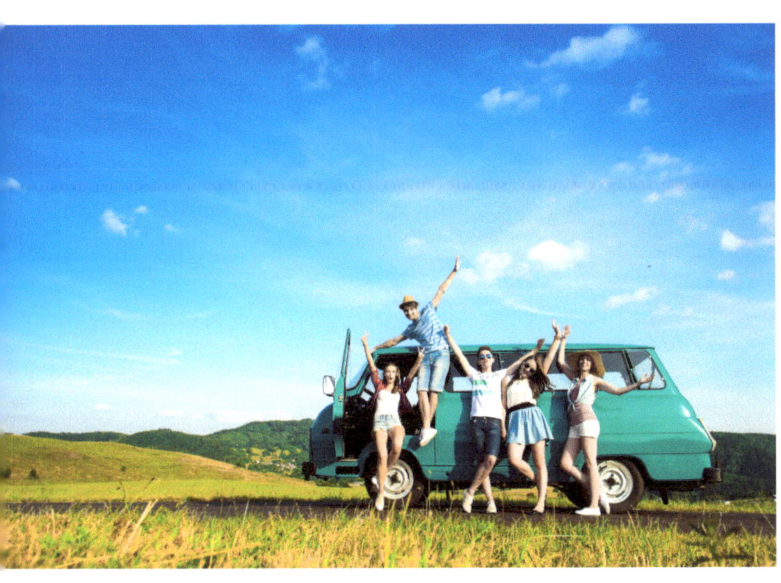
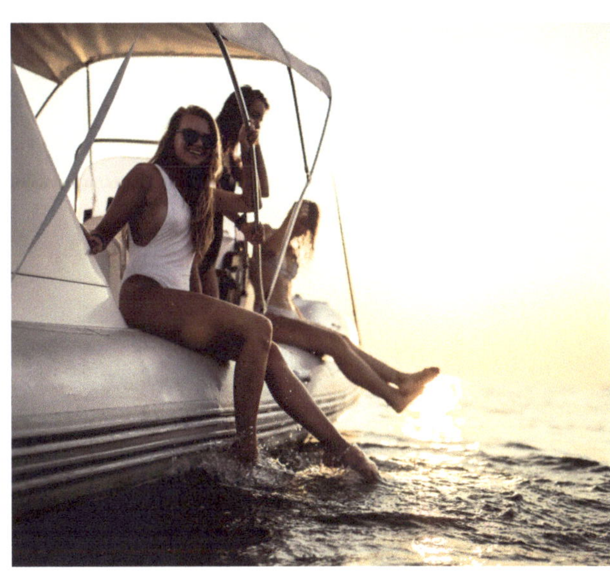
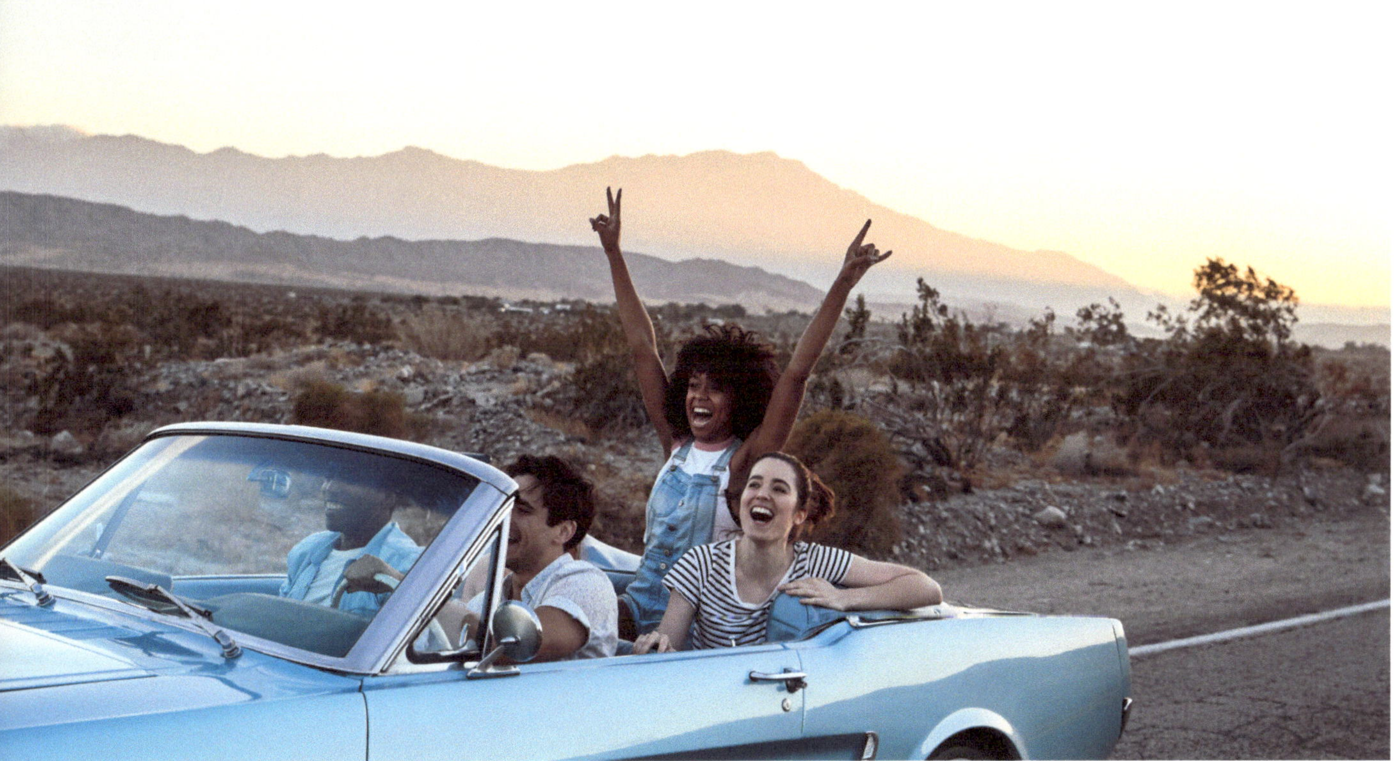
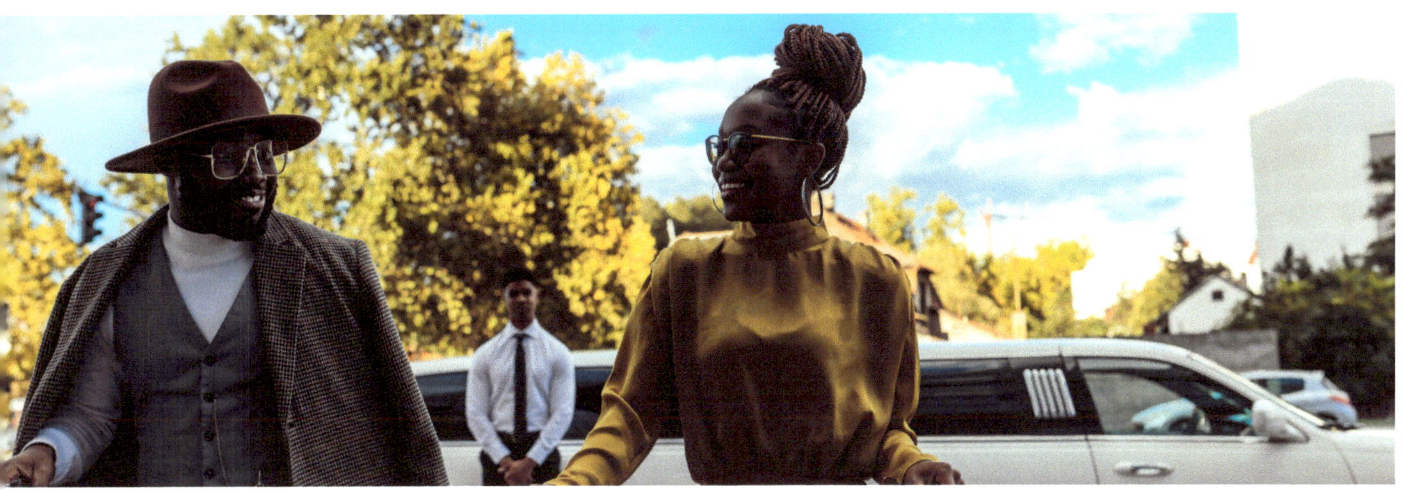

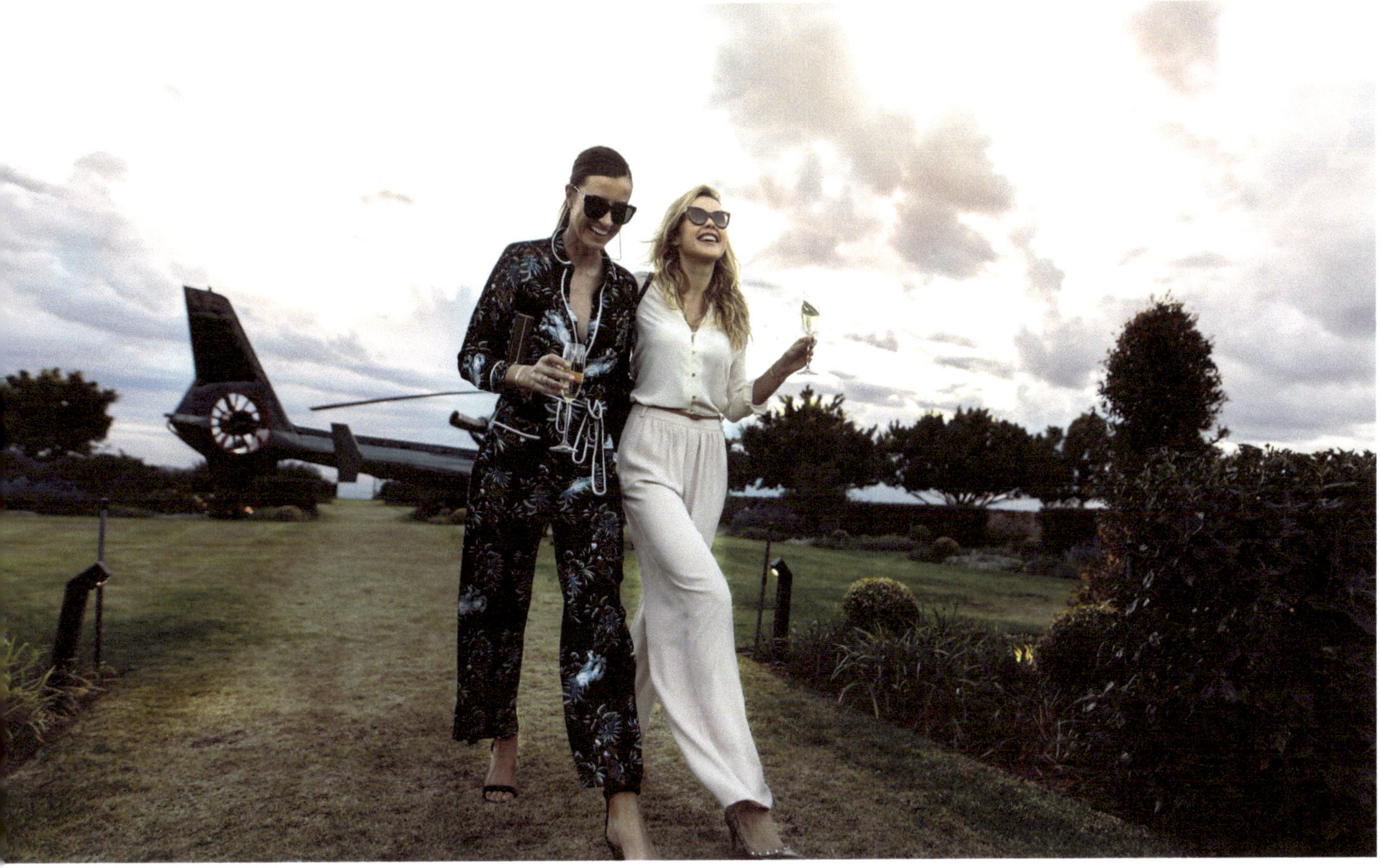

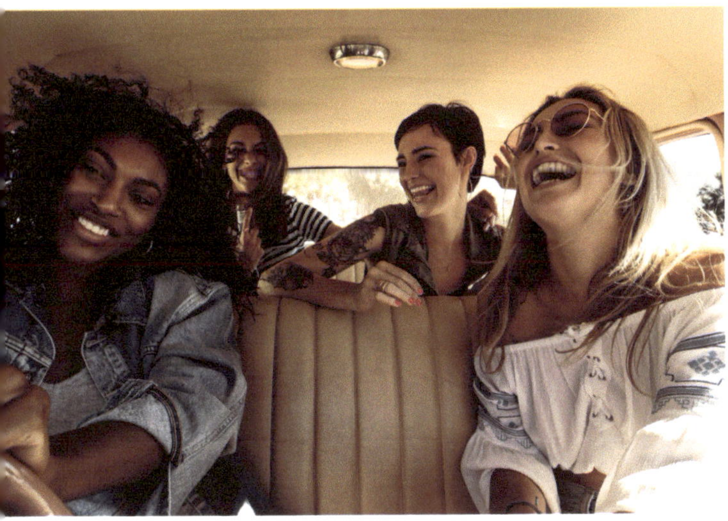
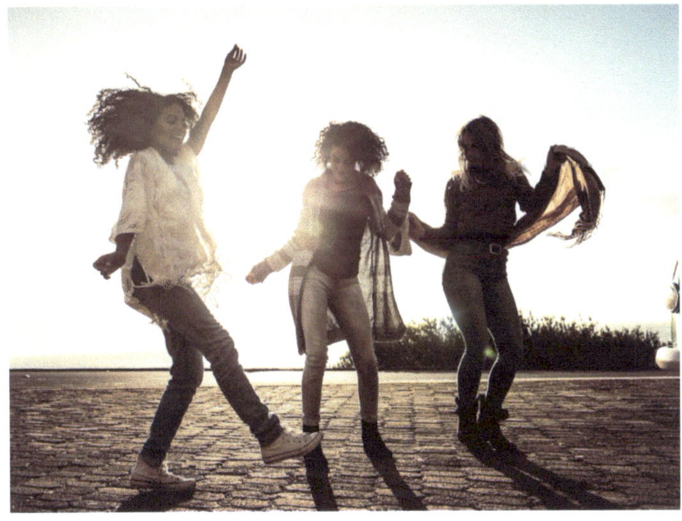
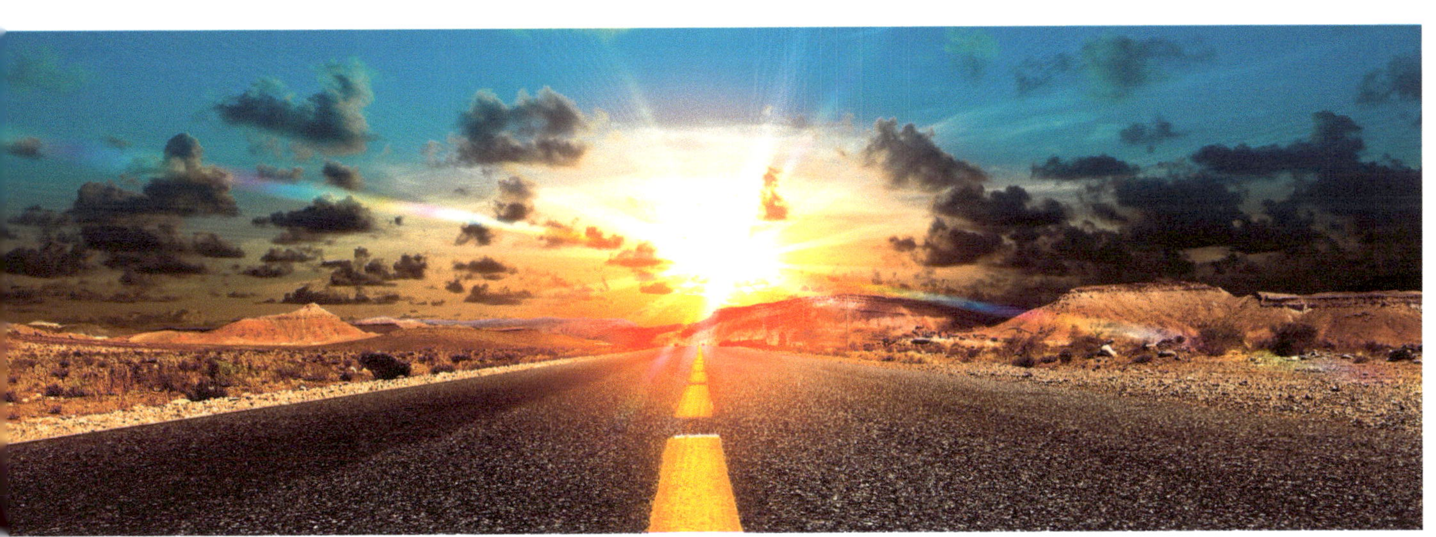

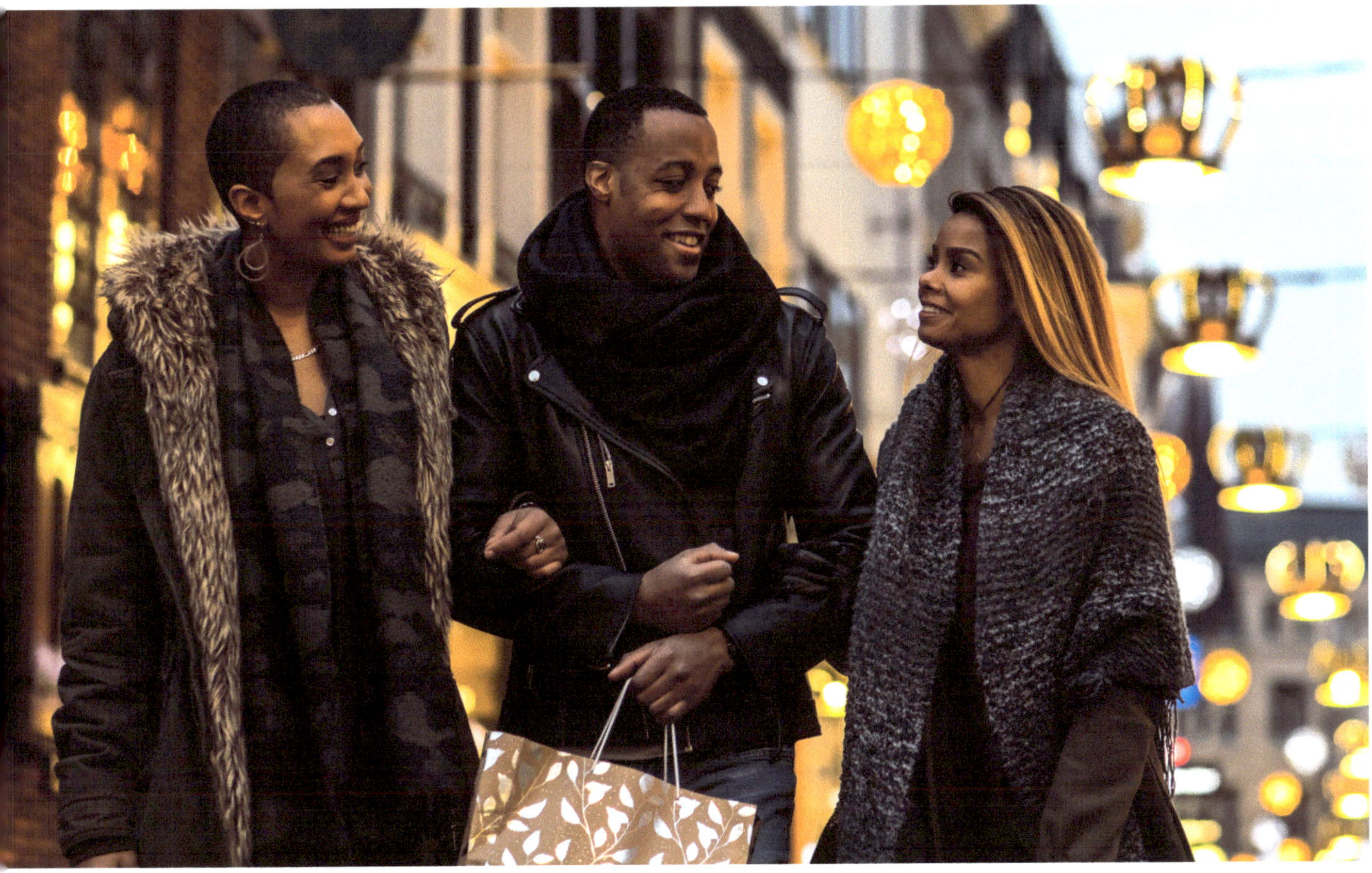

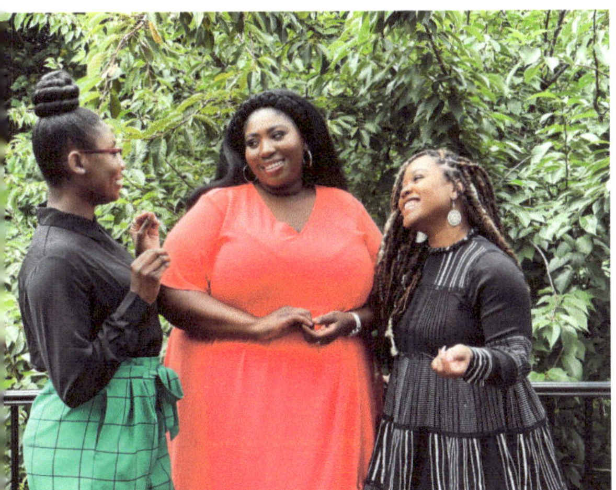

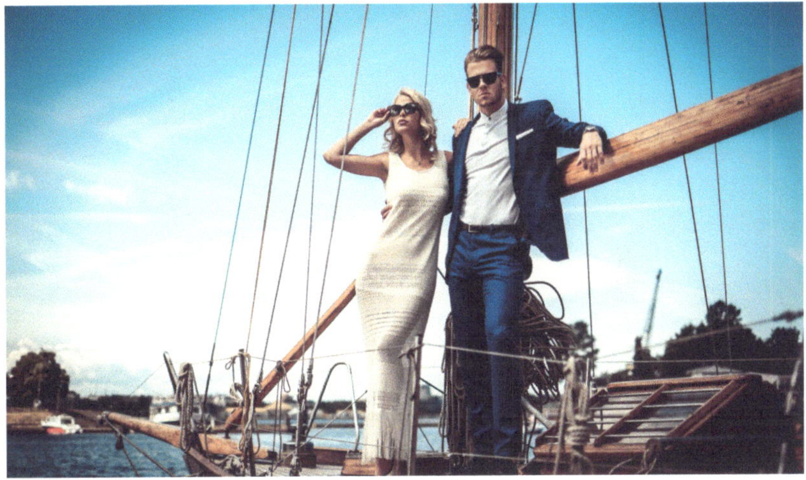

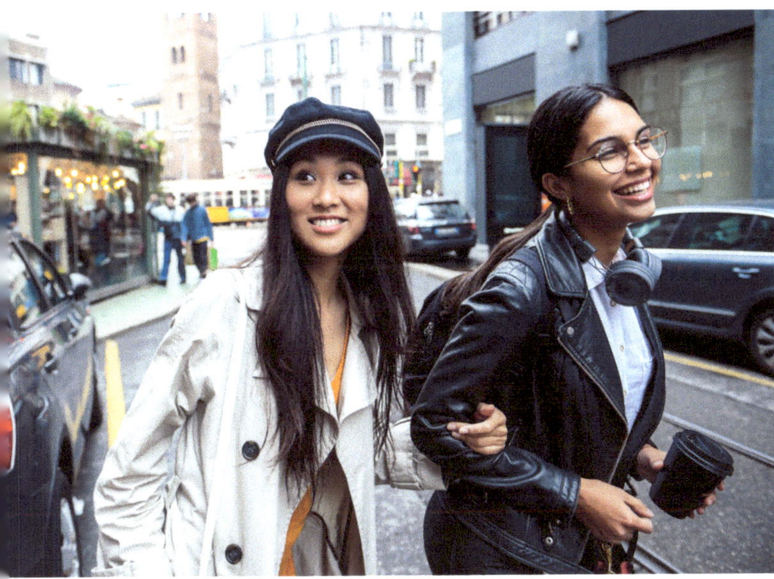

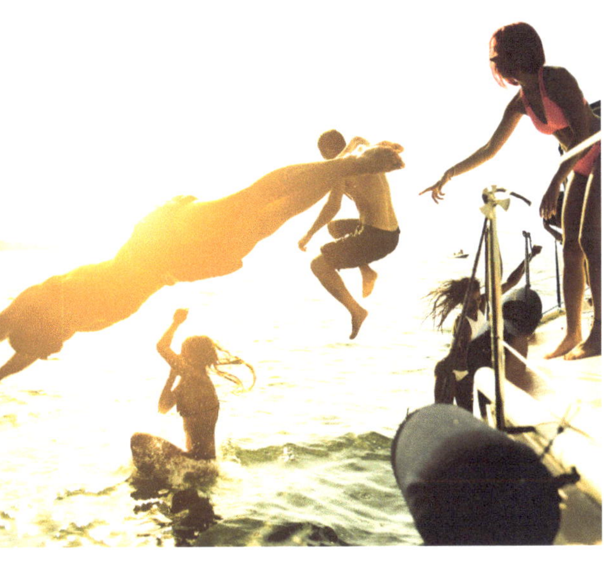

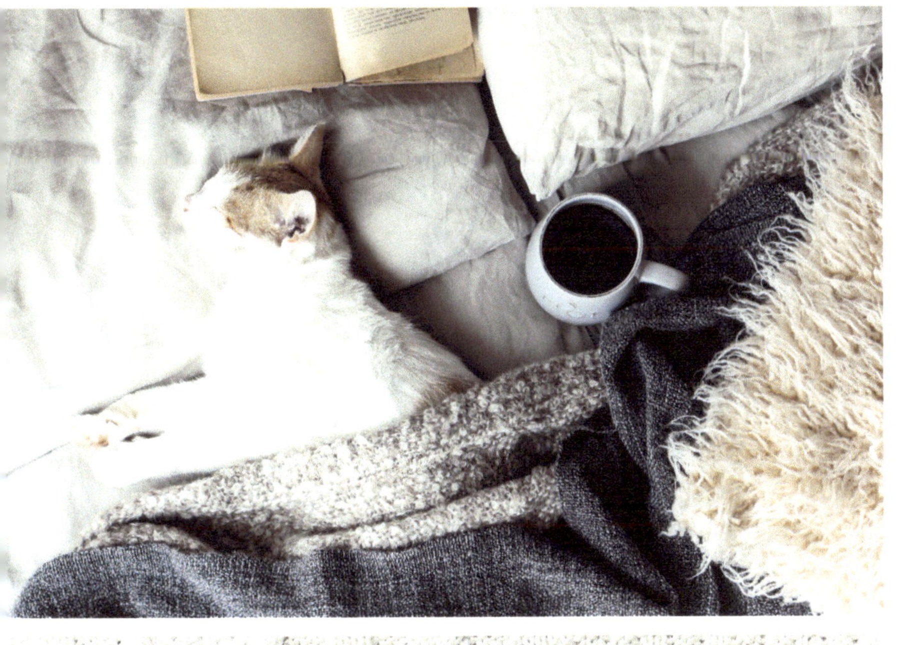

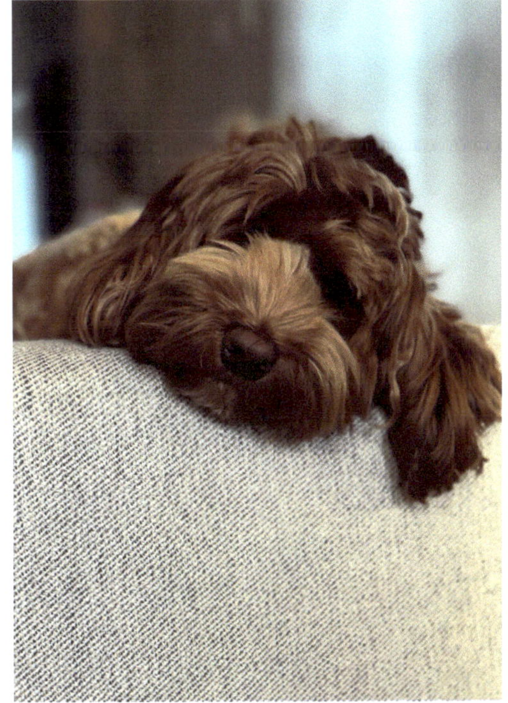

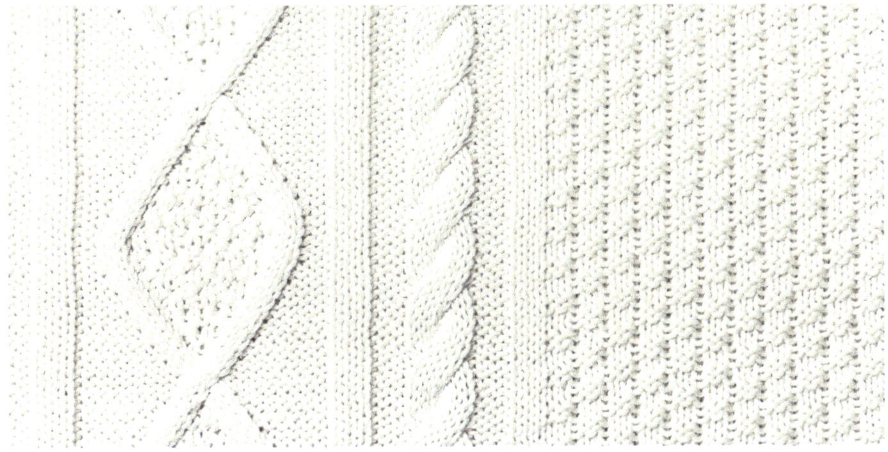

Home is where our story begins....

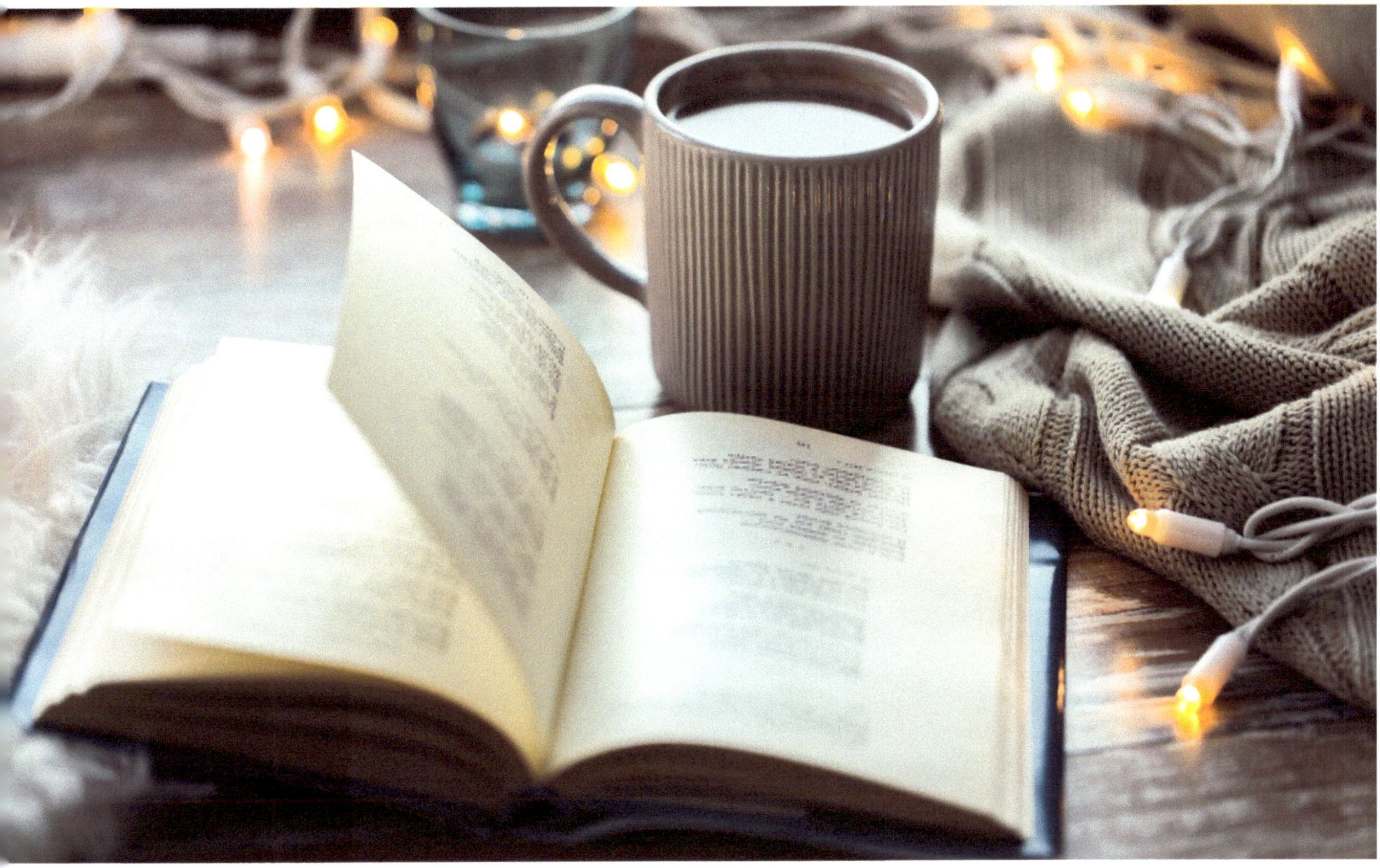

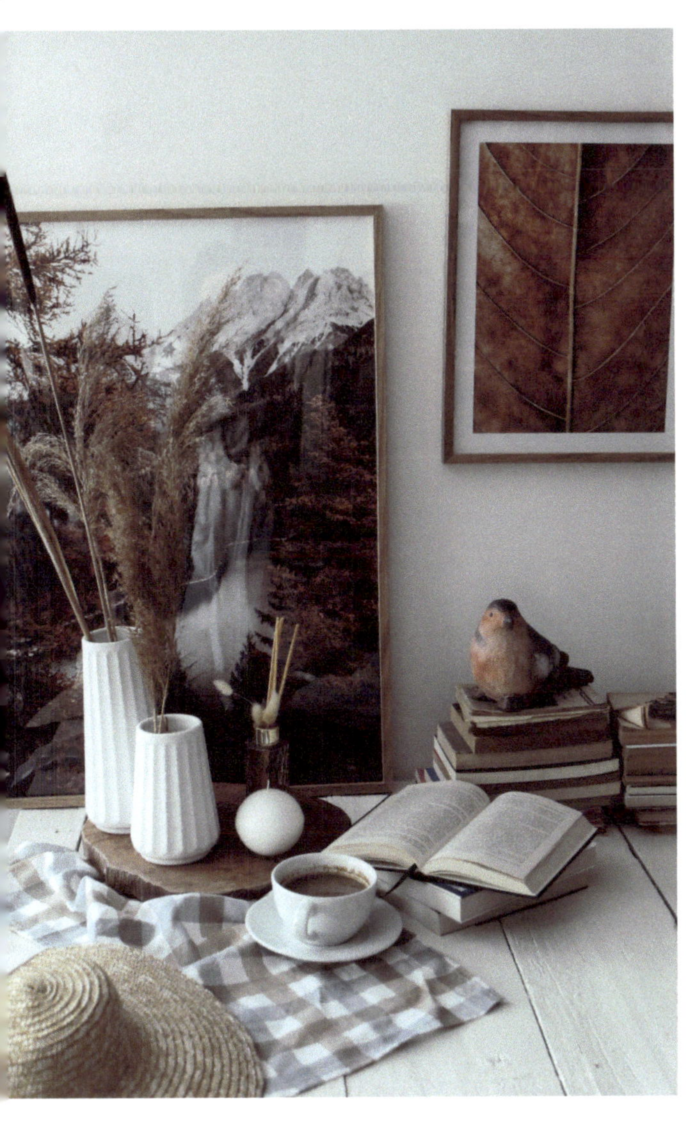
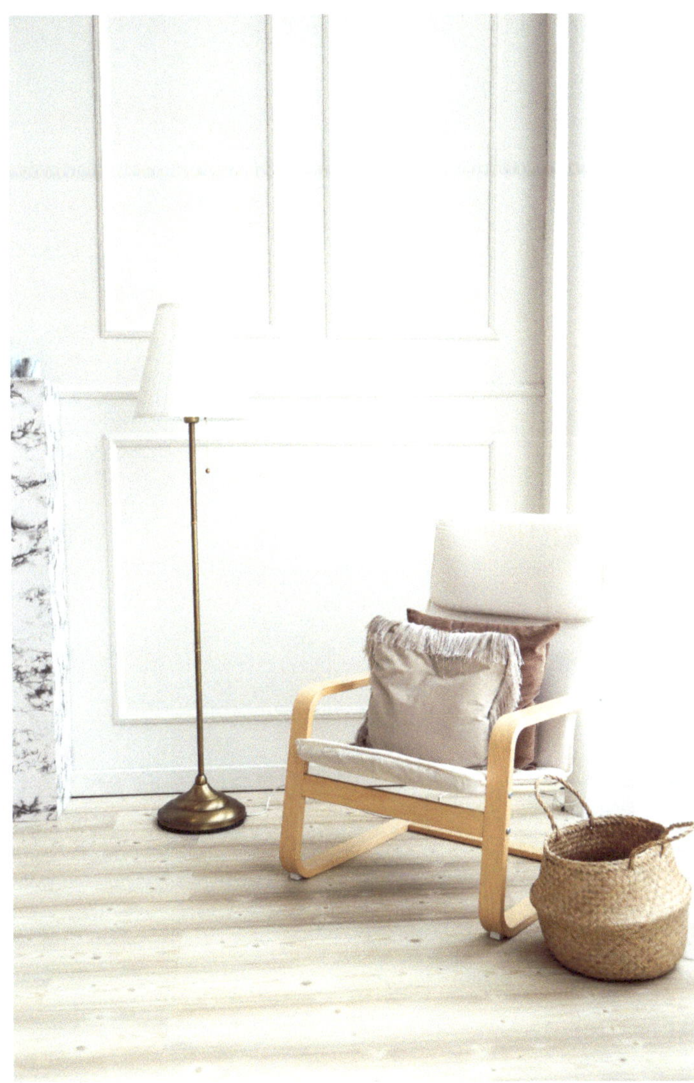
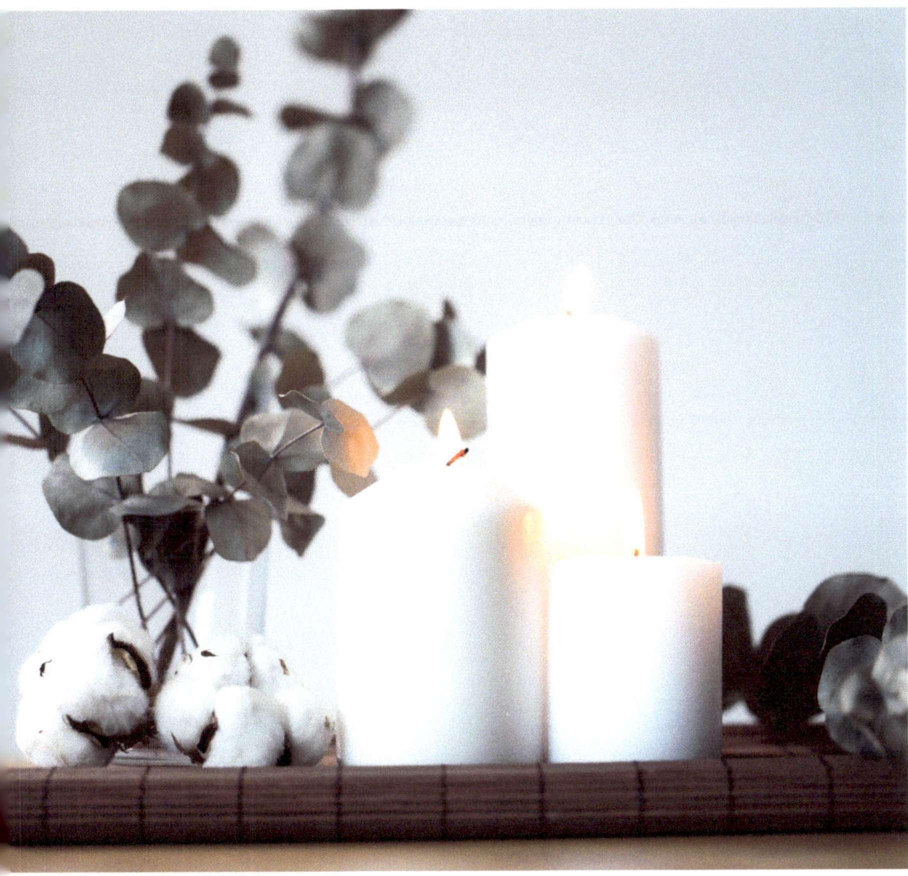
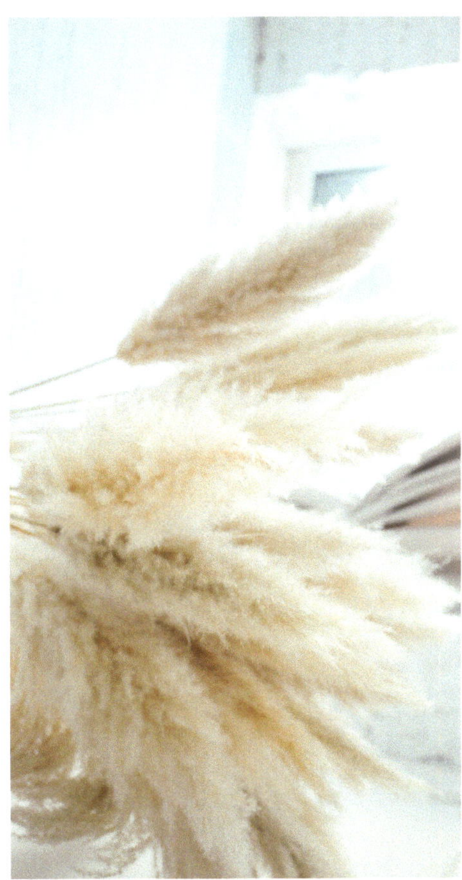

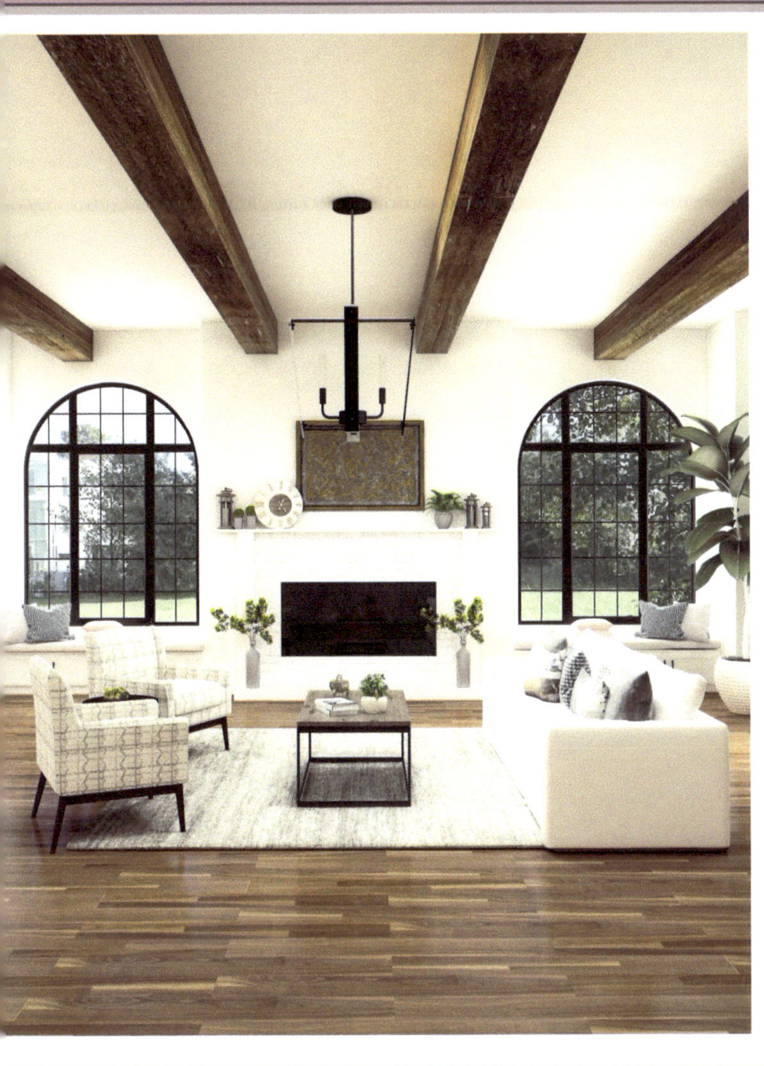
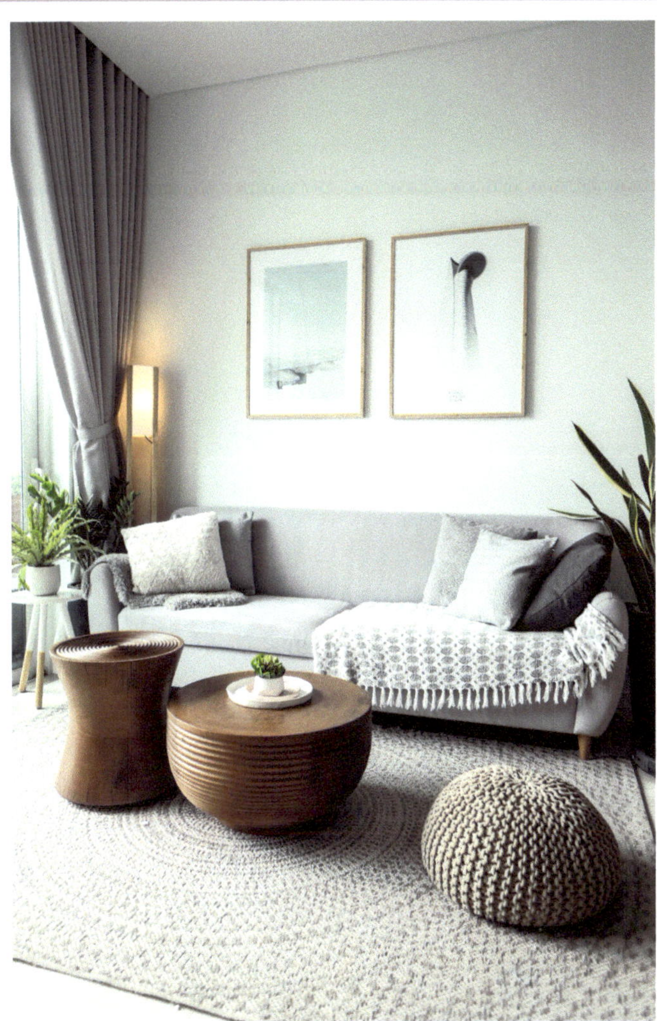
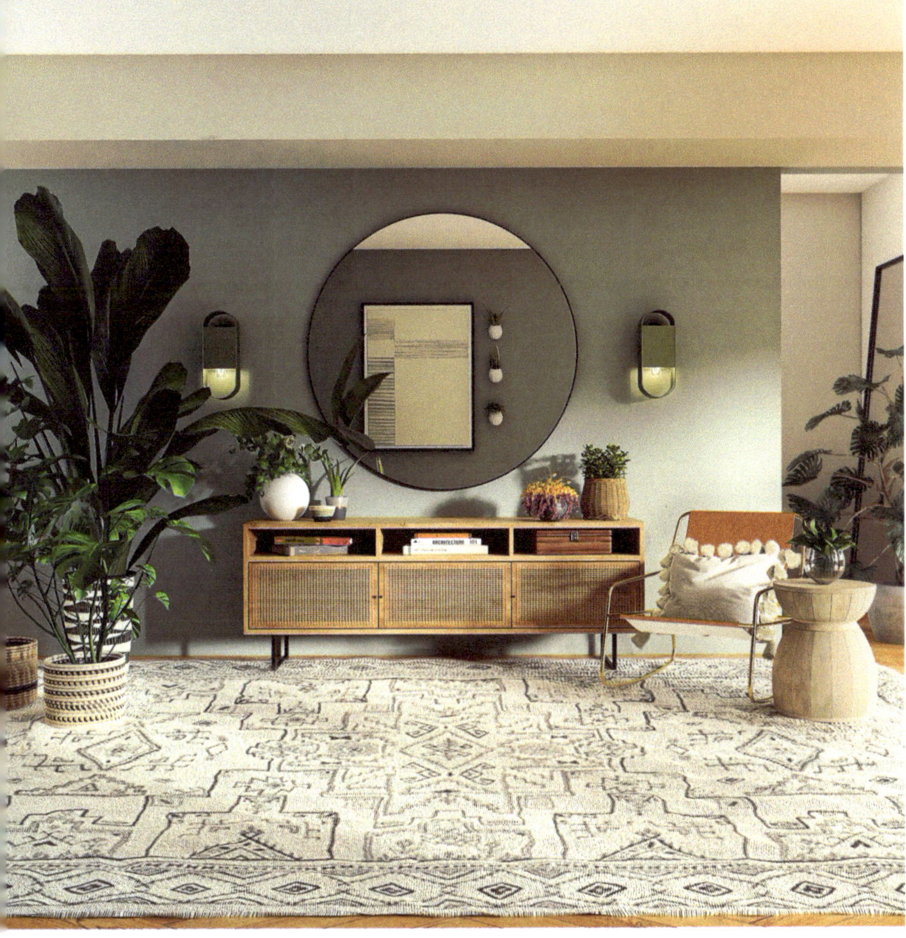
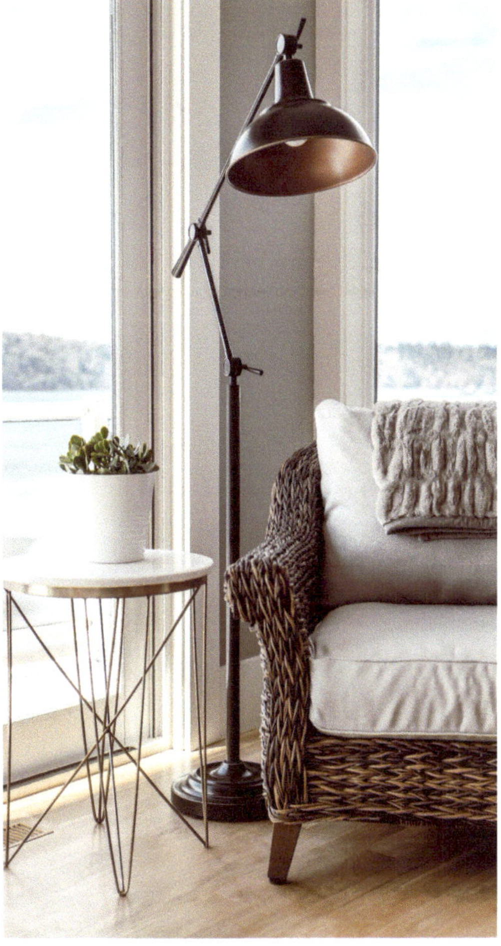

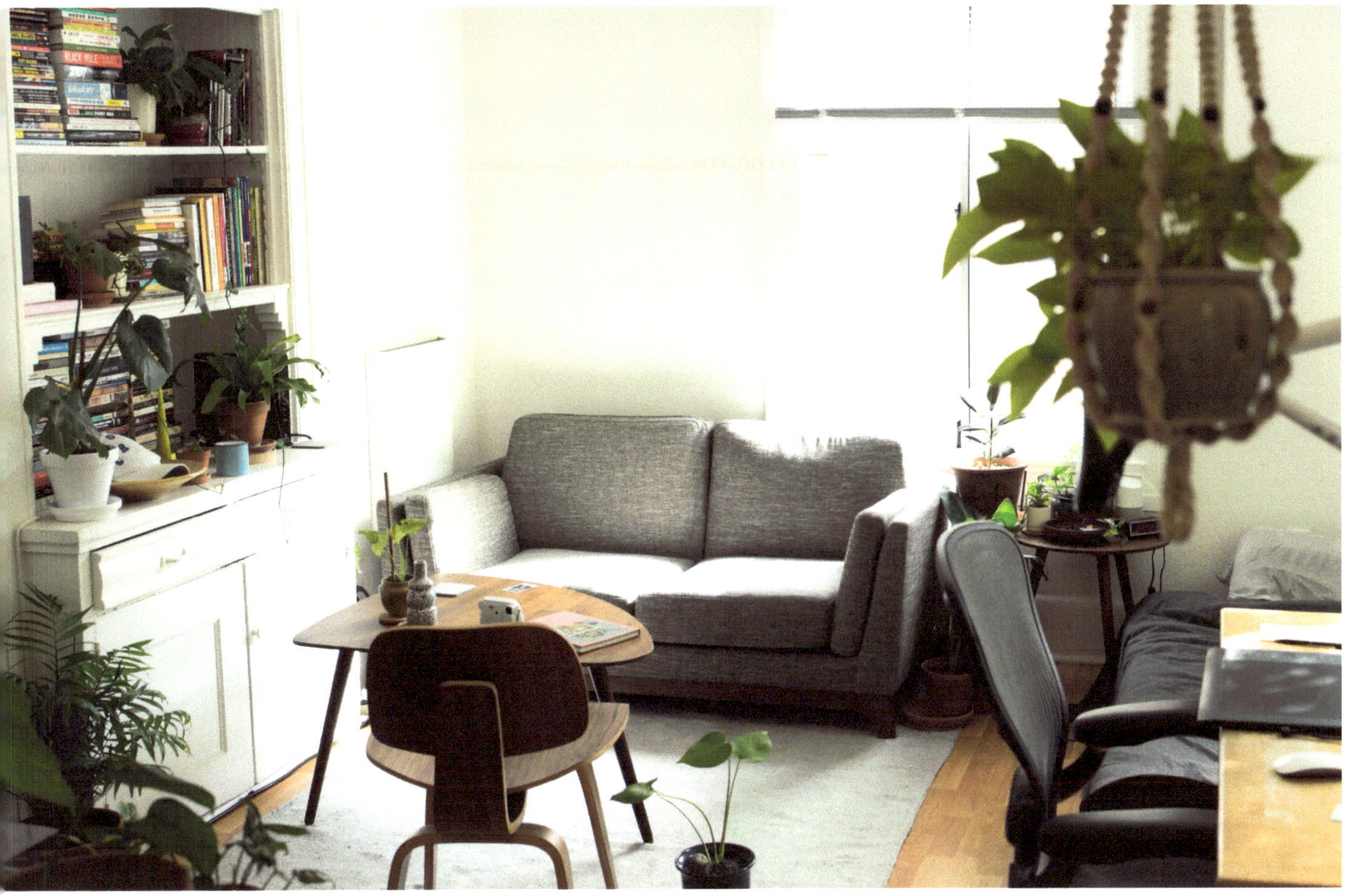

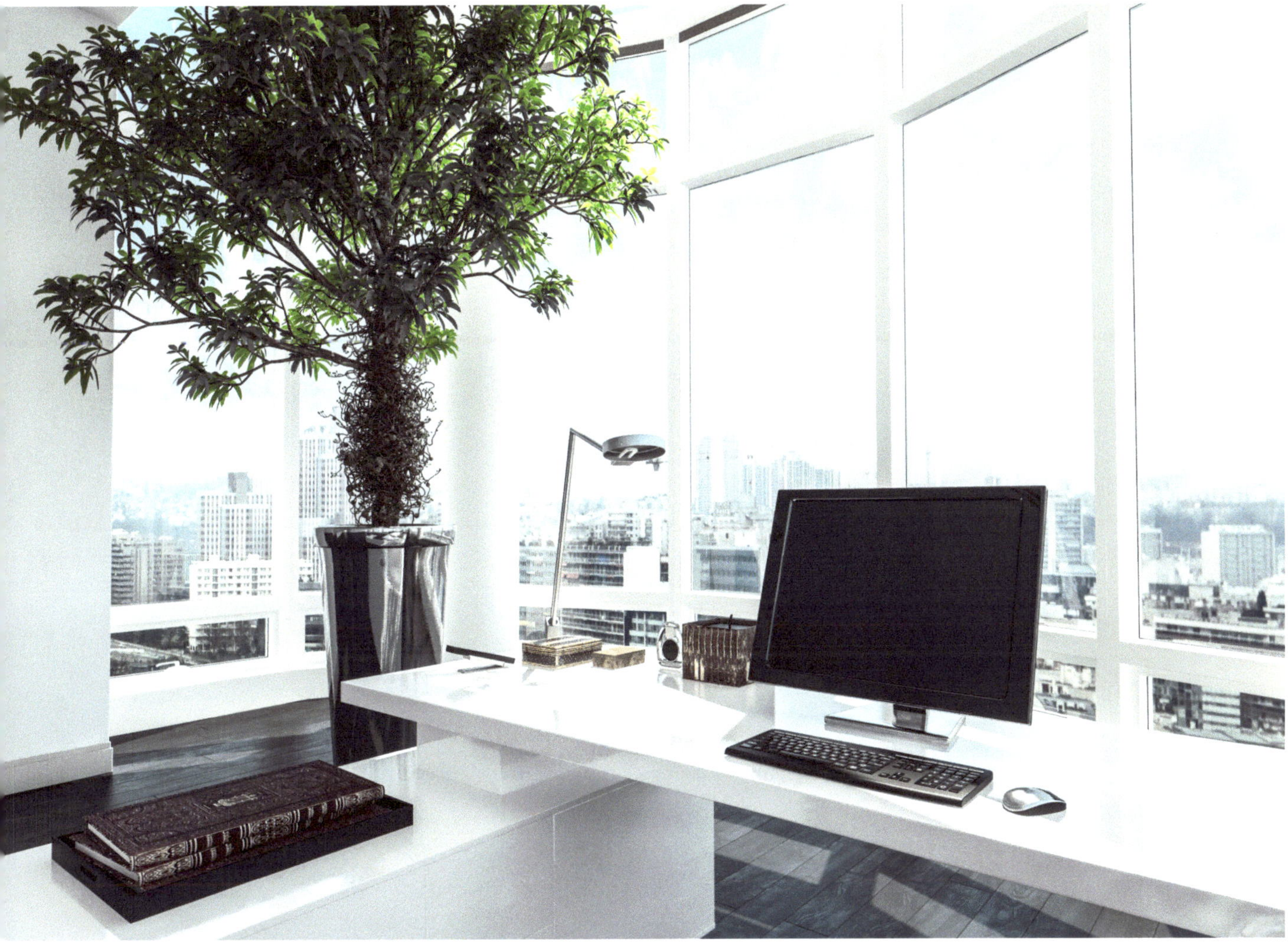

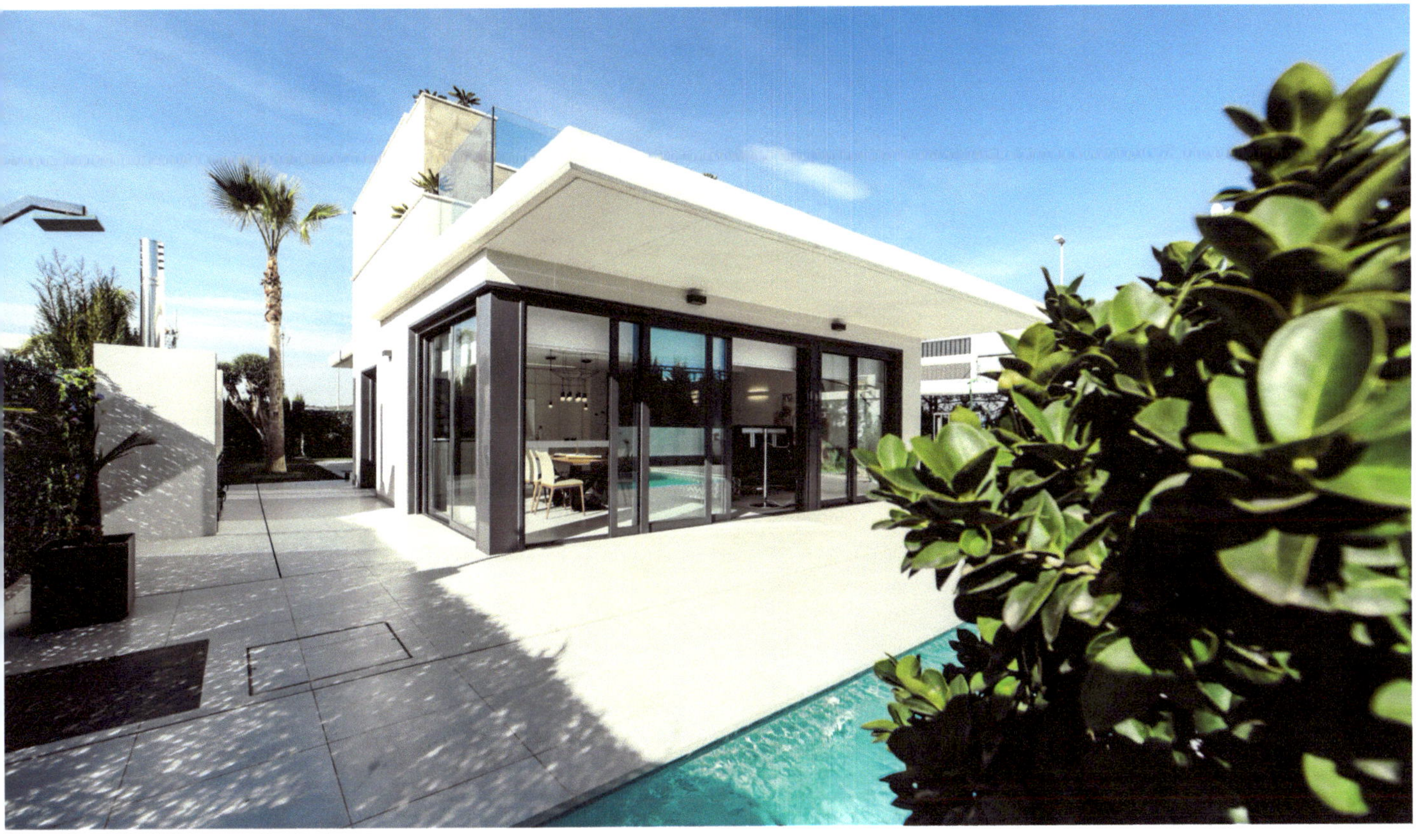

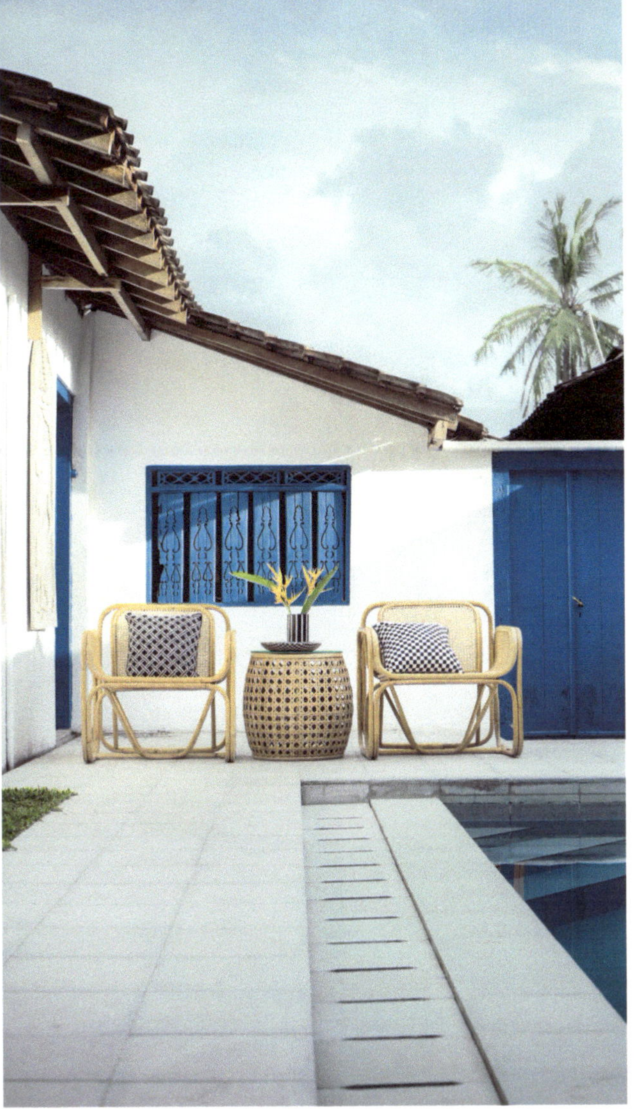

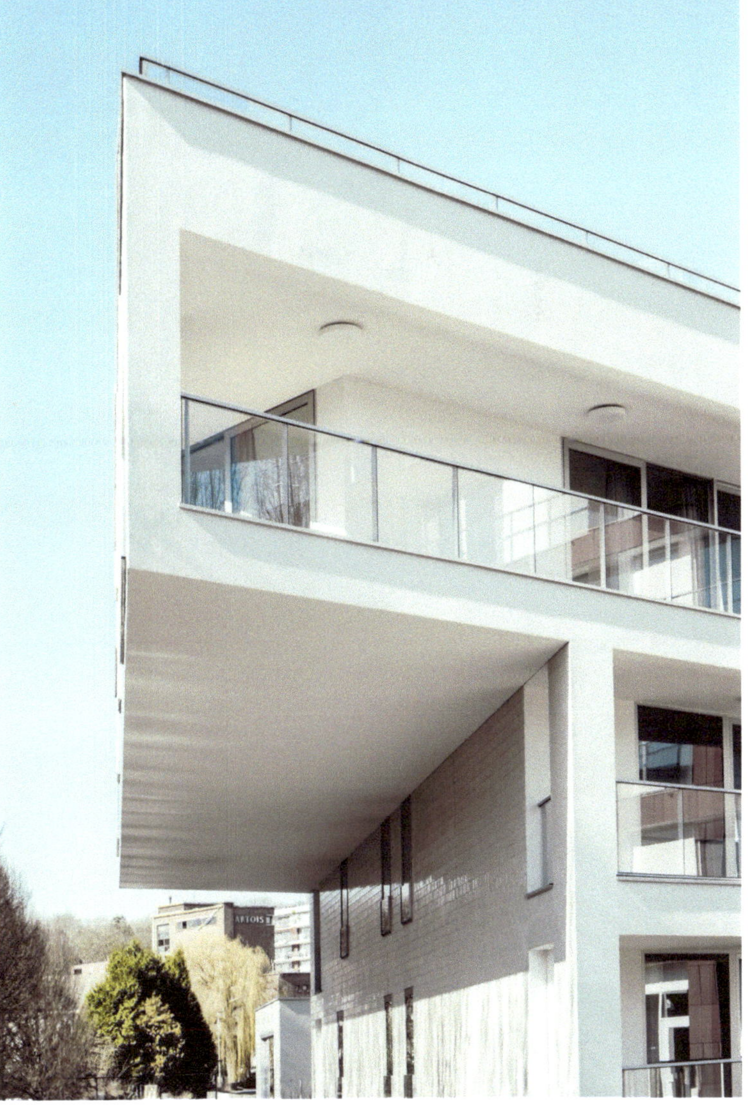

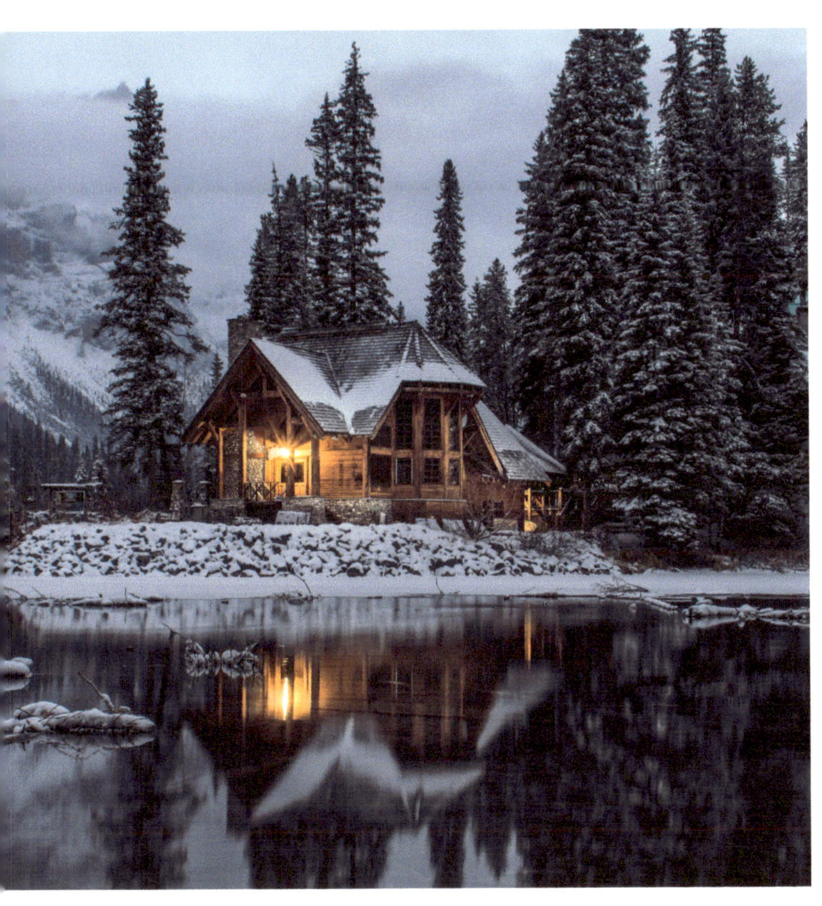

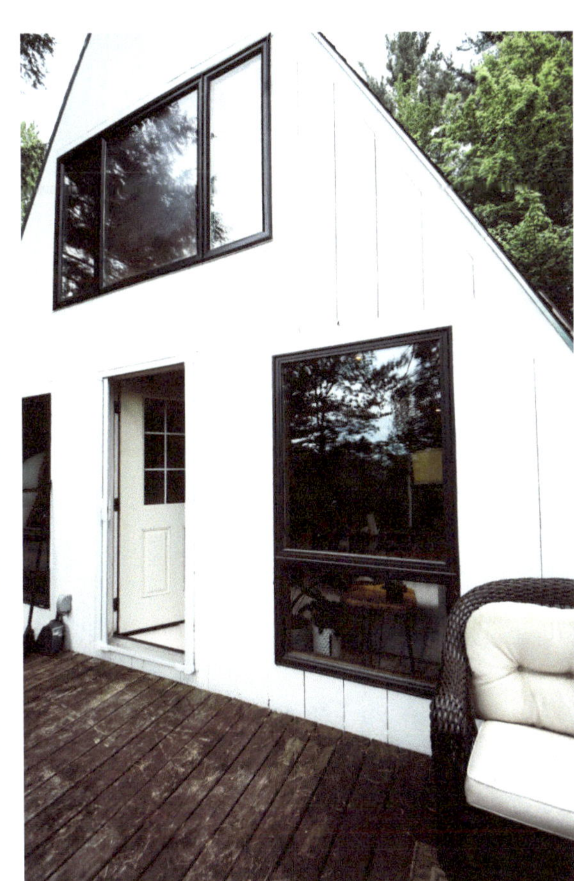

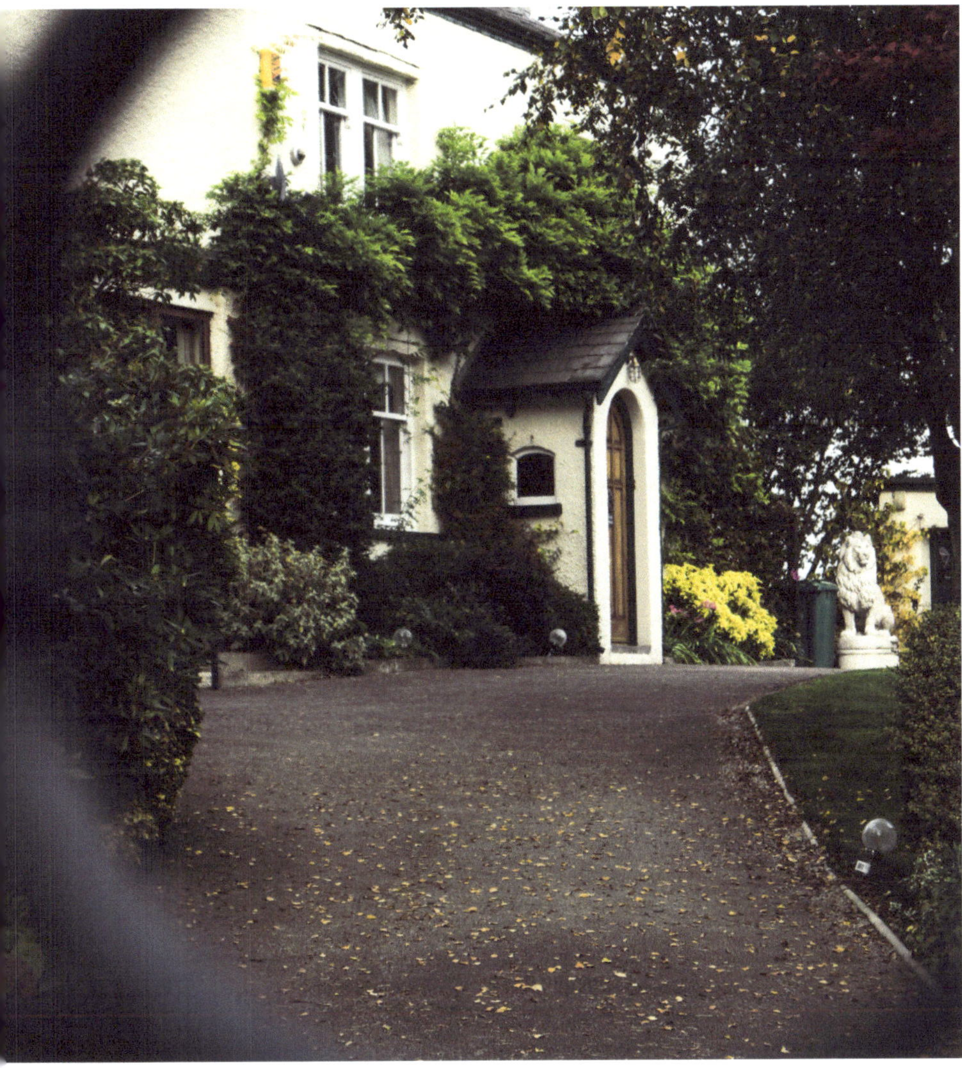

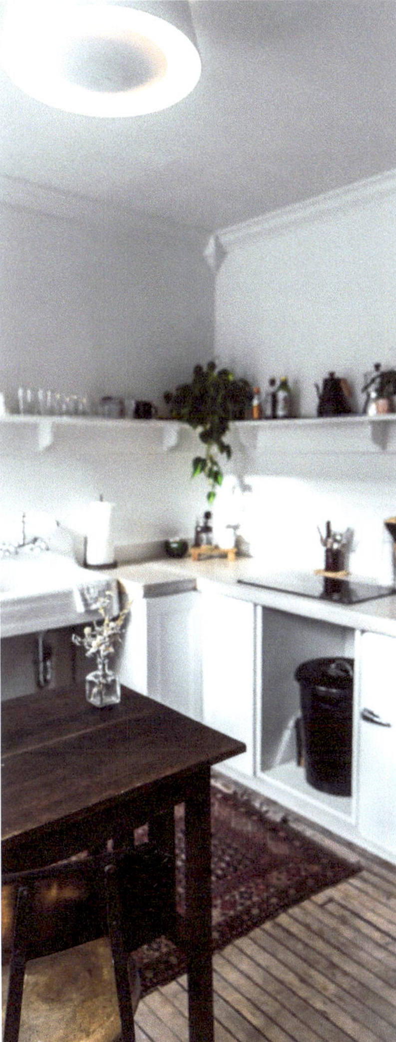

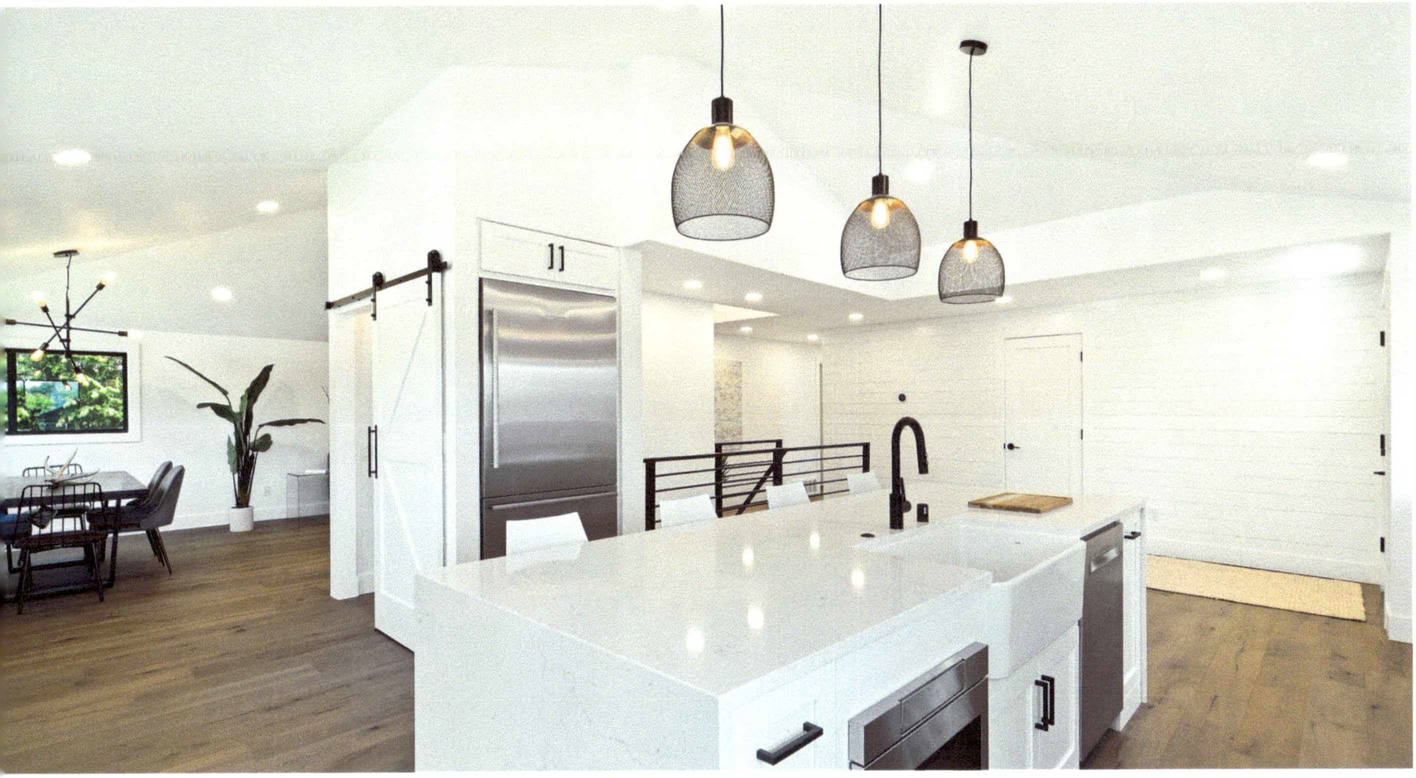

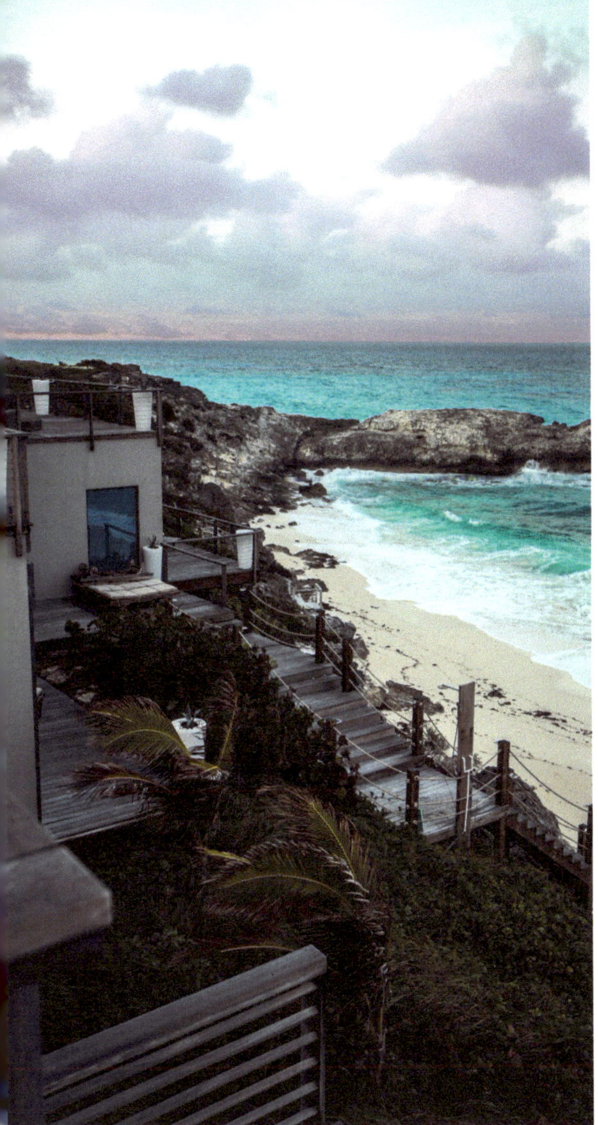

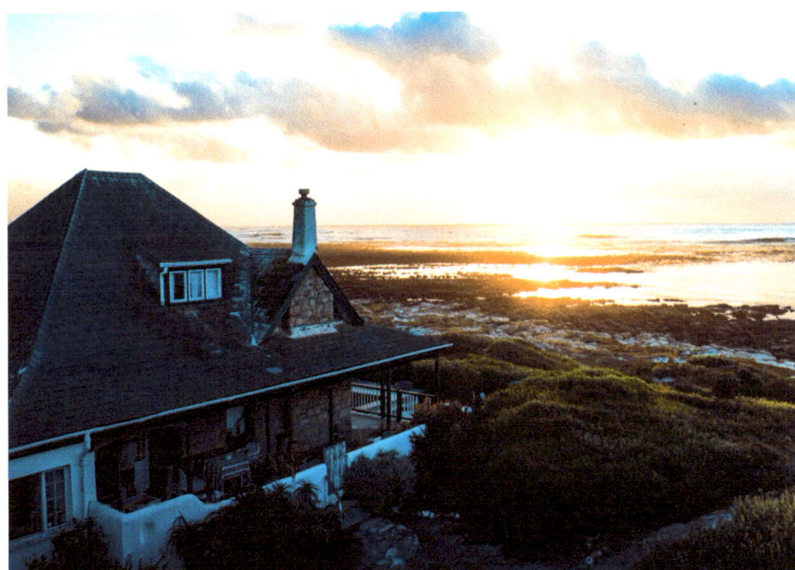

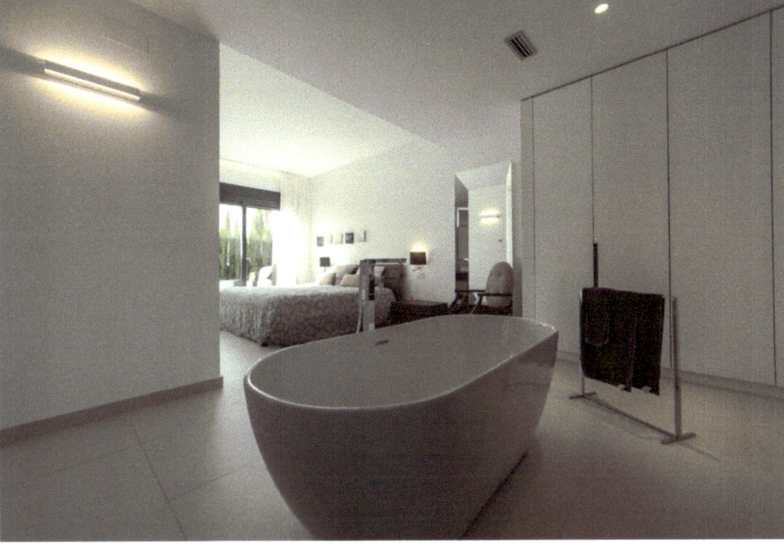

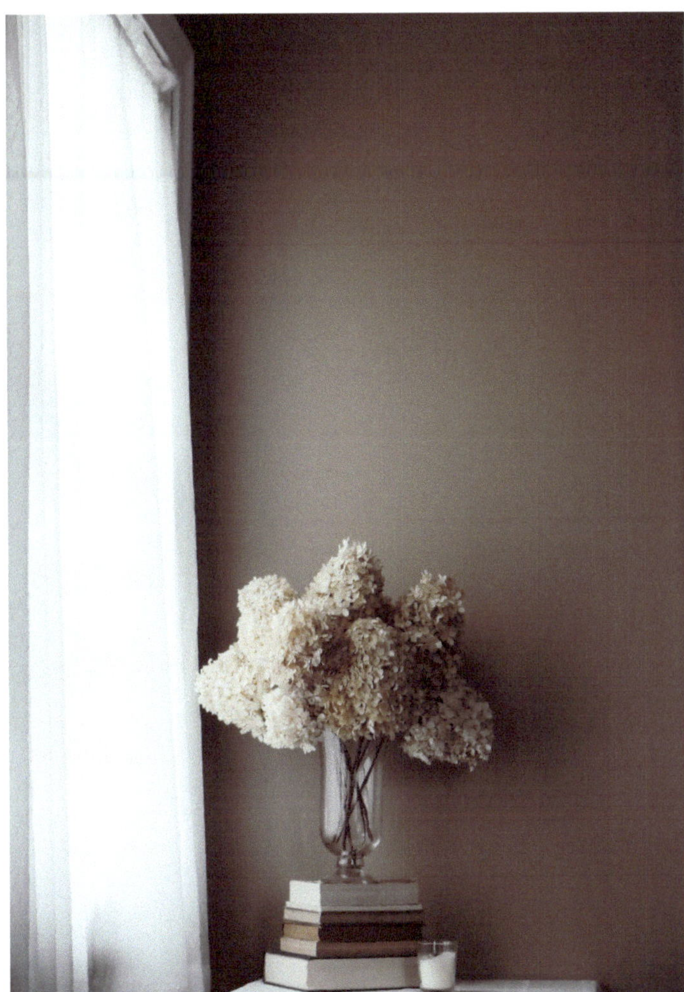
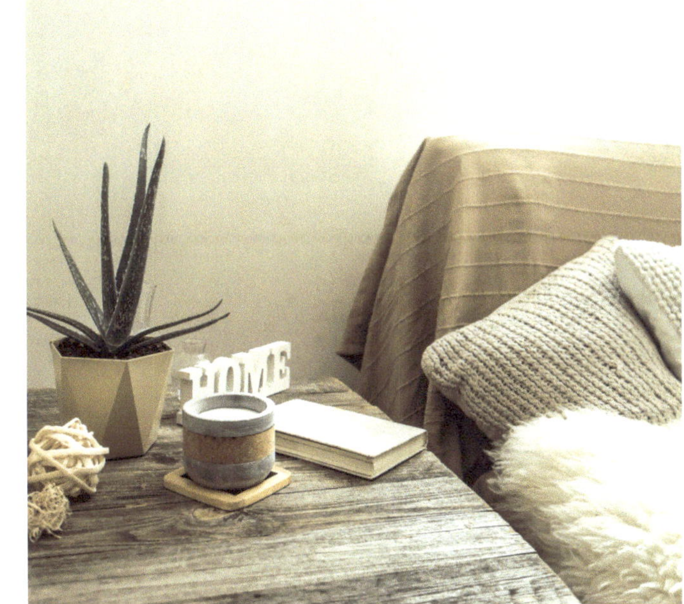
HOME
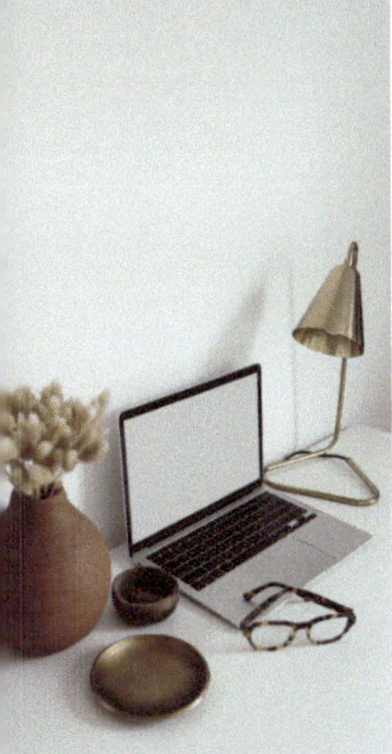
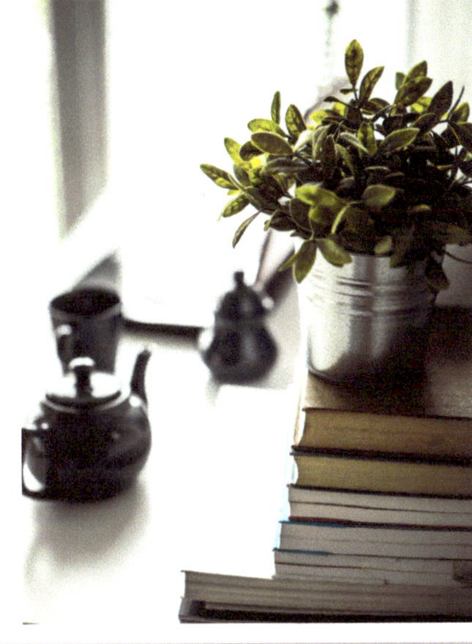
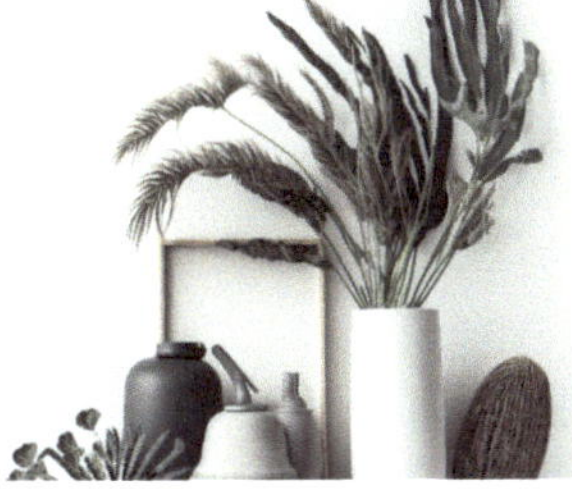

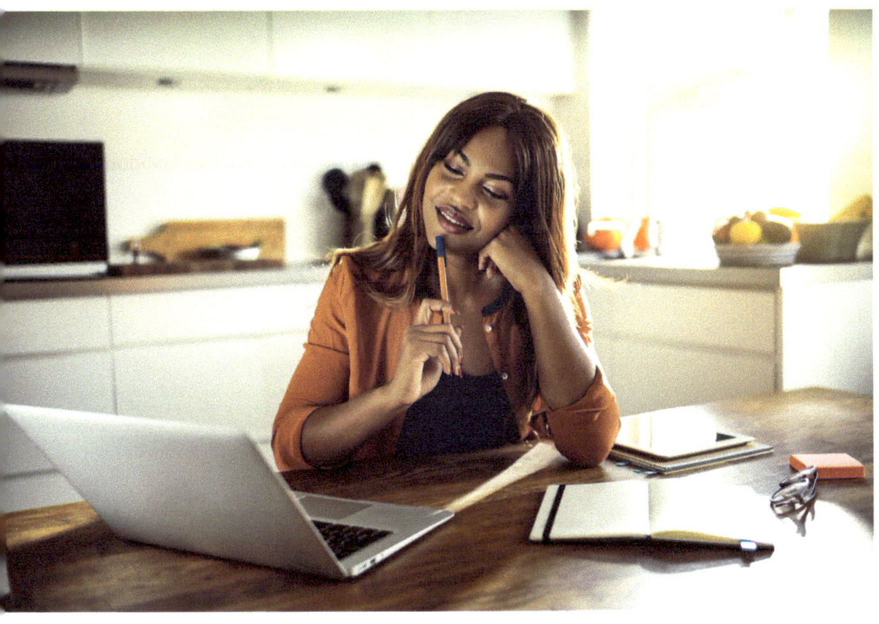

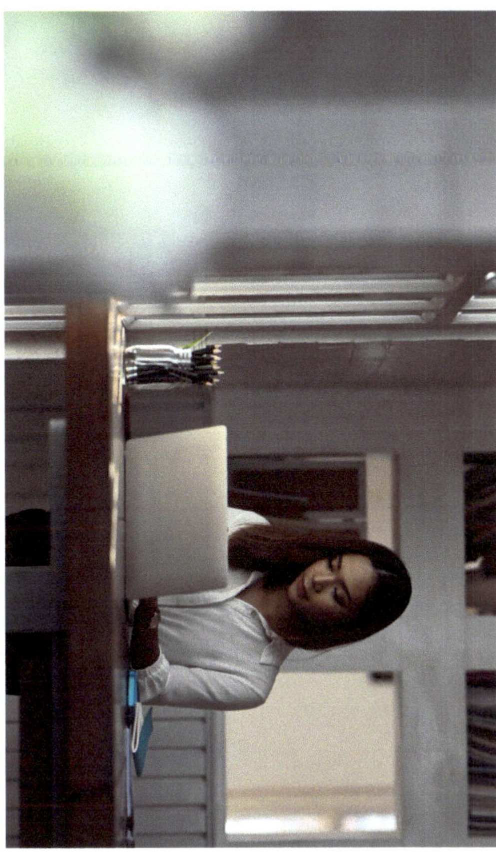

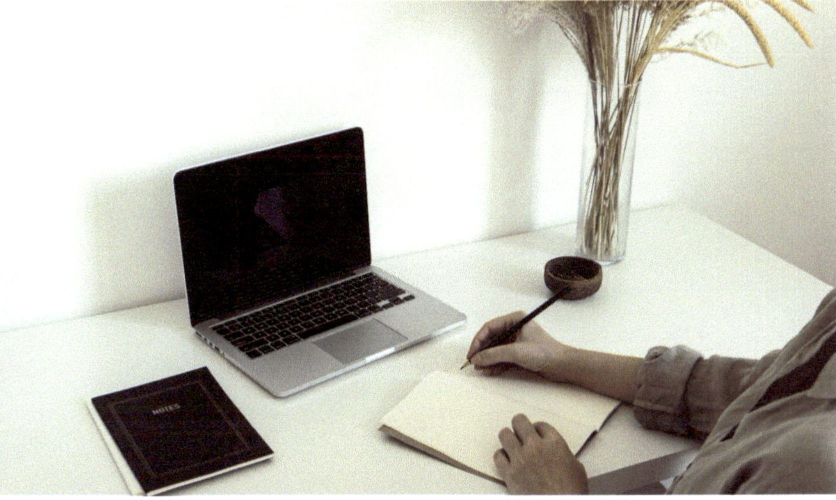

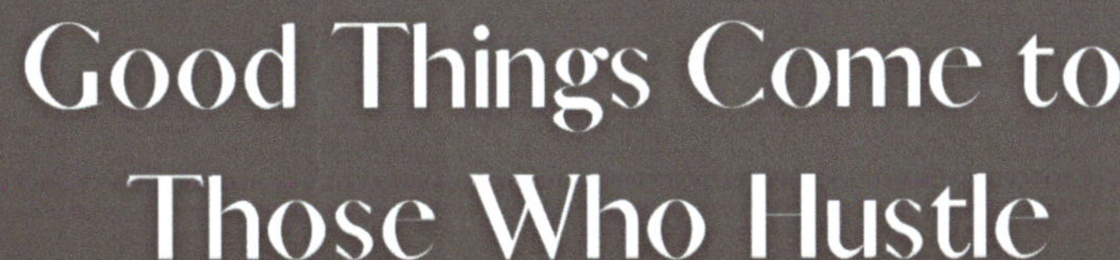
Good Things Come to
Those Who Hustle

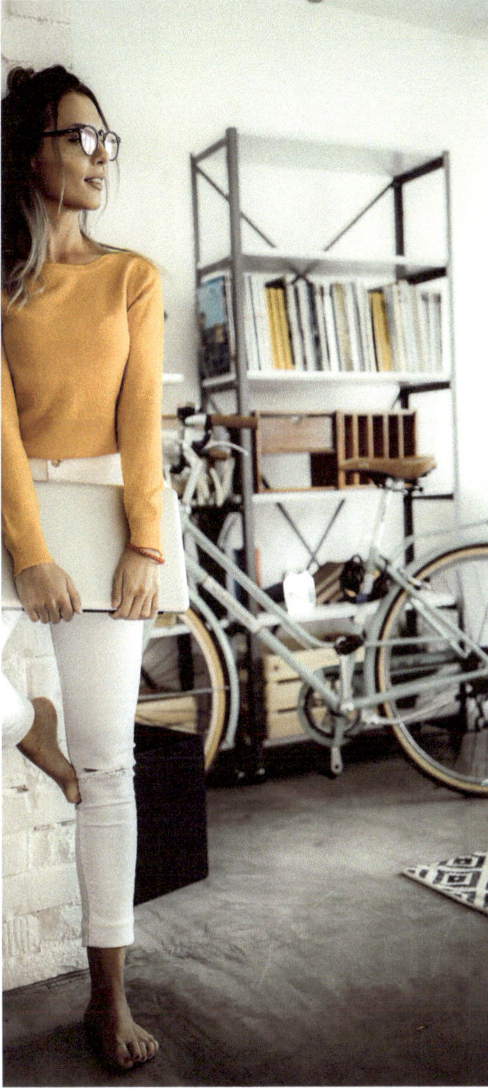

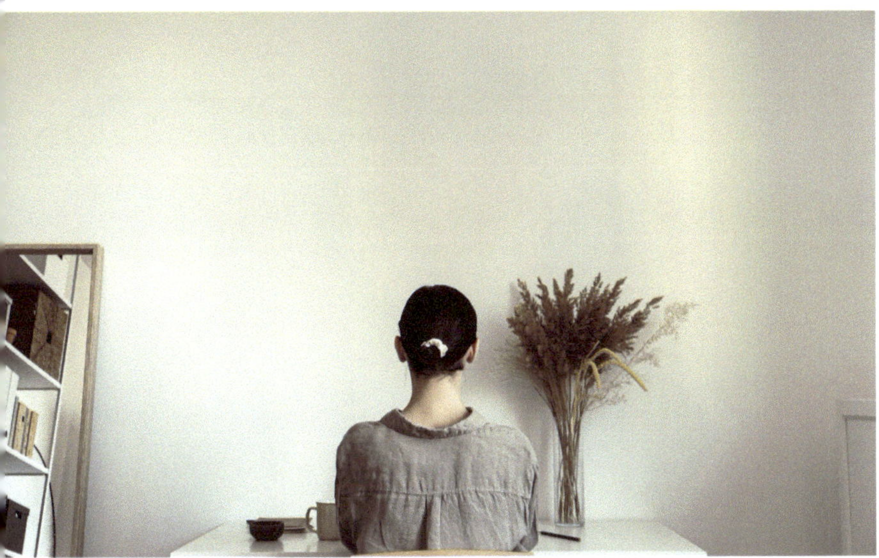

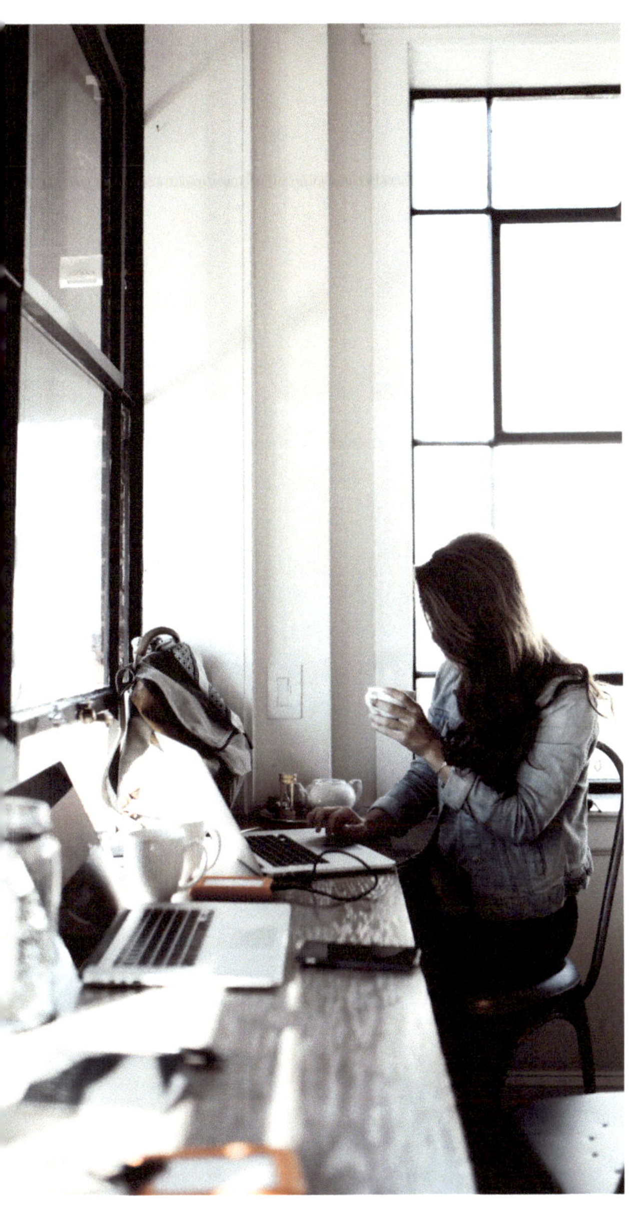

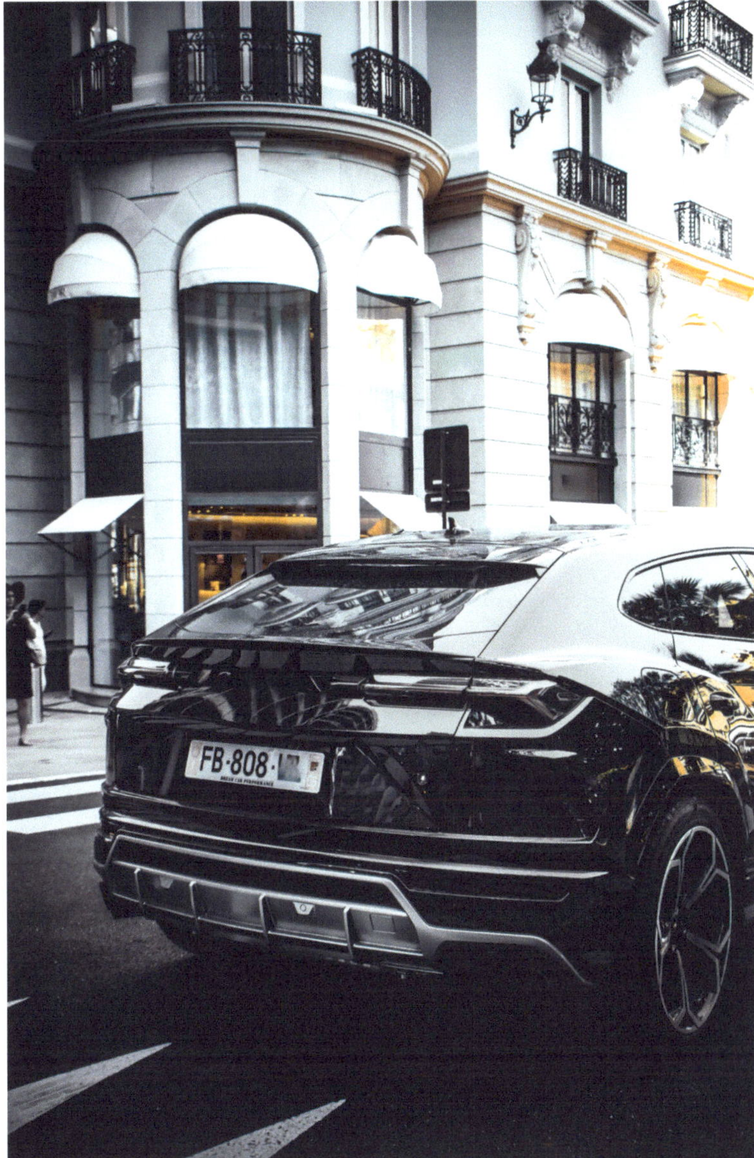
FB·808

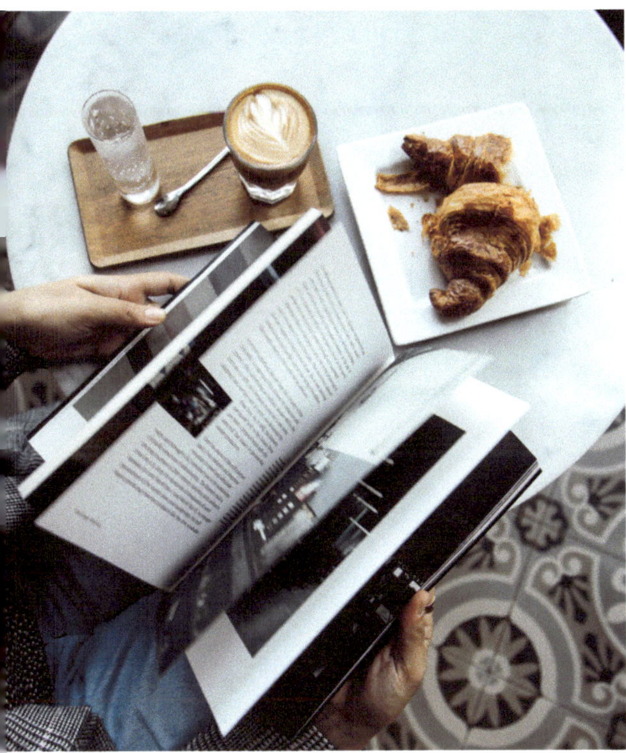

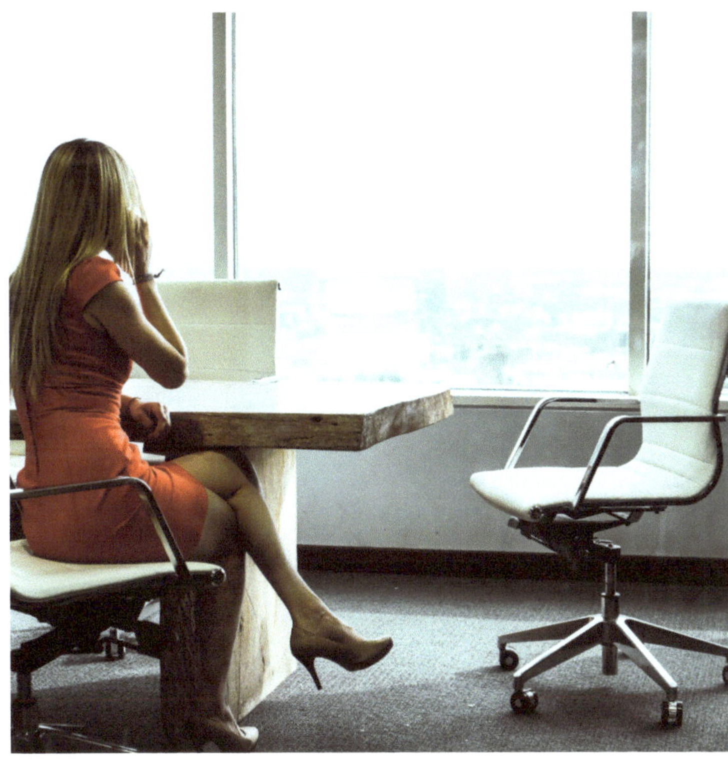

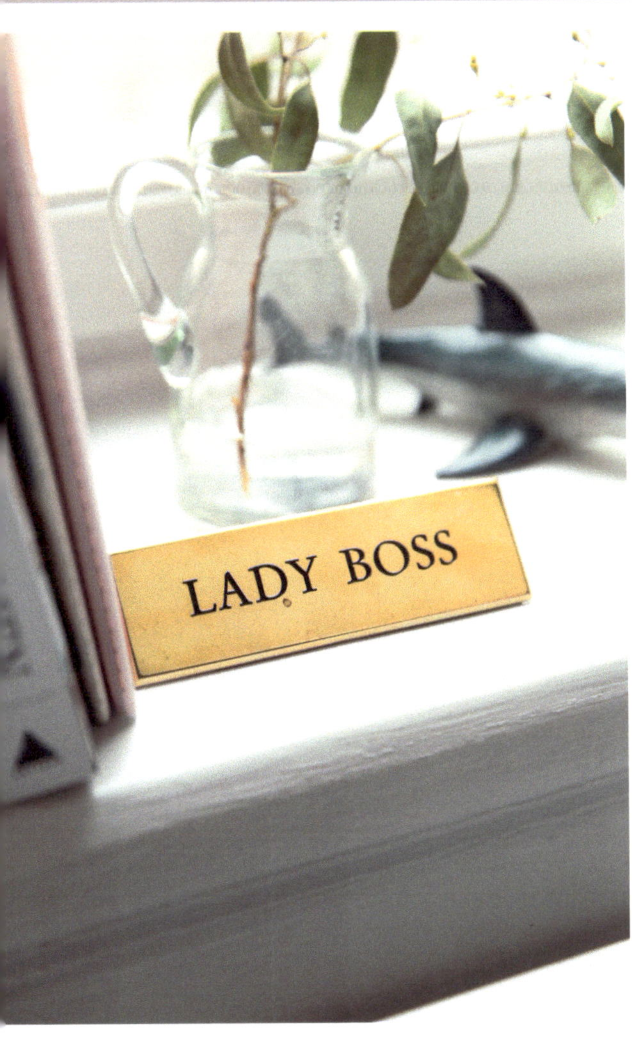
LADY BOSS
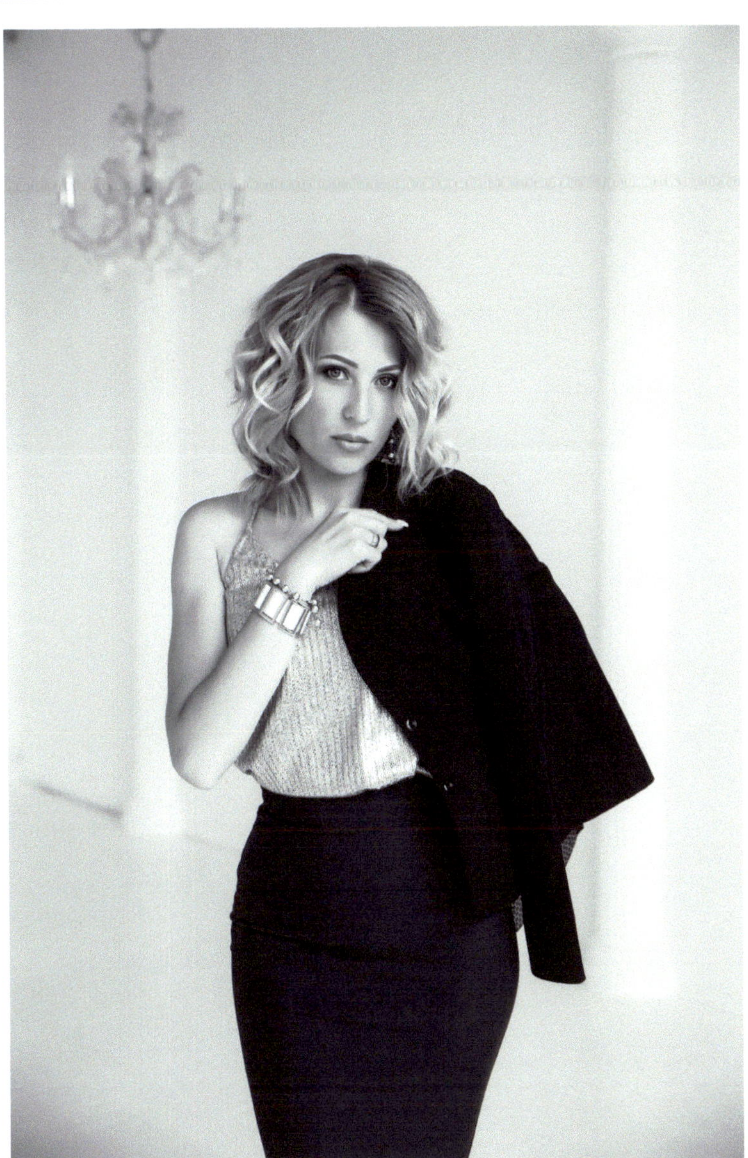
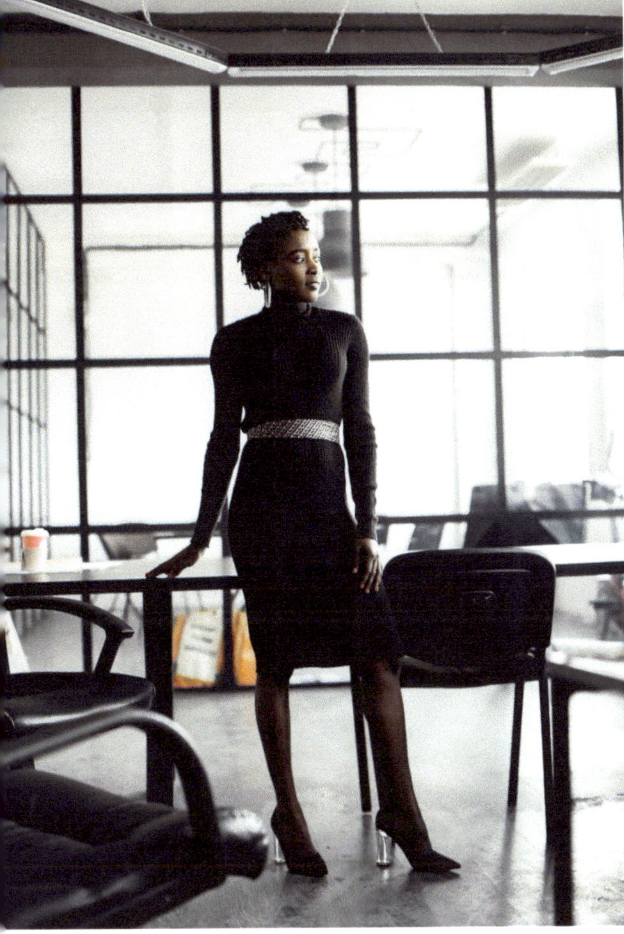
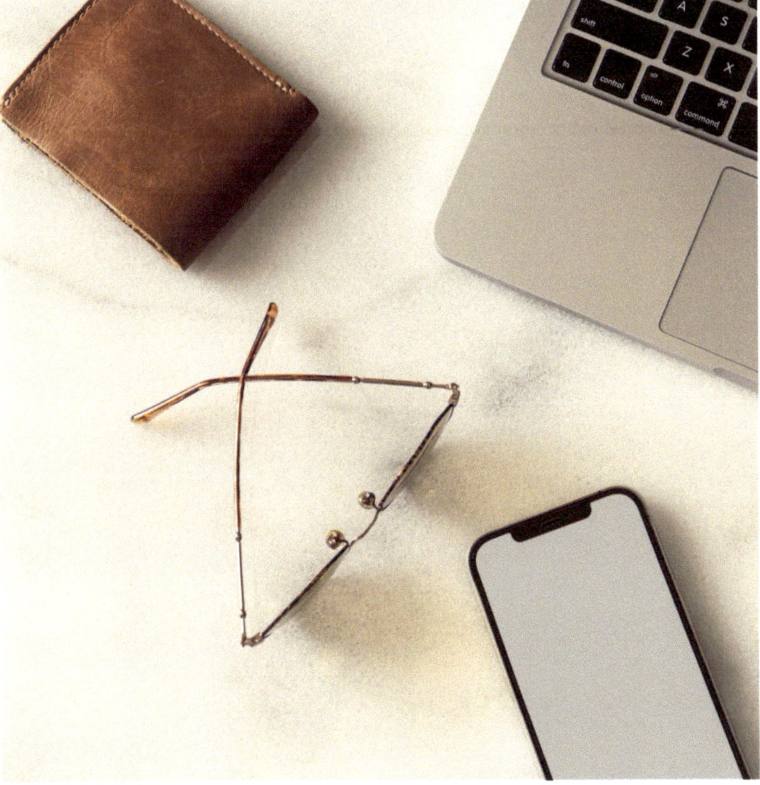

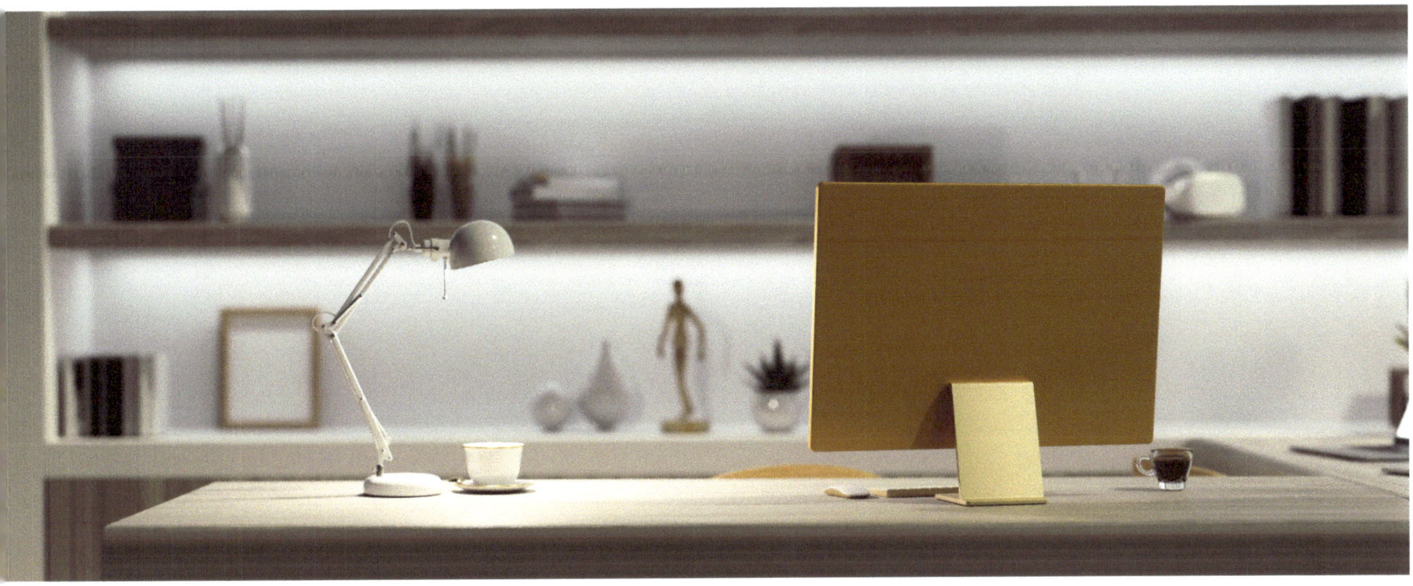

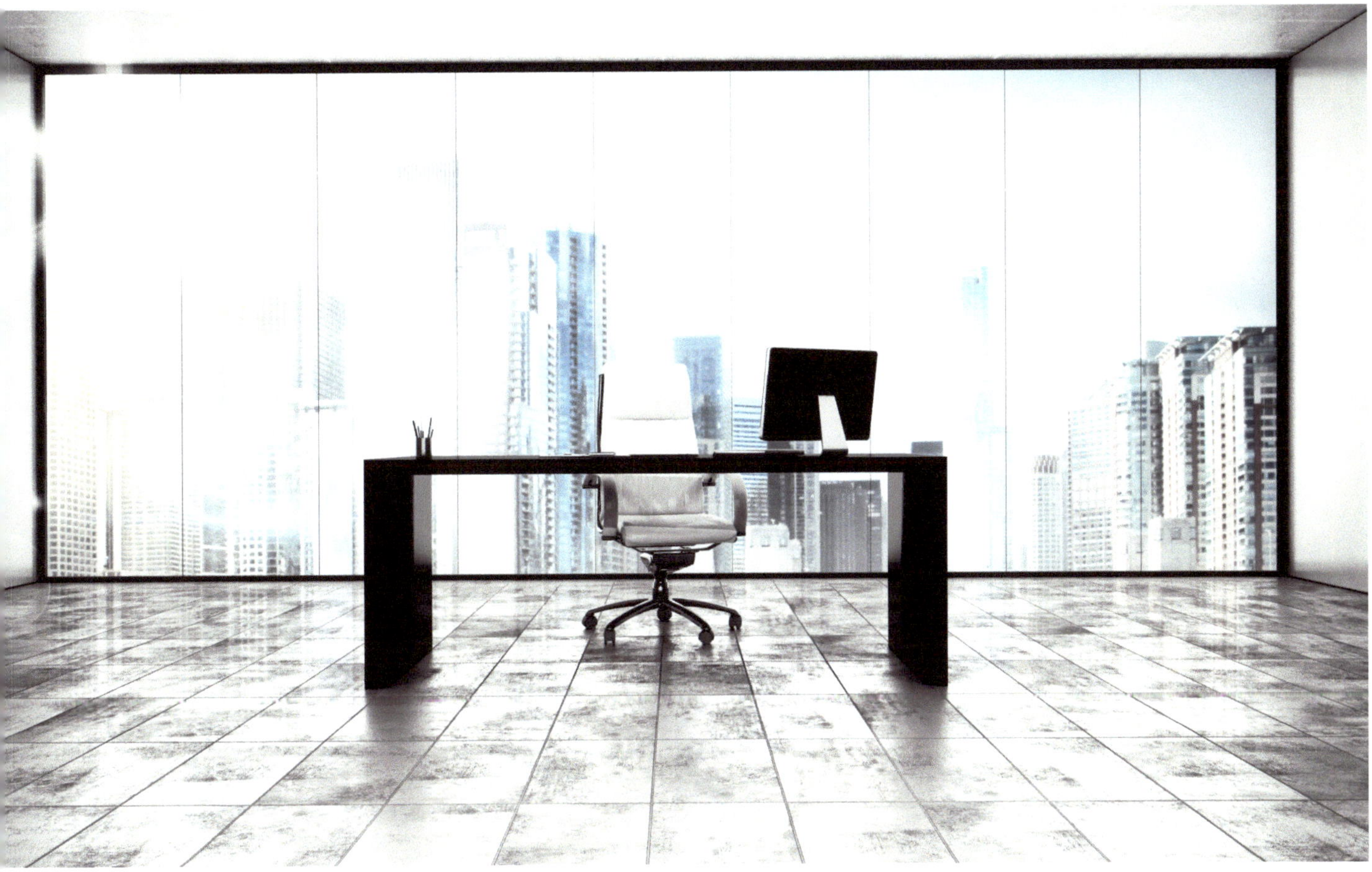

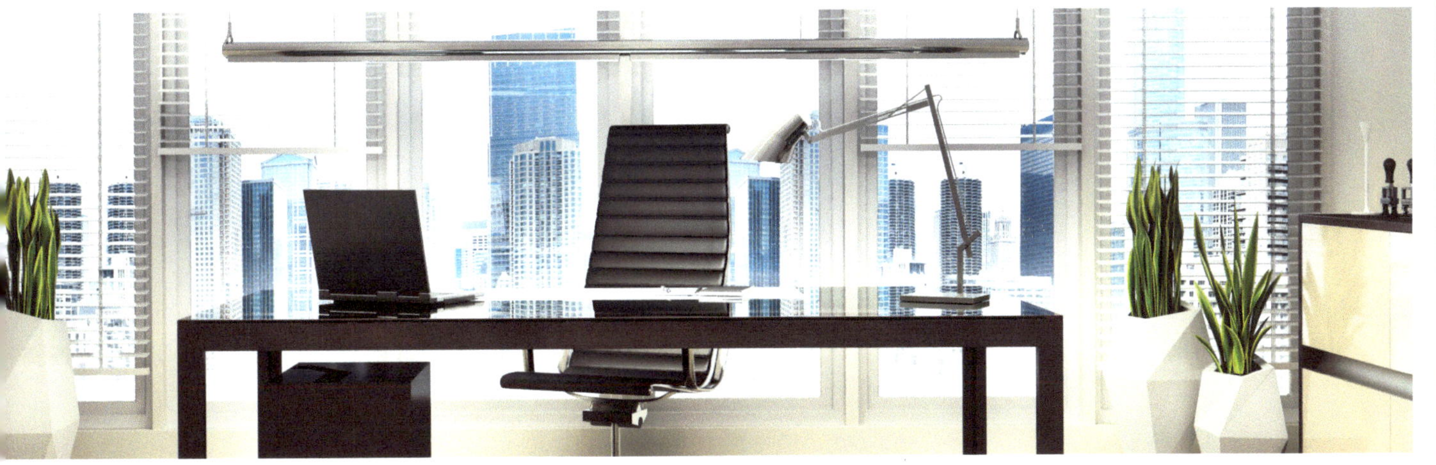

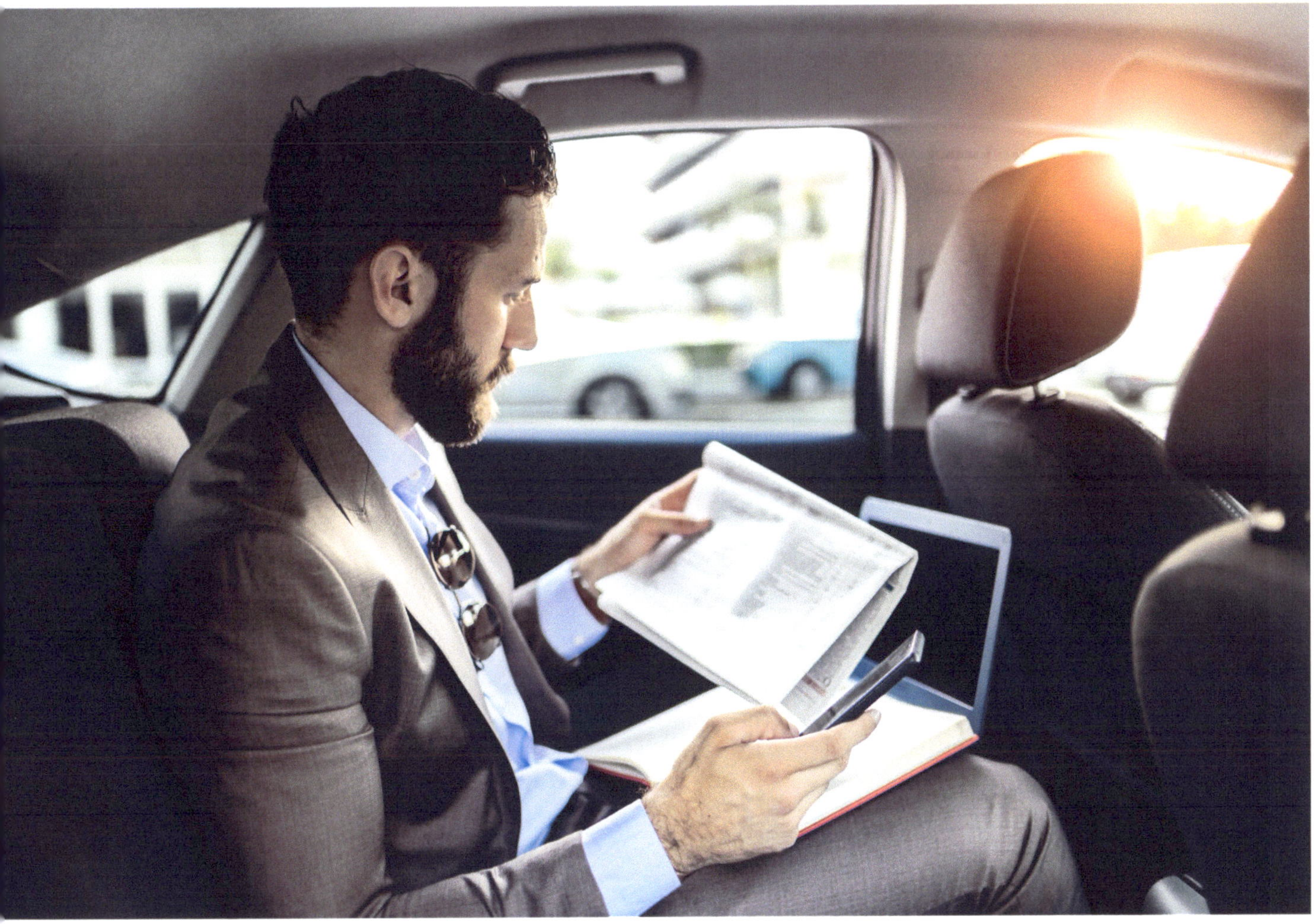

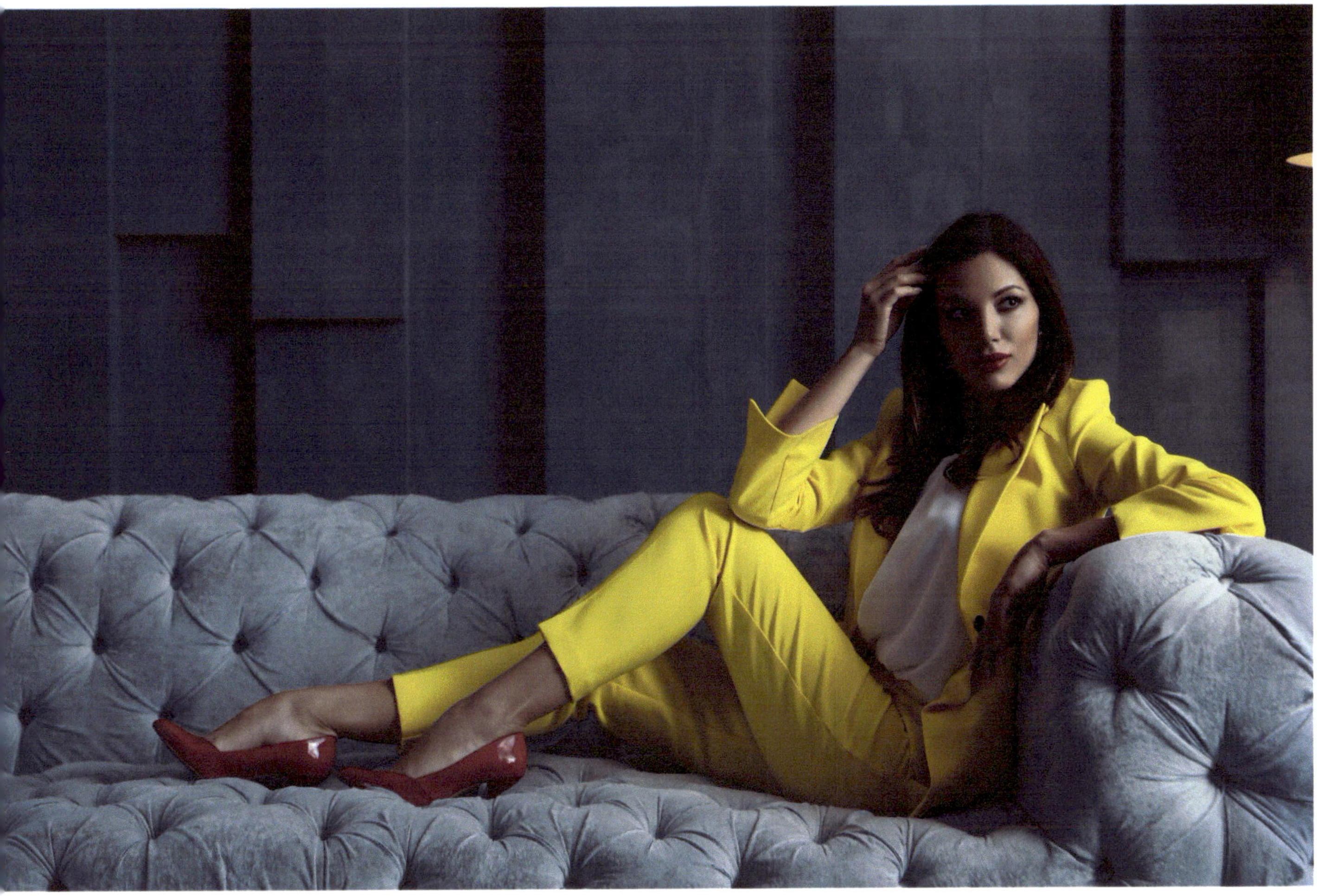

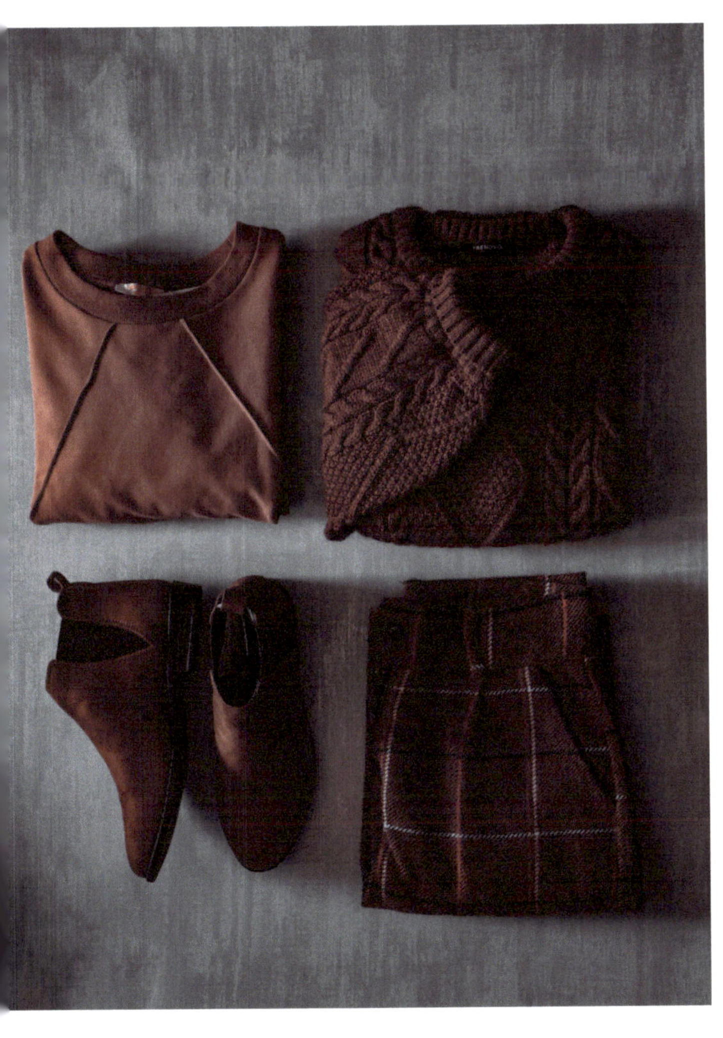

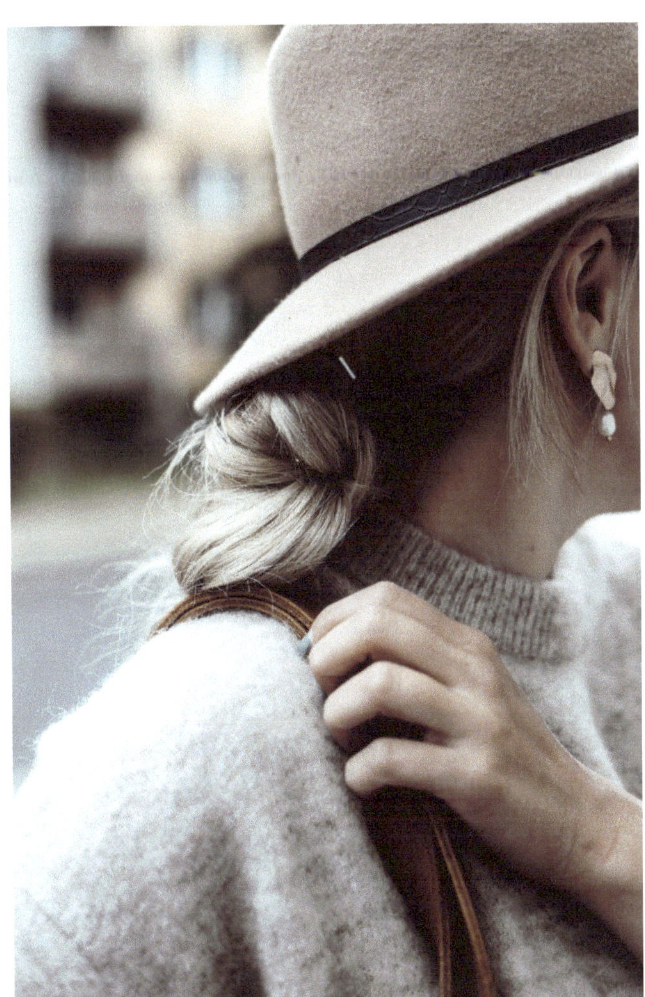

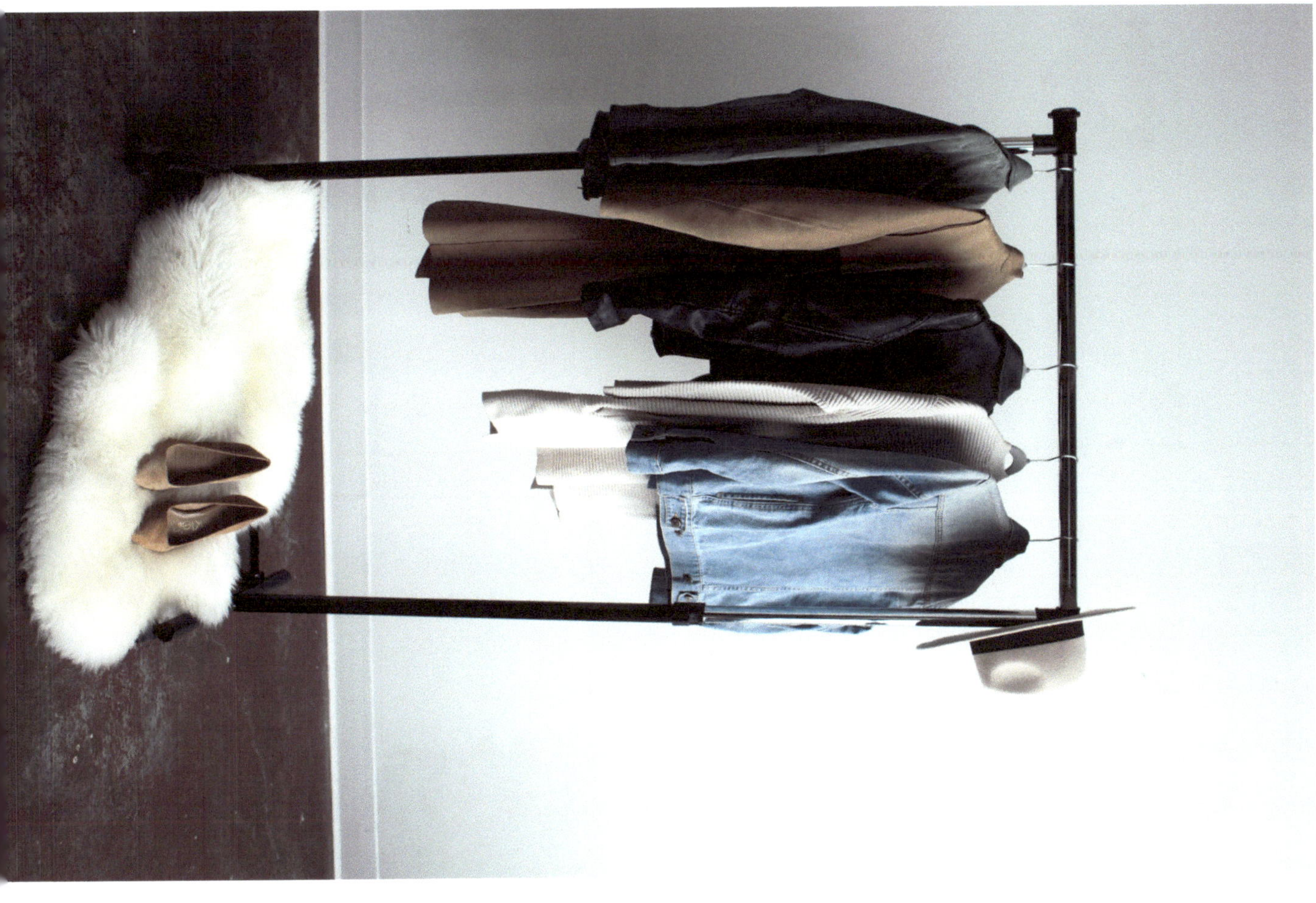

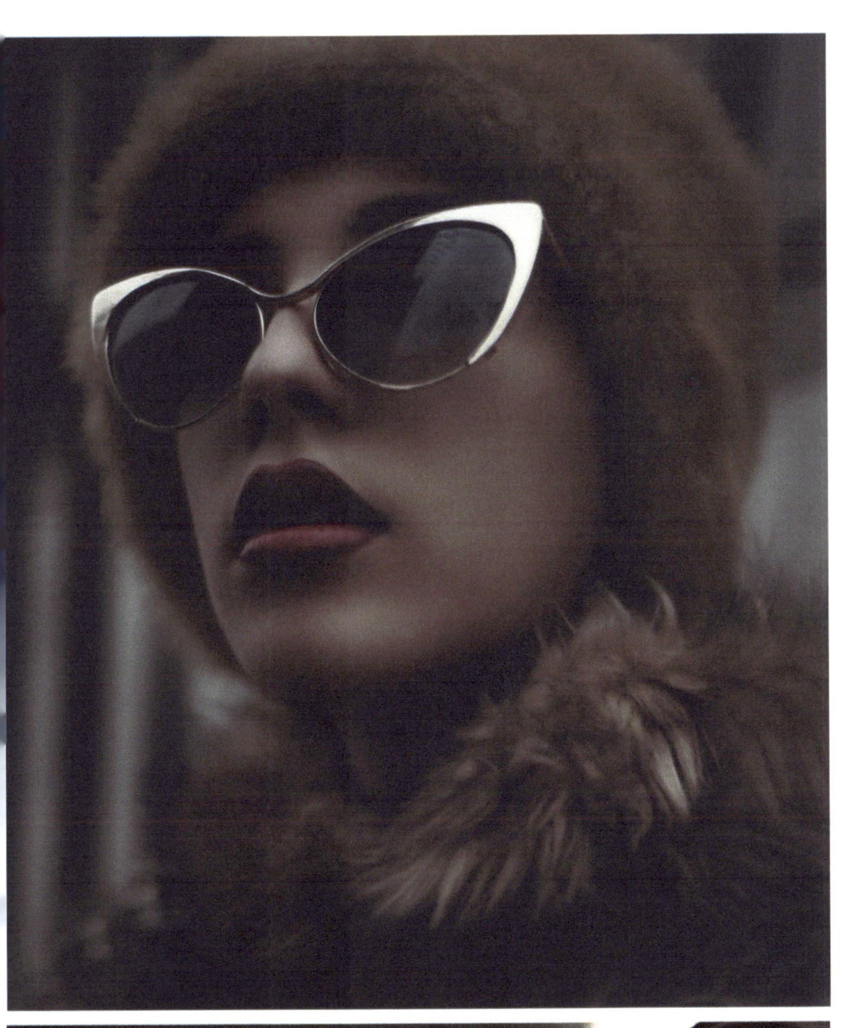

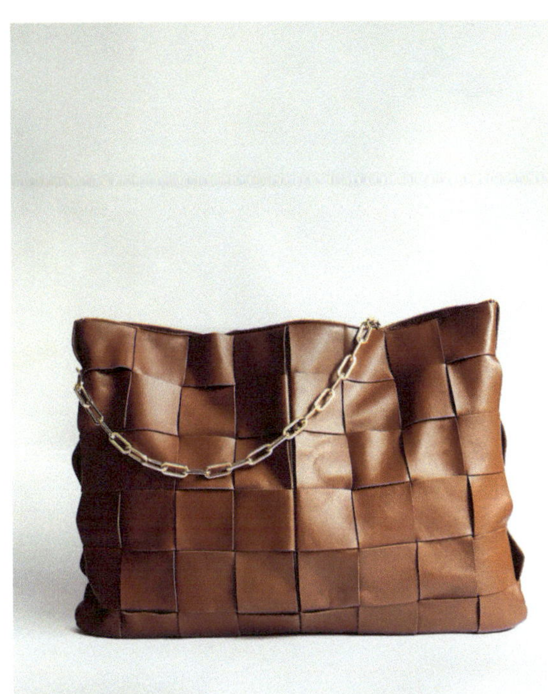

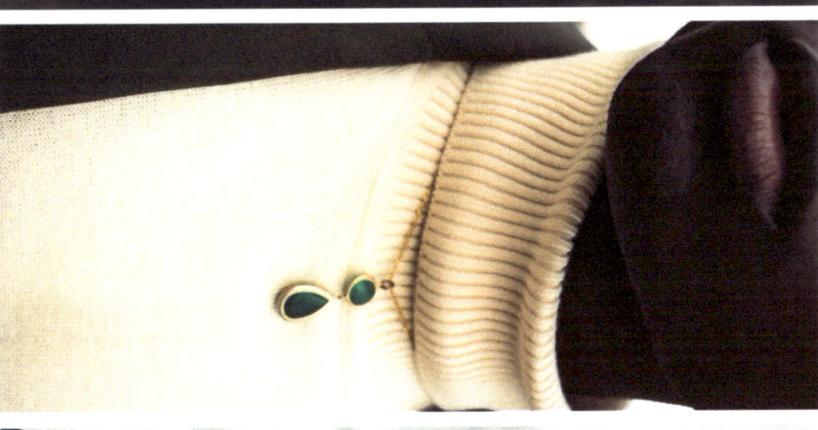

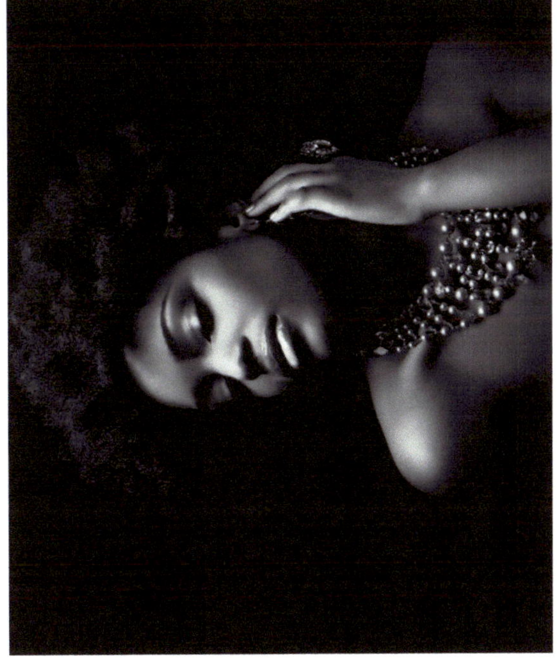

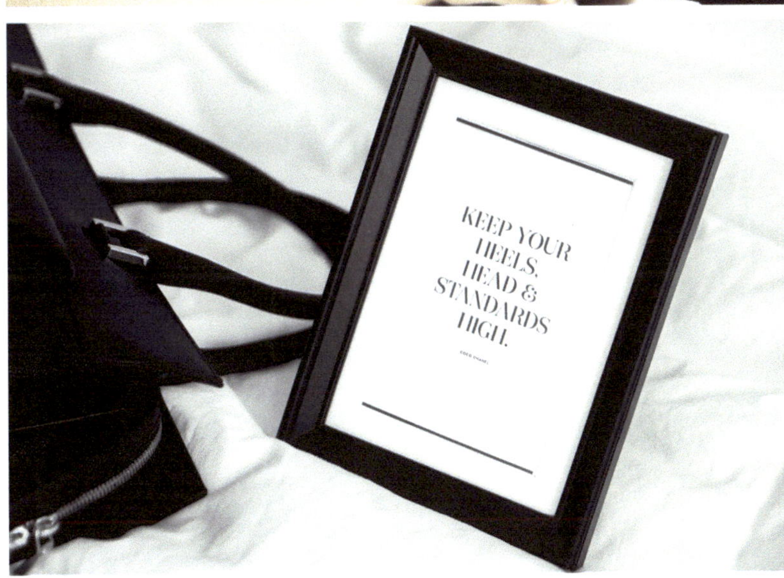
KEEP YOUR
HEELS,
HEAD &
STANDARDS
HIGH.

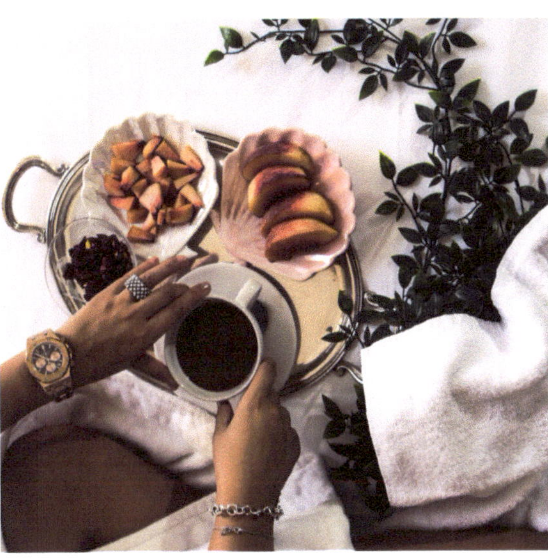

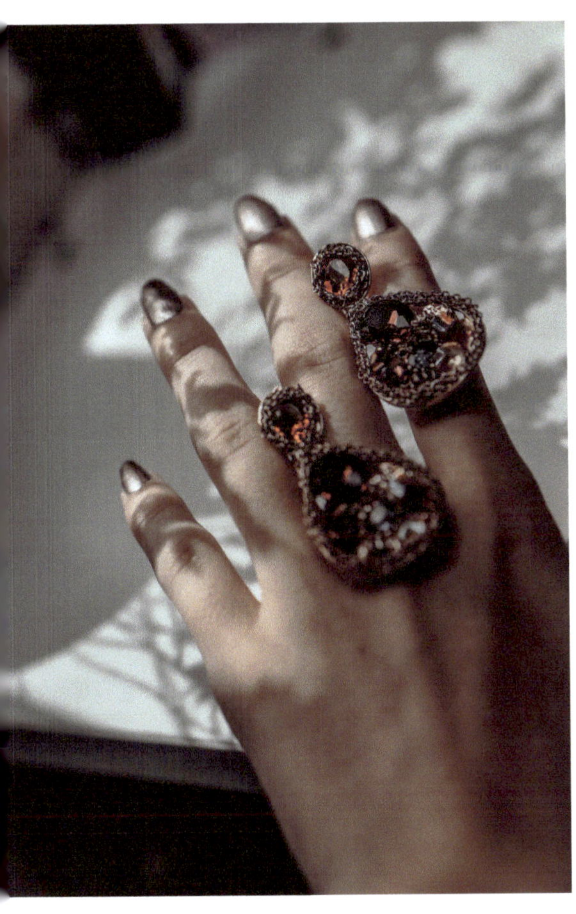

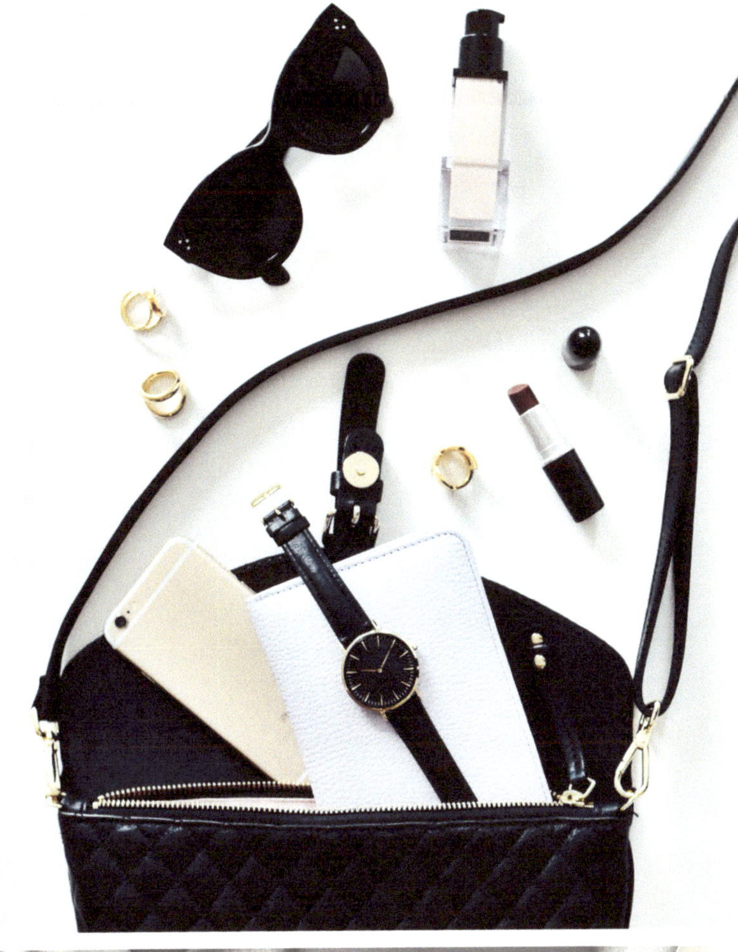

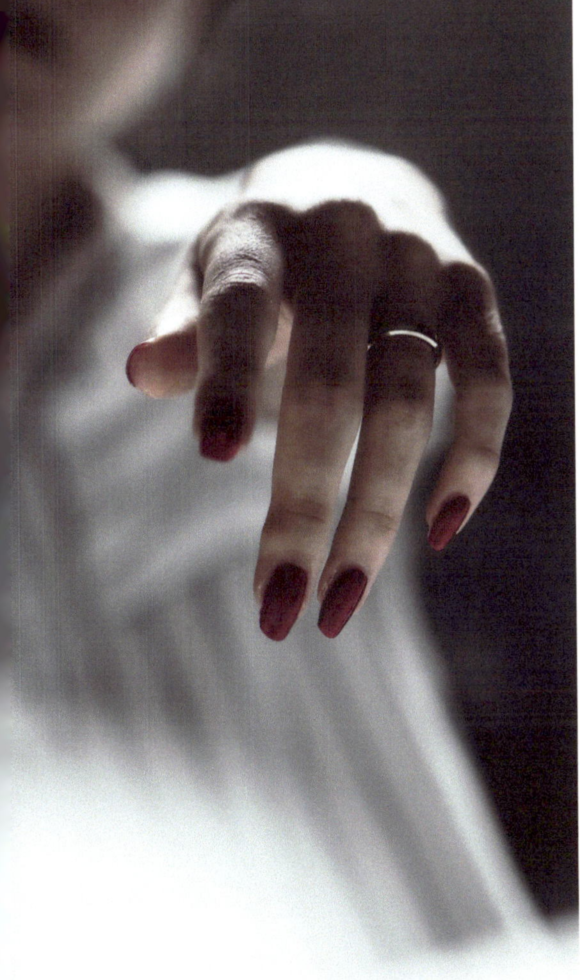

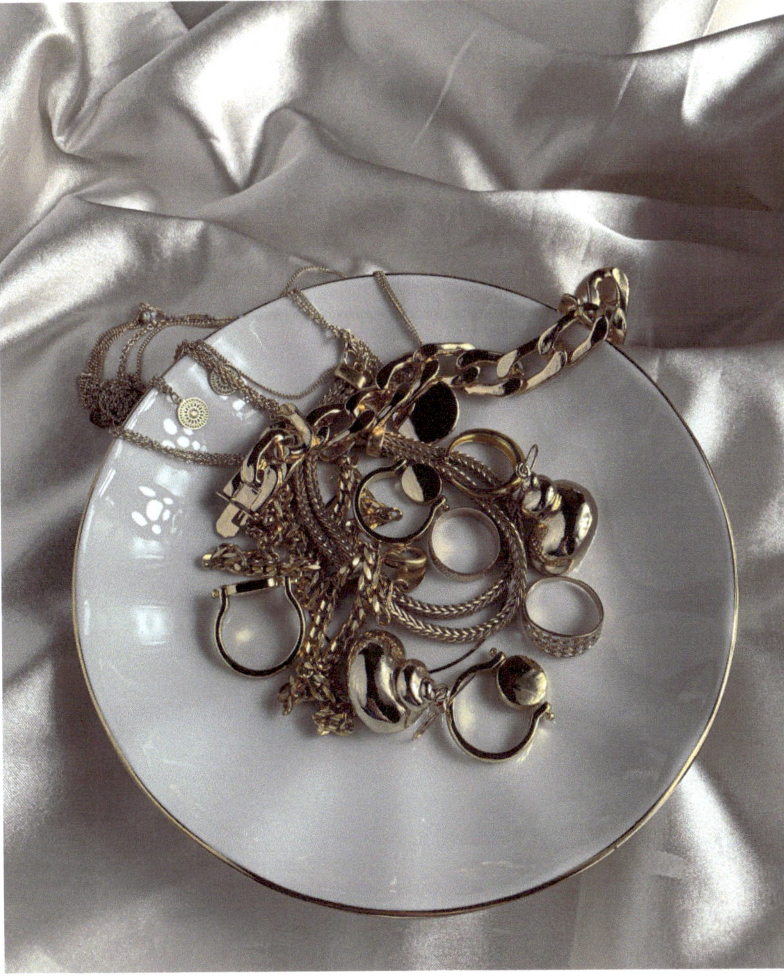

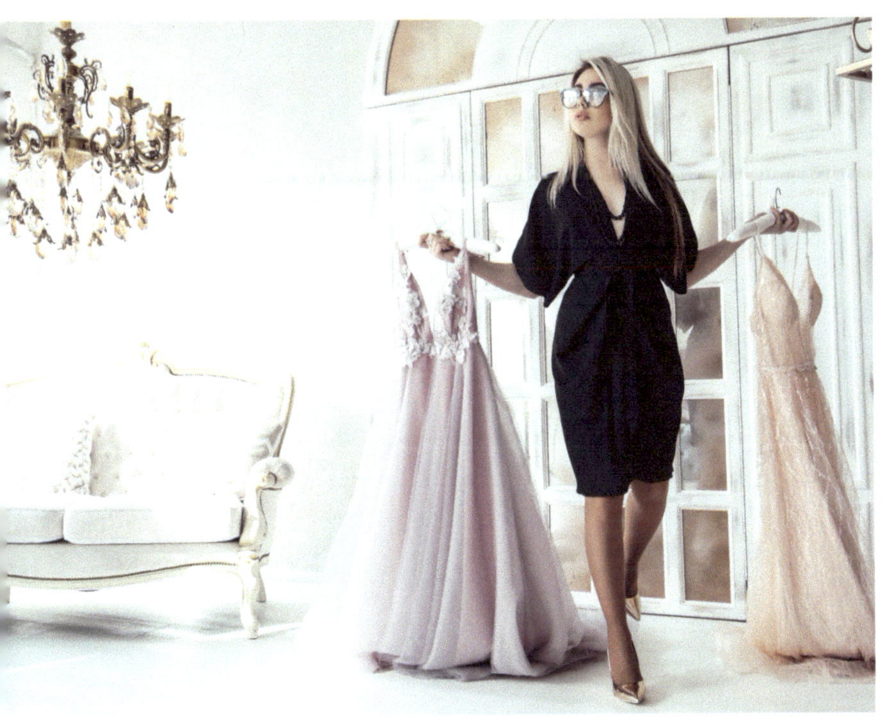
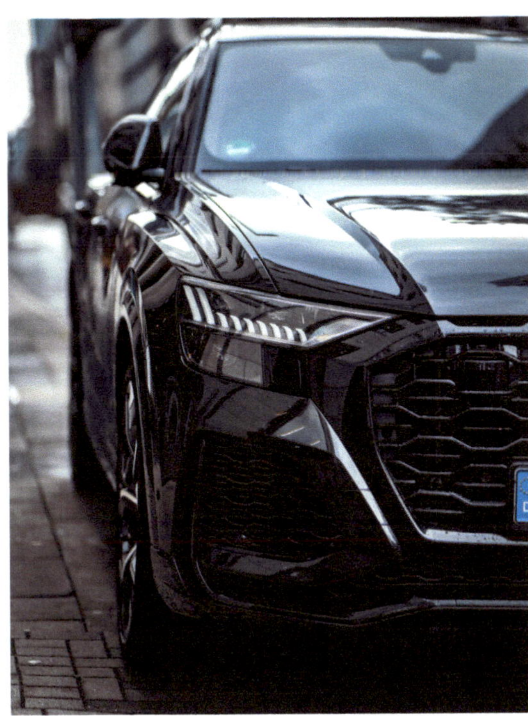
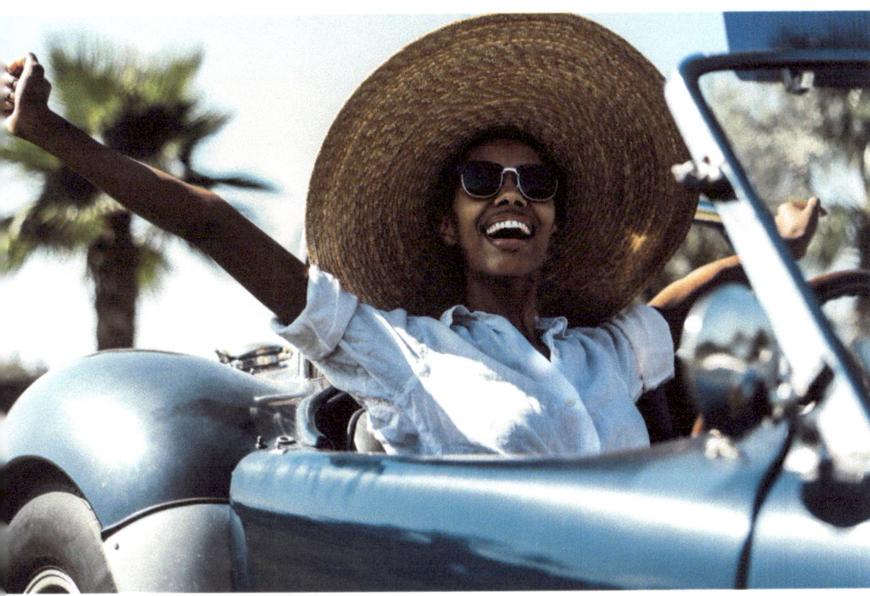
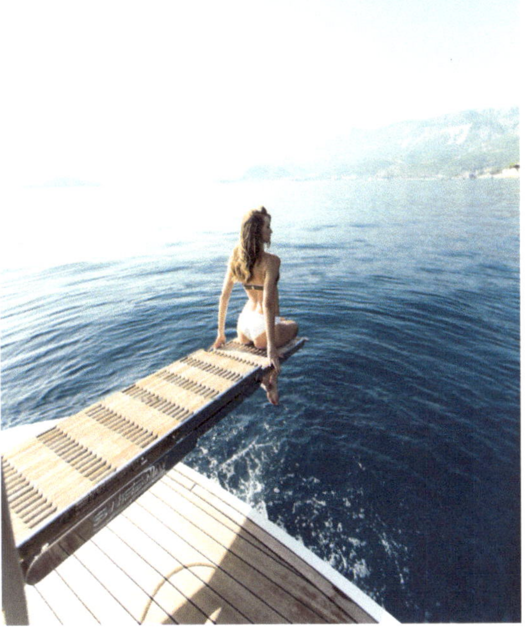
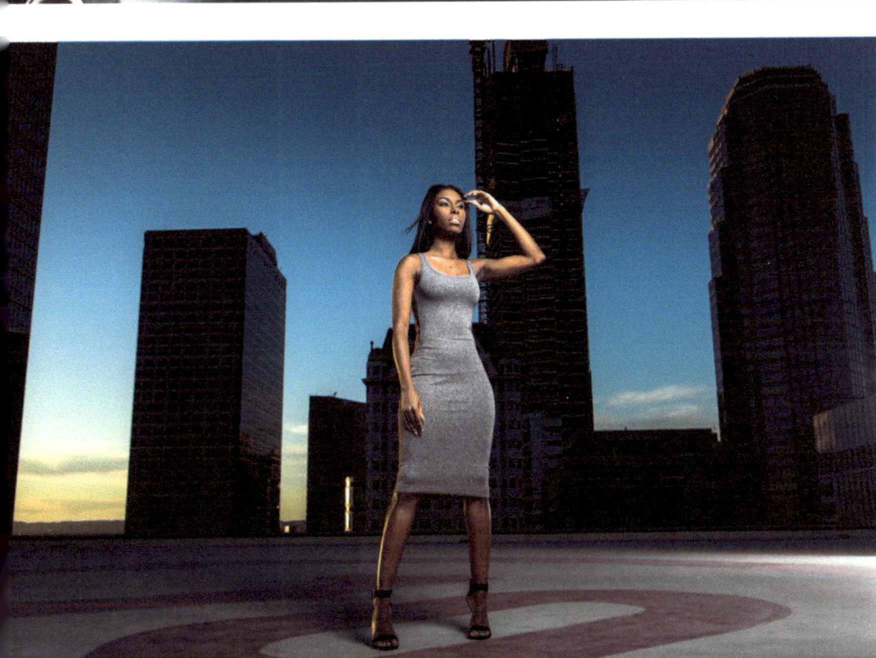
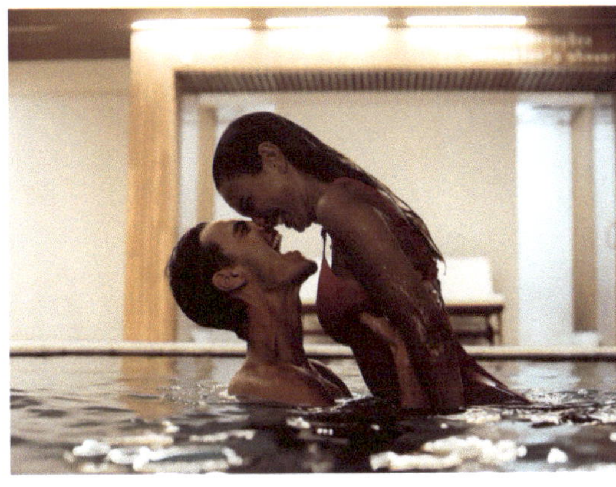

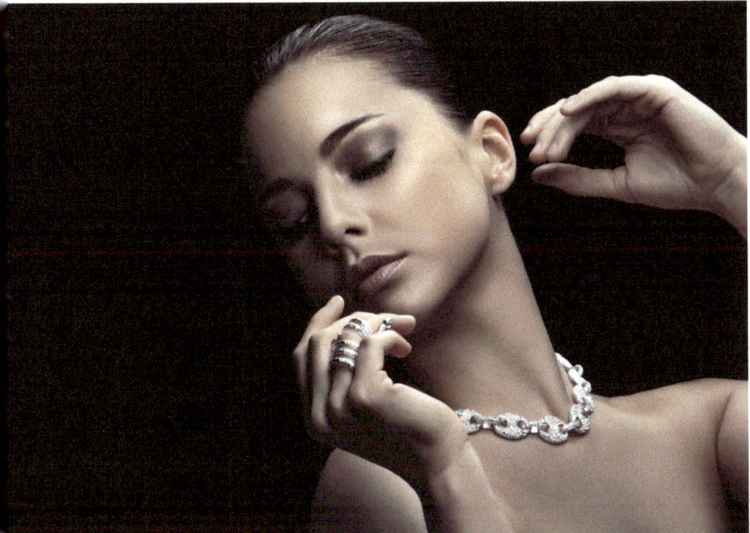

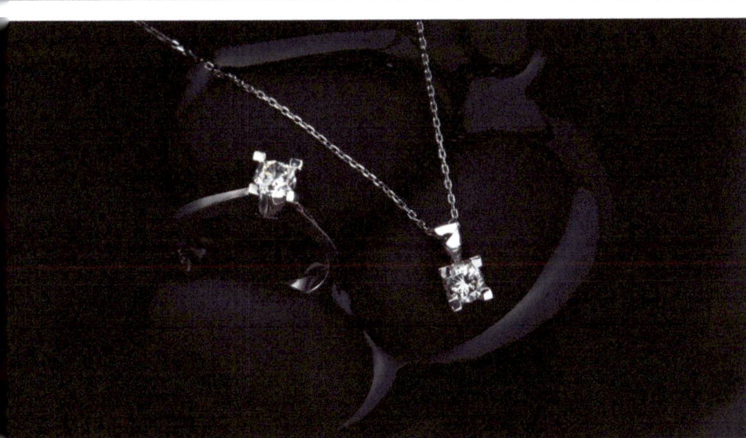

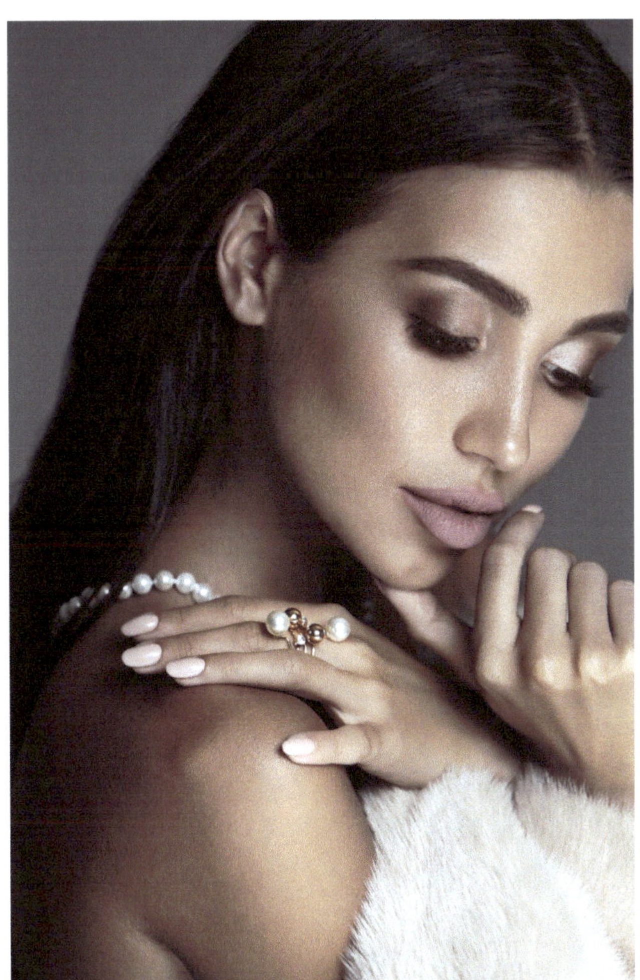

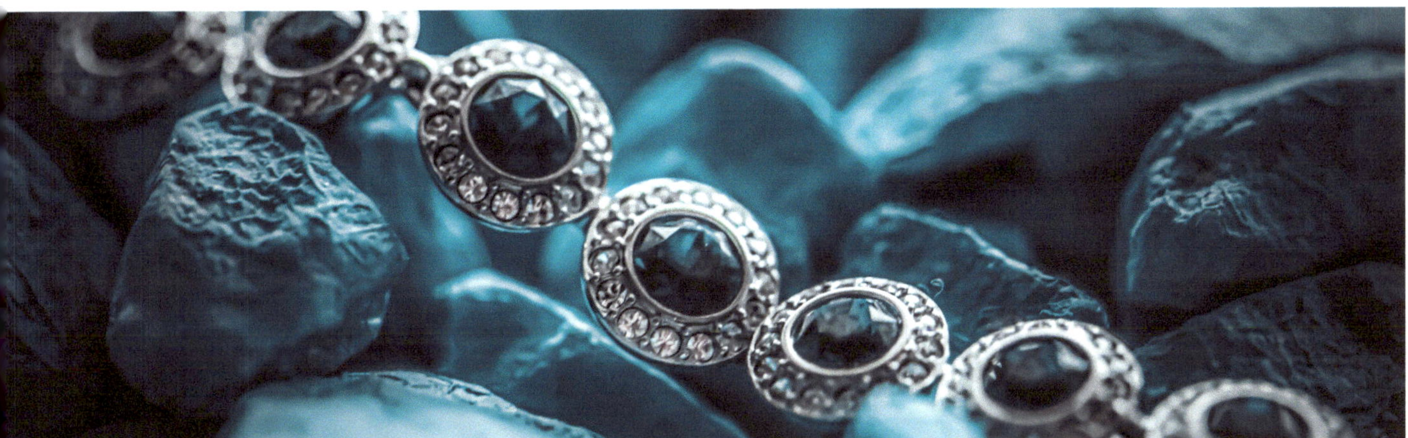

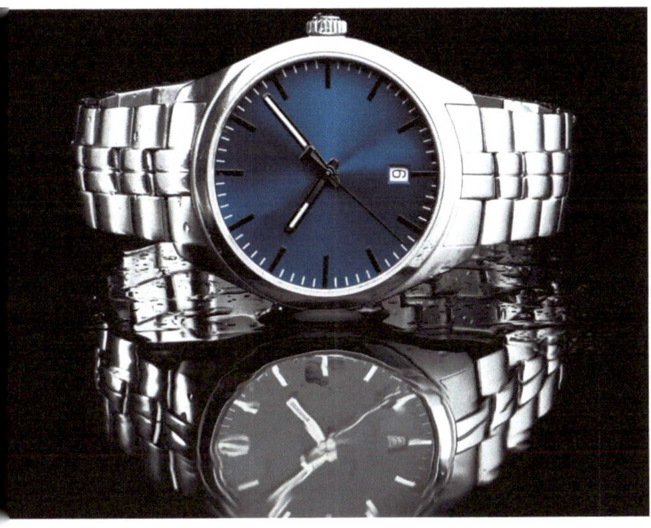

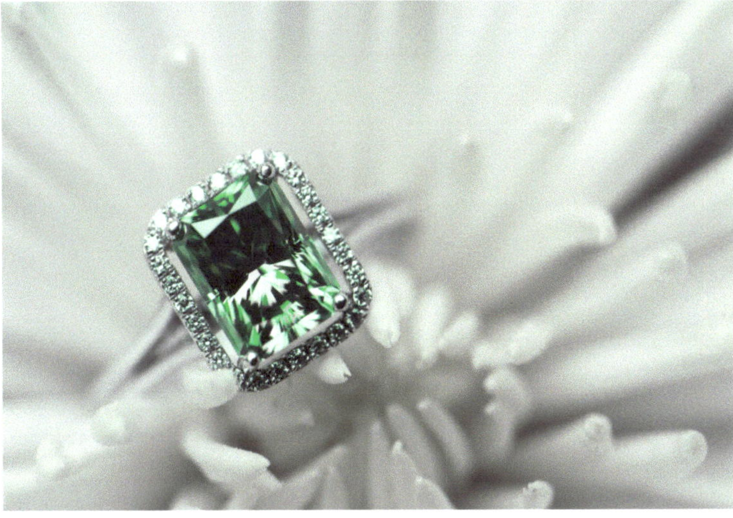

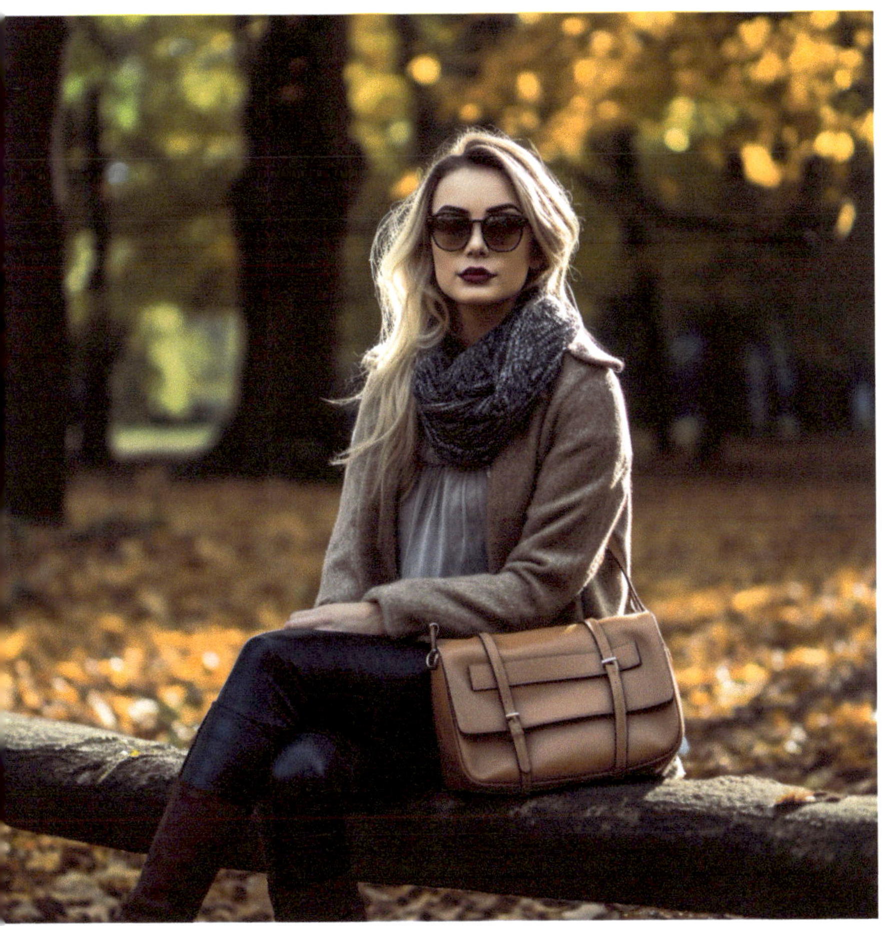

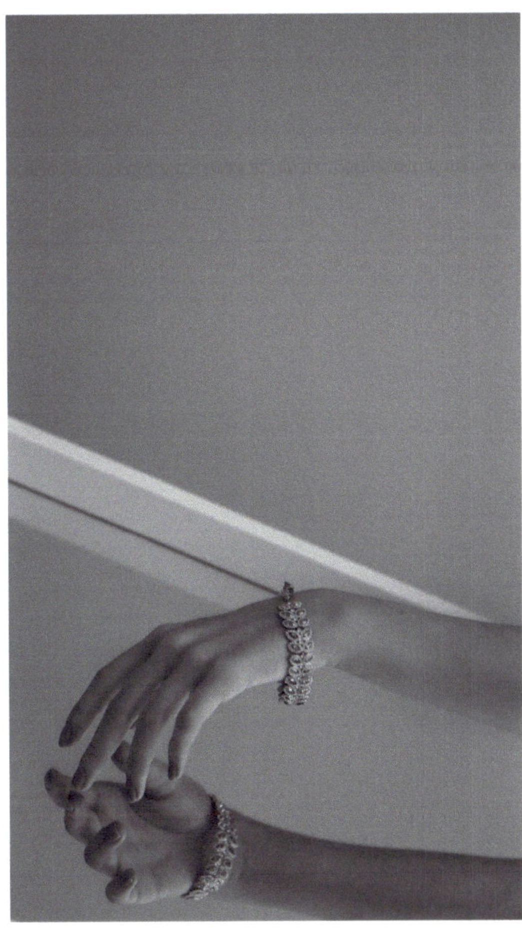

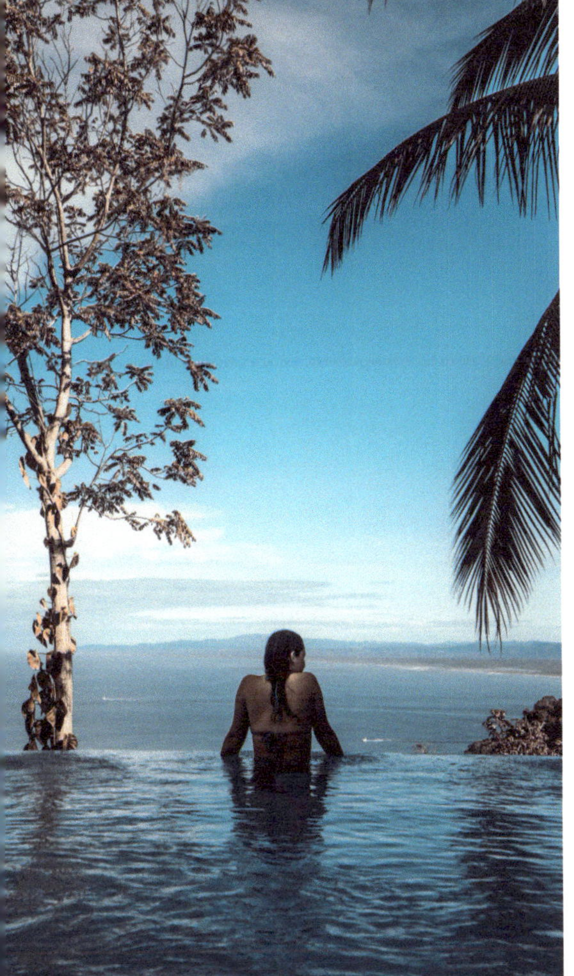

"Luxury is a state of mind."

-L Wren Scott

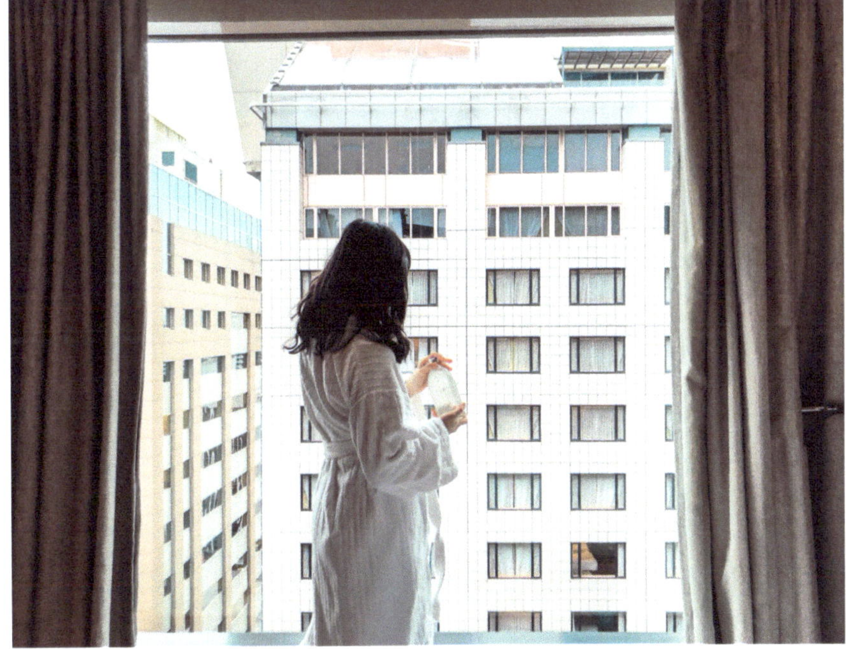

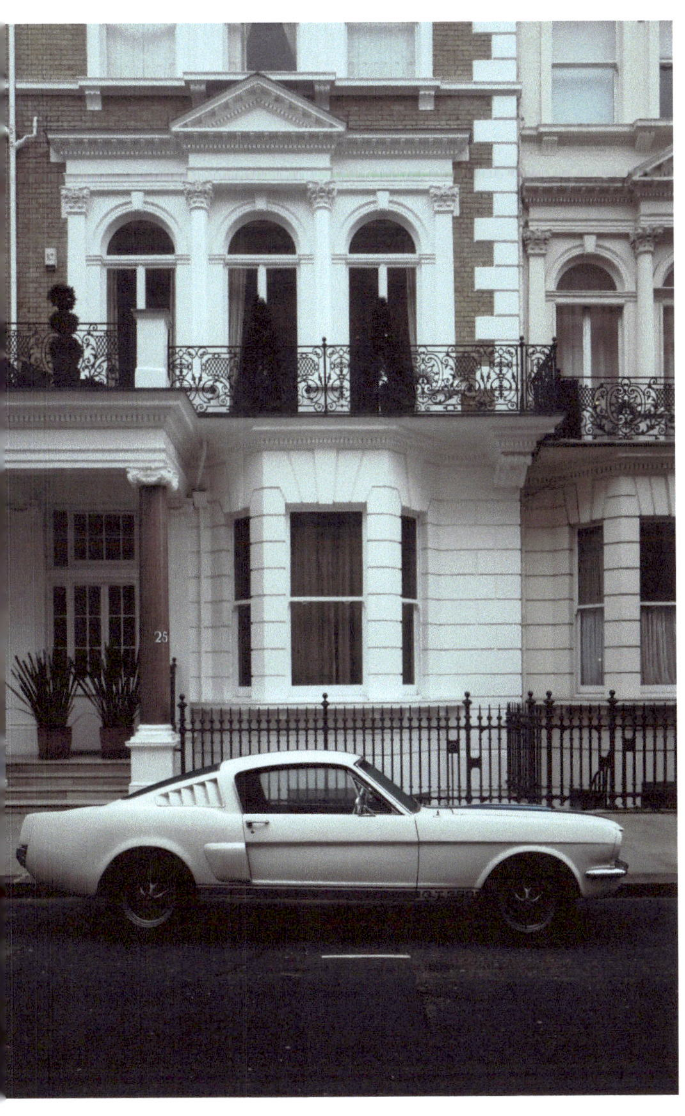
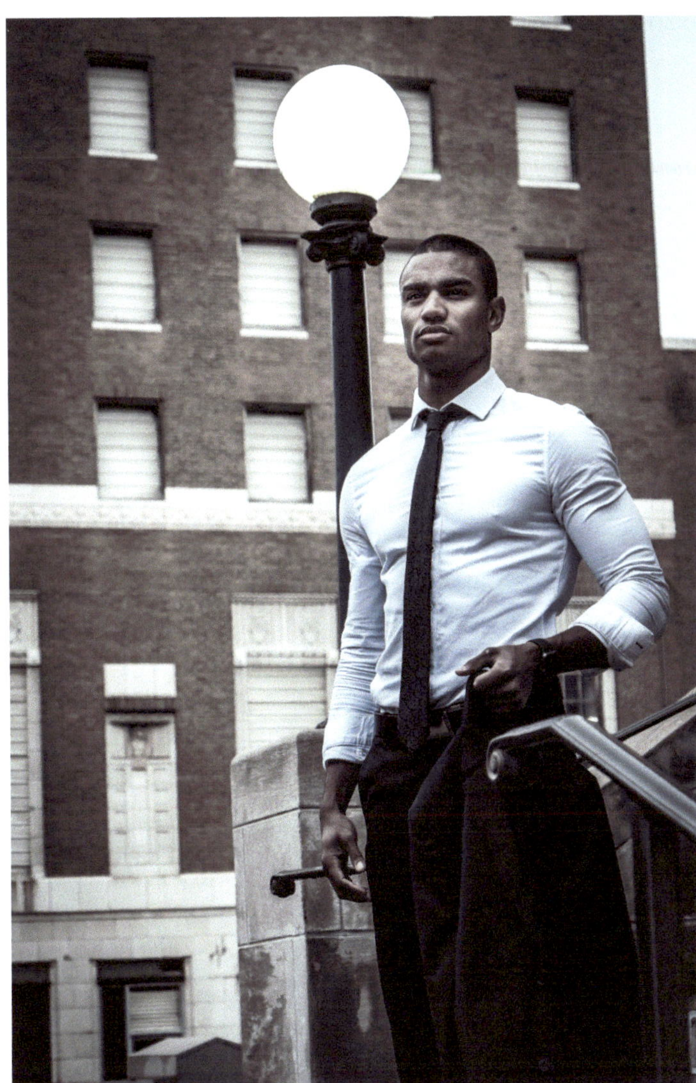
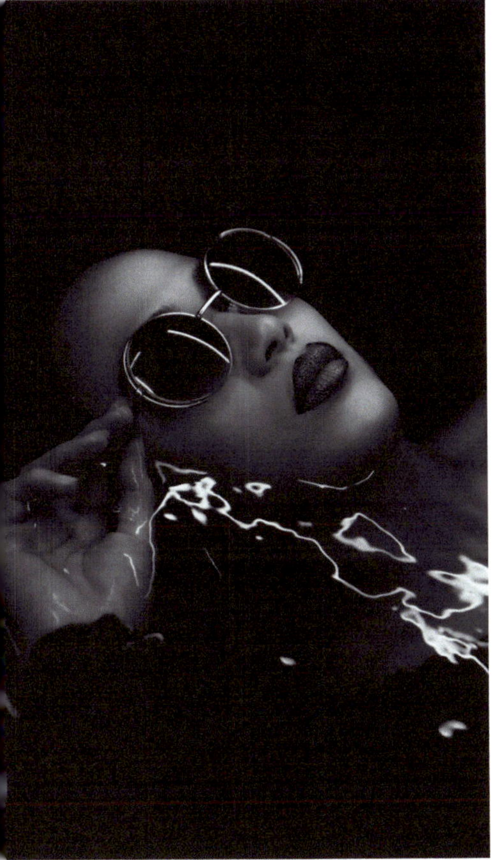
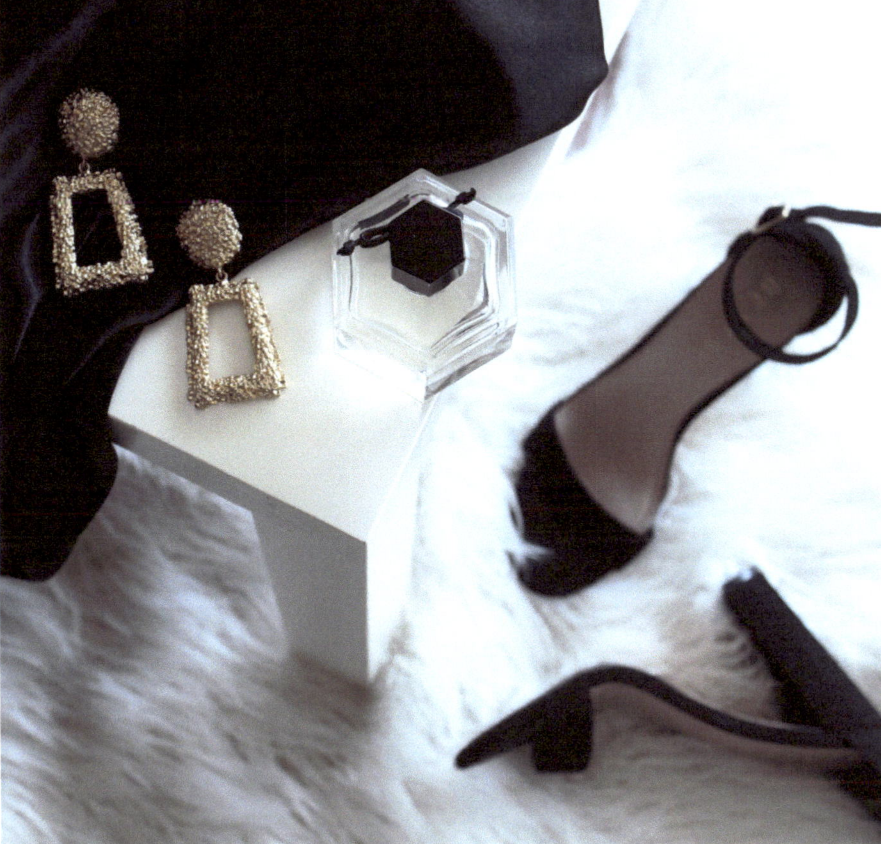

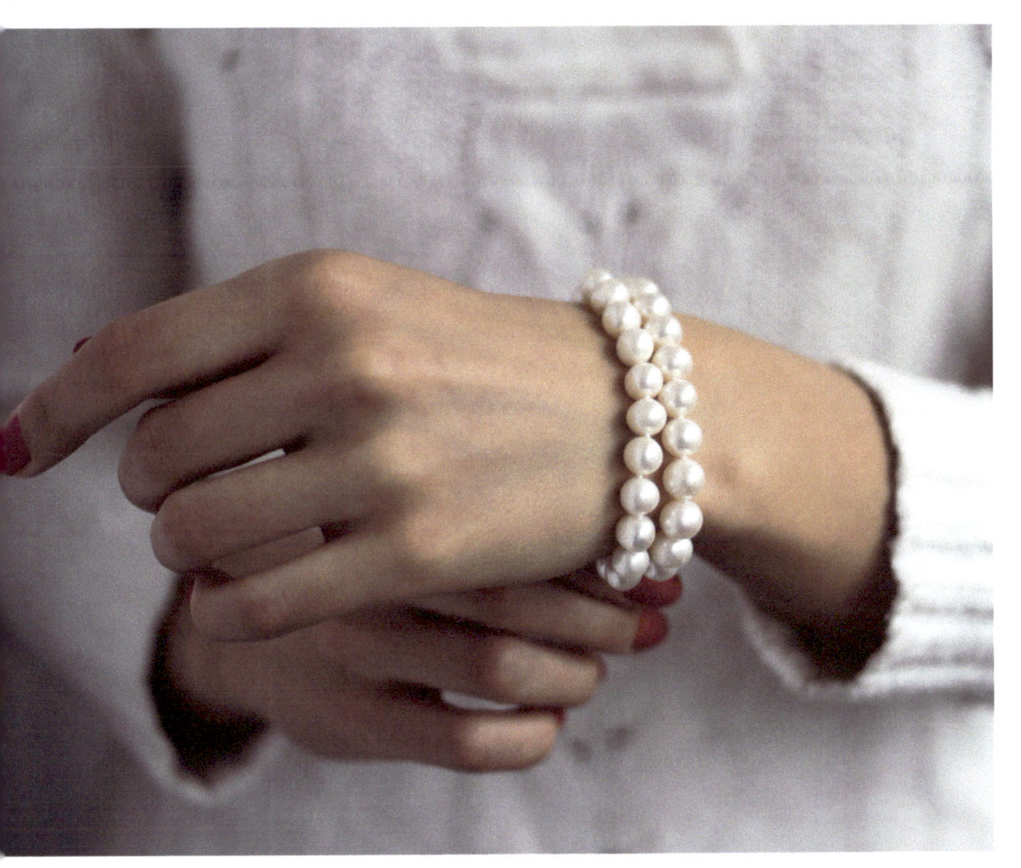
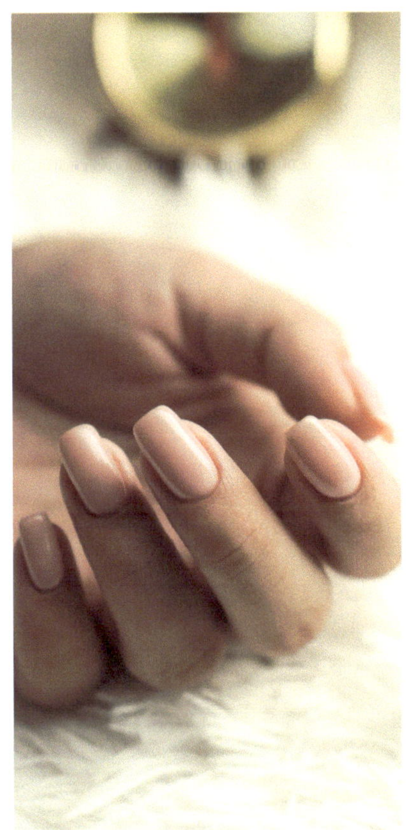
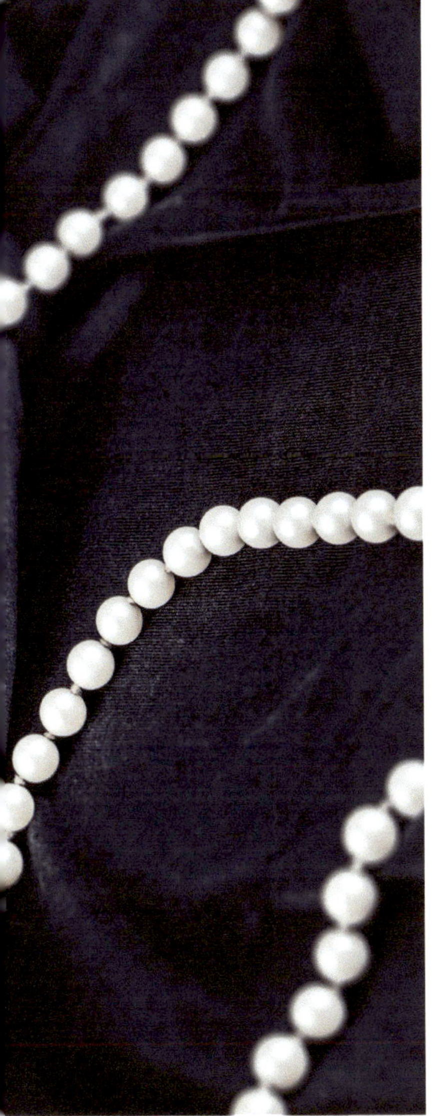

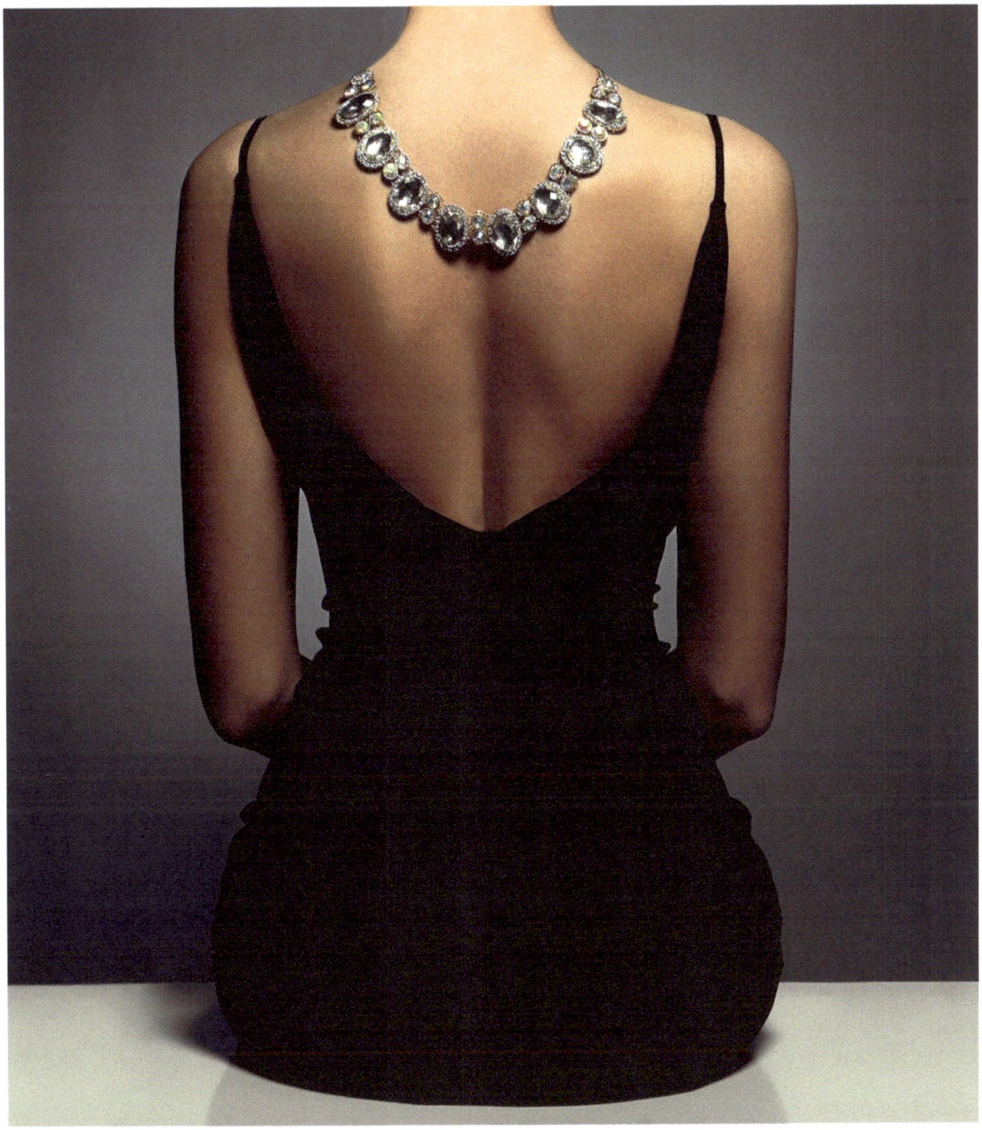

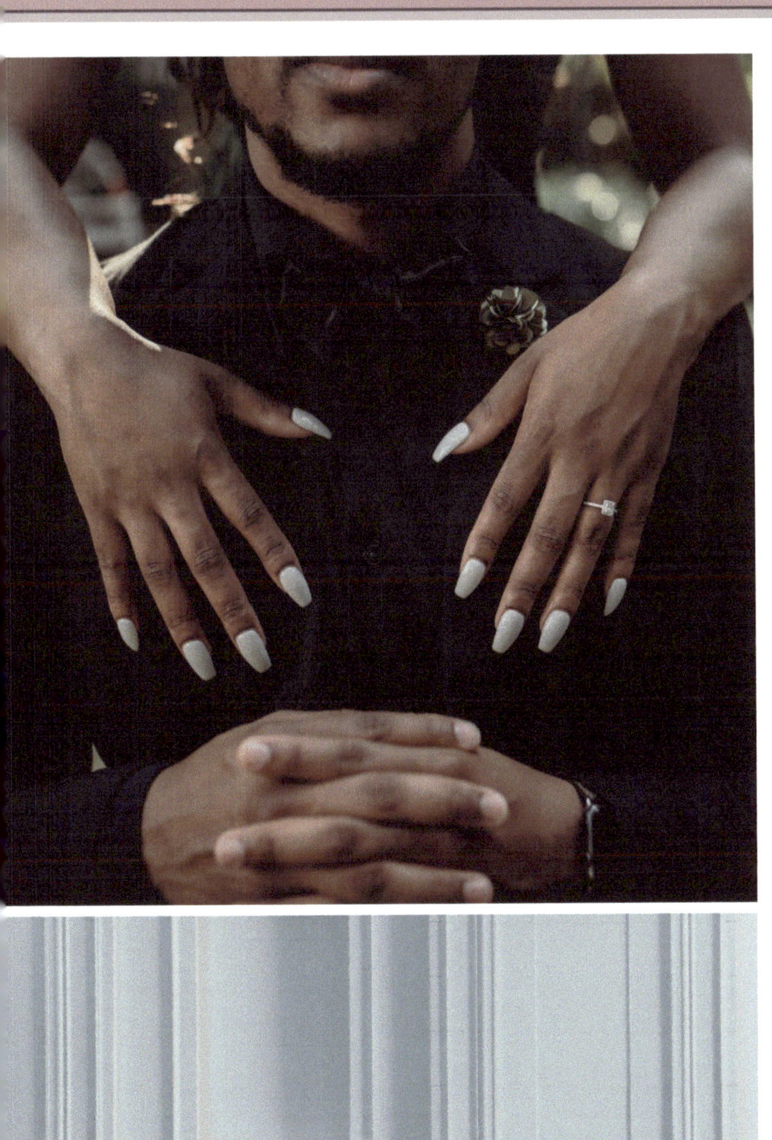
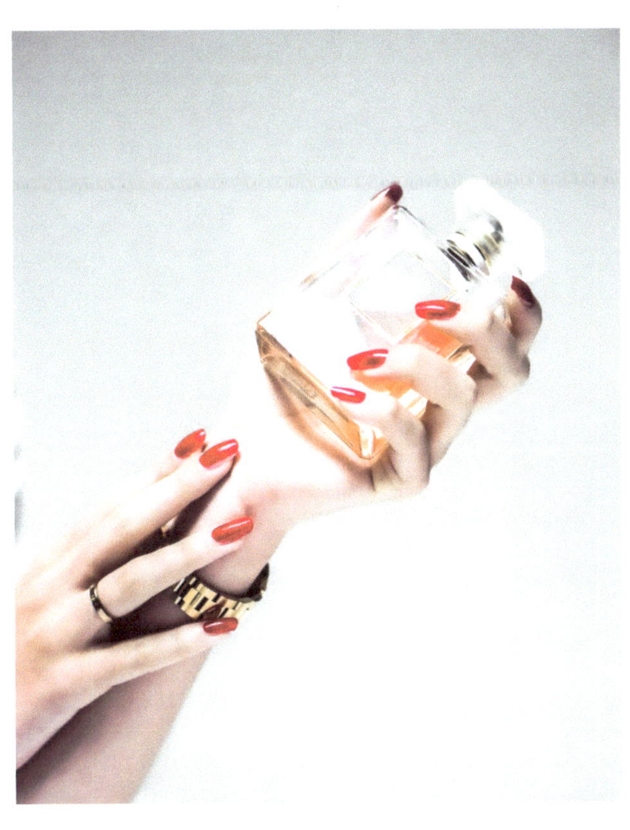
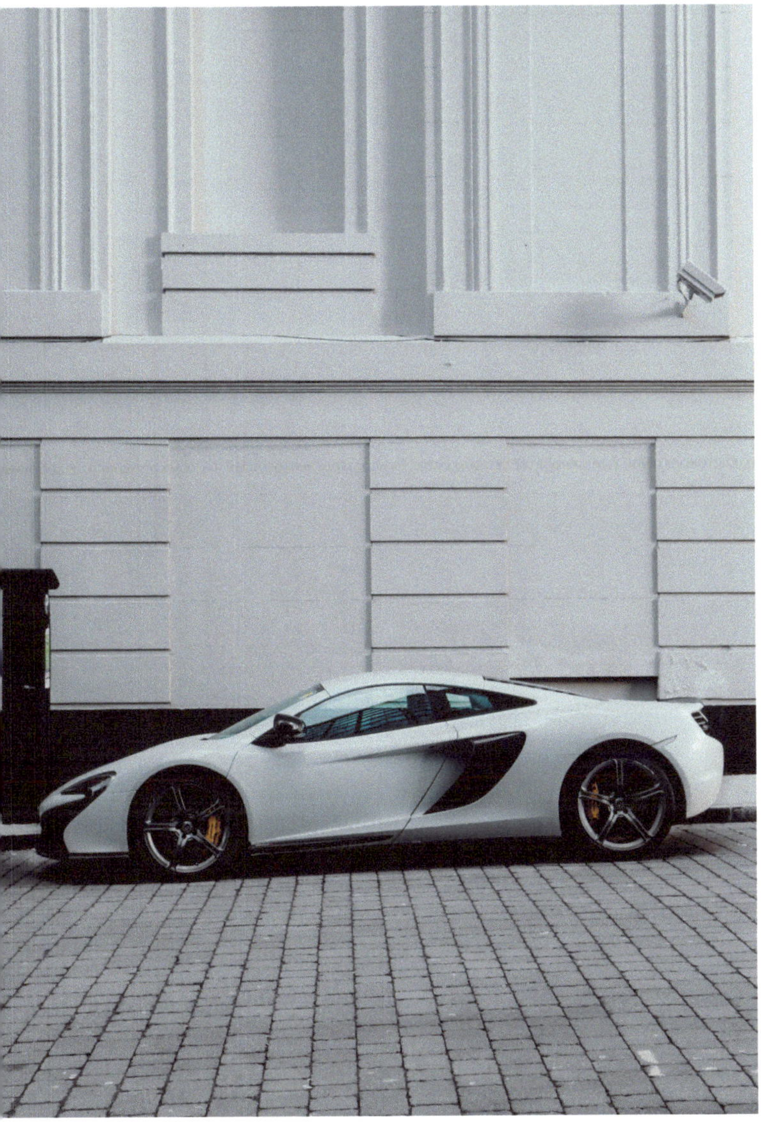
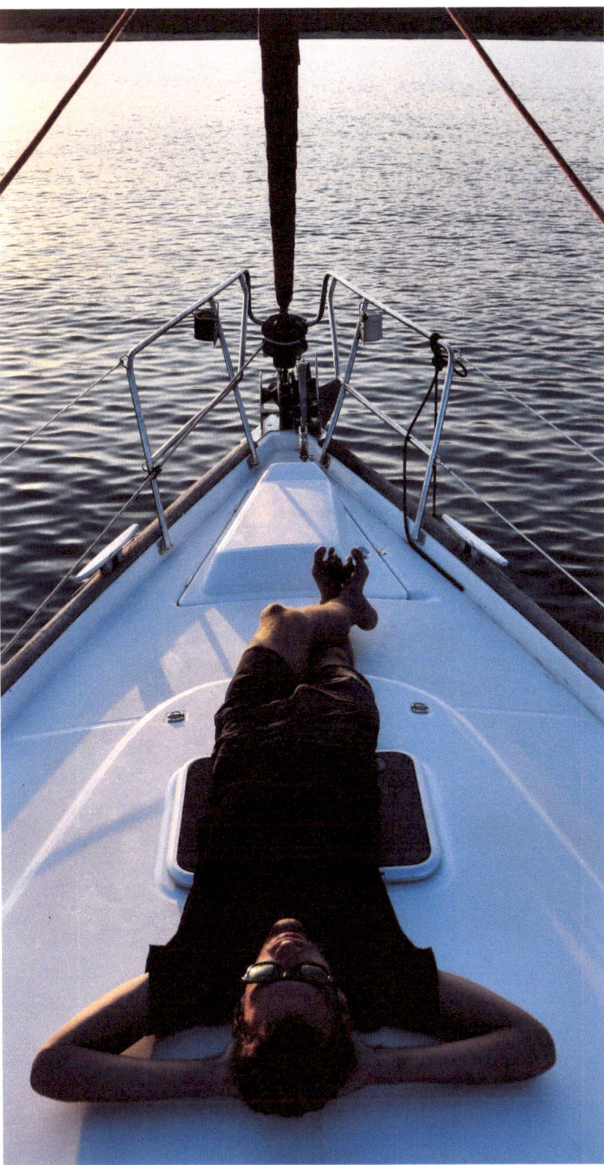

www.ingramcontent.com/pod-product-compliance
Ingram Content Group UK Ltd.
Pitfield, Milton Keynes, MK11 3LW, UK
UKHW060107300726
14090UKWH00003B/391

* 9 7 9 8 9 8 8 7 7 3 7 0 2 *